WHO SUCCEEDS IN SCIENCE?

WHO SUCCEEDS IN SCIENCE?

The Gender Dimension

▼▼▼▼▼▼▼▼▼▼▼▼▼▼▼▼▼▼▼▼

GERHARD SONNERT
with the assistance of GERALD HOLTON

R RUTGERS UNIVERSITY PRESS
New Brunswick, New Jersey

Library of Congress Cataloging-in-Publication Data

Sonnert, Gerhard, 1957–
    Who succeeds in science? : the gender dimension / Gerhard Sonnert
with the assistance of Gerald Holton.
        p.   cm.
    Includes bibliographical references and index.
    ISBN 0-8135-2219-6 (alk. paper). — ISBN 0-8135-2220-X (pbk. :
alk. paper)
    1. Women in science—United States.   2. Science—Vocational
guidance—United States—Sex differences.   3. Science—Study and
teaching—United States—Sex differences.   I. Holton, Gerald James.
II. Title.
Q130.S66   1995
305.43'5—dc20   95-8598
                                                                          CIP

British Cataloging-in-Publication information available

CONTENTS
▼ ▼ ▼

FOREWORD vii

PREFACE xi

CHAPTER 1   1
Science Careers for Women and Men
    Why Women Are Less Likely to Succeed: Two Models   1
    The Leaky Pipeline: A Chronology of Obstacles   8
    Thresholds and Glass Ceilings   11
    Who Cares? A Question for Policymakers   13

CHAPTER 2   16
Reaching the Top of Academe: Ten Who Succeeded
    Five Women   17
    Five Men   49

CHAPTER 3   80
Taking a Different Road
    Five Women   80
    Five Men   113

CHAPTER 4   138
Pieces of the Puzzle: Toward a Bigger Picture
    How Women and Men Are Treated in Science   139
    How Women and Men Act in Science   145
    Synchronizing Three Clocks: The Trials and Rewards
       of Marriage and Parenthood   157

CHAPTER 5   164

Mapping Scientists' Careers
> From High Chair to Department Chair: Stages and
>   Strategies in Scientists' Lives   164
> Kicks and Kicking Back: The Dynamics of a Career Path   179

CHAPTER 6   186

What Can be Done? Advice for Novices and Policymakers
> The Social System of Science: Now and Forever?   186
> Lessons for Aspiring Scientists   187
> Recommendations for Policymakers   189

APPENDIX   197

REFERENCES   207

INDEX   213

FOREWORD
▼ ▼ ▼

Our understanding of career choice—the factors associated with this choice and how these factors operate to influence this choice—remains quite limited. Our understanding of the progress of careers is also limited, based largely on a few biographies and interviews with high achievers and on longitudinal studies of doctoral degree holders' employment and compensation patterns. Little systematic study has been done of the complex dynamics of individual career paths. As a result, myths and stereotypes continue to flourish and expectations diverge from reality in ways that are dysfunctional for both individuals and society.

The long training period required for an entry-level degree for research and innovation in the sciences and the unpredictability inherent in the discovery process are distinctive features of scientific careers which influence the investments individuals and society are willing to make. It is therefore very important that we gain a better understanding of obstacles to the choice, access, and pursuit of such careers, and of the strategies that yield success or failure along career paths in science.

This is a particularly good time to examine obstacles and strategies in career paths in science because sufficient time has passed since science in the United States expanded from a small, elite community to a large, diverse, and diffuse enterprise. The experiences of the subjects in Sonnert and Holton's study have all been in this larger and more complex setting. Sufficient time has also passed since women were given greater access to higher education for there to be a large enough population of high-achieving women in science to study. This is also a good time for such an exploration because we are facing important changes in our population, our institutions, our position in the world—and consequently in the way we will need and conduct scientific research.

In this book Gerhard Sonnert and Gerald Holton provide the career path stories of twenty individual scientists, both men and women. These stories illuminate the mix of critical choices and day-by-day actions and attitudes that cumulatively affected the course of their careers. The voices of these individuals, some of whom persisted in scientific careers and some of whom chose to leave this career track, demystify the life of scientists and make real the ups and downs that are inherent in any significant endeavor. Through their stories we see the fascination and enthusiasm they feel about their work as well as the struggles with discouragement and obstacles. Their stories also reveal the variety of strategies that work. It will be reassuring to many who read this book to learn that success can be achieved by both a straight arrow path and a spiral path.

The authors place these specific stories in the larger context of our changing expectations about women's participation in the workforce in general and in science in particular and in the context of changing patterns in the way men's and women's careers intersect with family responsibilities. This latter issue is powerfully communicated in the authors' metaphor of the challenge of synchronizing three clocks: a woman's biological clock, her career clock, and her spouses's career clock. The role of luck and the influence of the social components of science—that is the mores or folkways, the implicit rules of the game and styles of interaction—are identified as important but often overlooked dimensions of careers in scientific research.

The full value of the individuals' stories derives from their being illustrative of the career-path information obtained from the authors' study of the much larger sample of seven hundred lives. Some significant similarities and differences in the experiences of men and women scientists become clearer and the ways these experiences intersect with the organizational structures in science are described. From this foundation, the advice offered for both novices and policymakers derives its validity and usefulness.

The people who participated in the work described in this book are all very high achievers. They have cleared with ease many hurdles that slow the progress of other competent, but less extraordinary persons. By identifying the obstacles and strategies in the careers of high achievers, Sonnert and Holton have brought into much clearer perspective how institutional structures and practices can advance or interfere with our goals. Our continuing challenge then is to make our institutions and our practices in science work well for a wider range of talent in our population. Our objective must always be to tap talent more fully, to encourage aspirations, and to develop the creative potential.

Linda Wilson
President, Radcliffe College

PREFACE

What does it take to succeed in science? Brilliance? Hard work? Connections? Favoritism? Good luck? Every year, about a quarter of a million young men and women in the United States receive their first academic degree in science, mathematics, or engineering. A small fraction will eventually become research scientists. But many who start out with that goal drop out along the way—for reasons that may have little to do with their scientific ability. The path to a successful career in science is often filled with unexpected and occasionally serious obstacles as well as opportunities that are not always easy to recognize. A chief aim of this book is to enable aspiring scientists to spot opportunities, steer around roadblocks, and achieve the satisfying life of a scientific researcher.

Most scientists, especially those still on the lower rungs of the ladder, know little about the way their careers are helped or hindered by their actions in the laboratory and classroom, their relations with departmental colleagues, their choice of institutions or research programs, or their methods of presenting research. You may excel in your science; but if you do not know how to direct your career, you may miss the chance to do your best work and reap the rewards for it.

The reasons for this ignorance are not difficult to find. Beyond your training in scientific skills and intuition, your education as a scientist rarely concerns itself with "the rules of the game." But building a career depends on many decisions that may have little to do with science. Where should I take a postdoctoral fellowship? Who might make the best mentor? Should I work alone or with a team? What kinds of collaboration work best? Should I try to maximize the number of articles I publish or concentrate on fewer, longer, synthesizing papers? How will being married and having children affect my chances for advancement? Such questions can be as urgent in the actual course of a career as the fate of a particular experiment or theoretical calculation; yet during your formal education you are unlikely to hear anyone explicitly acknowledge their importance.

Clearly, no set of answers could possibly apply to every practicing scientist. But we have taken a close look at the actual lives of contemporary scientists and have found that certain strategies and characteristics, on average, favor or hamper the chances of advancement. Decisions that look obvious at the time can turn out to have quite unexpected career effects later.

The results we present in this book are the product of *Project Access*, a large-scale research project based at Harvard University. It was organized to investigate the detailed career paths of men and women scientists, with a special emphasis on women's careers. We examined the careers of hundreds of young researchers who seemed to be poised for distinguished careers in science, mathematics, and engineering. They had received prestigious postdoctoral fellowships from the National Science Foundation (NSF), the National Research Council (NRC), or the Bunting Institute at Radcliffe College; or they had been Bunting finalists. If members of this select group did not do well or did not stay in science, the reason was certainly not lack of talent or lack of institutional recognition at the conclusion of their formal training. Our data base, the largest and richest of its kind, includes answers to lengthy, field-tested questionnaires from 699 former NSF and NRC fellows (508 men; 191 women). (The smaller number of women is owing to the relative dearth of women among the fellowship recipients.) Additionally, we conducted open-ended individual interviews that lasted two to three hours each with two hundred former NSF, NRC, and Bunting fellows and Bunting finalists (92 men; 108 women).

Their responses allowed us to see to what extent career outcomes could, for better or worse, be predicted by individual characteristics. We paid particular attention to the difference that gender makes in scientific careers. In this book, we present our most significant results in a way that we believe will be interesting and useful to a wide audience: above all to women and men who are now, or who are planning to be, scientists, mathematicians, or engineers. We also believe it will be useful to teachers, science administrators, and policymakers. In one sense, it is a how-to book, a source of ideas and insights that may be valuable in a variety of situations. (If you are curious about the detailed statistical results and analyses of Project Access, see our *Gender Differences in Science Careers: The Project Access Study* [Rose Book Series, published for the American Sociological Association by Rutgers University Press, 1995].)

We must stress that this book does not contain sure recipes for guaranteed career success. The career path to science is a complex dynamic system, and this clearly limits the effects on career outcomes of personal strategies and institutional intervention. To a large degree, for instance, career success depends on luck—being in the right place at the right time and prepared to recognize an opportunity. Moreover, individual choices and policy programs are sometimes powerless in the face of environmental conditions, such as labor-market fluctuations.

Although we are confident that our work will be of use to men in science, we focused especially on those characteristics and events that seem to have a positive or negative effect on women's careers. It is well known that women scientists, especially in the later stages of their careers, are less likely to attain distinguished positions in their profession. Although institutional discrimination has been outlawed in the United States since the 1970s, impediments for women scientists have continued to exist, albeit in increasingly subtle patterns. Jonathan Cole (1987, 368) noted that it is "in the domain of informal activities in science that the biggest gaps between men and women remain. It is in the more intangible set of experiences associated with doing science from day to day that women rightly feel most excluded."

These changes in the structure of gender disparities required us to adjust our approach to examining them. We thought studying a cross-section of the vast population of scientists and scientists-in-training would be too coarse-grained and superficial for us to discern those increasingly important subtle differences in career decisions and career paths. We expected differences—small, with the potential to lead to major differences in career outcomes—to be more easily identified and examined within a relatively homogeneous subgroup of the population of scientists—those who have started their professional careers on a more or less equal footing.

We chose to concentrate in depth on the men and women who had been identified early in their careers as promising scientists, mathematicians, and engineers by virtue of having been awarded a coveted postdoctoral fellowship. Part of the rationale behind selecting such an elite population was our desire to examine whether the relatively few women in this subgroup had overcome a threshold beyond which their careers paralleled those of their male cohorts or whether these women hit a glass ceiling that made it harder for them to enter the top echelons of their profession.

All the people in our sample had relatively successful career paths through the first stages of a science career—that is, up to the doctorate.

But after their postdoctoral fellowships, their career paths fanned out in different directions; some of them became extraordinarily successful scientists, while others left science altogether. The many obstacles that confronted these promising scientists in their later careers should be even more worrisome and threatening to the many scientists without the initial advantage of a prestigious fellowship. Thus, our subgroup's career trajectories and strategies should contain useful lessons for anyone interested in pursuing a science career or administering programs that involve policy decisions about careers.

Because of the increasing subtlety of gender disparities in science careers, we chose to perform a sort of "triangulation" using different methodological vantage points. The population on whom we focused our attention was large enough for standard quantitative methods but small enough to let us study a sizable proportion more qualitatively—that is, through interviews. Adopting this unusual and burdensome research model, we gathered and statistically analyzed our questionnaire data and, through the interviews, also sought for the insights that only personal life histories can offer. From two hundred face-to-face conversations we chose twenty examples for particular attention in this book. One group of ten consists of those who achieved very successful careers as academic research scientists; the other ten abandoned research science, even though their postdoctoral fellowships initially marked them for probable success in that profession. Each group of ten includes five women and five men. The accounts we present of their career paths, often in their own pungent words (and, of course, with their permission), allow us to compare the strategies and experiences of those who achieved academic success and those who left research science as well as clarify some of the differences in the strategies and experiences of men and women. They let us glimpse the dynamics and details of the great variety of real lives in science today.

We should address two potential misunderstandings that might arise from our selection of groups for presentation in this book. First, our concentration on academic scientists does not imply that we consider non-academic scientists inherently less important. Rather, we simply felt we lacked the criteria for quantifying the success of research scientists outside of academe (those working in industry, for example, or for the government) because the nonacademic sector is much more heterogeneous than the academic sector. Within academic science, the criteria of success are fairly conventional and widely acknowledged—chiefly academic rank, prestige of institutional affiliation, and publication productivity.

Hence, it is easier to develop a success rating for academic scientists. (The Appendix spells out the details.)

Second, those who have left research science do not automatically incur the stigma of career failure, and such a characterization is not implied in our selection of the two groups. In fact, as you will see, some of the people presented here who did not stay in research have been very successful in their careers outside of the profession and have continued to make valuable contributions to society from their positions.

Personal stories about careers in and out of science are rarely encountered in the literature, yet they have a special meaning and usefulness for the aspiring scientist. We tell the actual stories of highly successful scientists and those who left research science. We note the variety of barriers, listen to how these men and women tried to overcome them, and reveal how they dealt with the advantages or ill fortune that came their way. We ask whether gender differences exist even in career paths that have roughly similar outcomes and focus on the important common ingredients that characterize these biographies. Thus, we offer aspiring scientists some tools for preparing for the professional side of a science career.

Although this book focuses on difficulties, problems, and obstacles that scientists, especially women scientists, encounter during their careers, we do not intend to overshadow the fact that most scientists, certainly most of the people we interviewed, find great excitement and joy in science. By pointing to potential problem areas, we do not aim to discourage anyone from entering science careers. On the contrary, we want you to succeed in that noble endeavor. The best service we can render is to alert hopeful scientists to some of the often-neglected social and political aspects of a science career. If you are aware of potential problems and strategies you can use to counteract them, you can make informed decisions that may increase your chances of success.

We end the book by making specific recommendations to individual scientists and people who set science and human-resource policy. Although these recommendations are intended to improve career development in the sciences, they are not a quick fix. Nevertheless, as Albert Einstein once remarked, while it is unrealistic to expect sudden and radical changes in a complex system, it will be sufficient "if the good is made more likely, and the bad less likely."

A draft of this book was circulated among administrators and policymakers in academic and nonacademic science, and we greatly benefited from their comments as we prepared the final manuscript. Several members of our informal advisory committee—Jill K. Conway, John E. Dowling, Carola Eisenberg, Nathan Glazer, Kenneth Hoffman, Matina Horner, Lilli S. Hornig, Ellen J. Langer, Margaret L. A. MacVicar, Mary Bunting Smith, Shirley M. Malcom, Elizabeth McKinsey, Benson R. Snyder, Betty M. Vetter, and Dean K. Whitla—were kind enough to suggest improvements at early stages of the work, as were the directors of the Bunting Institute. We gratefully acknowledge the financial support that Project Access received from the National Science Foundation, the Office of Naval Research, and the Ford Foundation. In no case did the advice or the award of grants imply an endorsement of our results.

The design and testing of our questionnaires owed much to suggestions from Daniel Yankelovich and Dean Whitla. Sara Laschever conducted the interviews throughout the United States, and Mabel Lam developed the coding scheme for the interviews. Joan Laws ensured that the project was kept on track administratively. Among the other fine members of our project staff, special thanks go to Kate Schmit, Robert Stowe, Sarah Tasker, and Sally Thurston.

Last but not least, we thank the hundreds of people who responded generously and frankly to our requests to submit themselves to detailed questionnaires and interviews. And to those of you embarking on a science research career: Godspeed!

Gerhard Sonnert
Gerald Holton
Jefferson Physical Laboratory, Harvard University

WHO SUCCEEDS IN SCIENCE?

CHAPTER 1
▼ ▼ ▼

Science Careers for Women and Men

> The beginning was difficult for her.... The director of the Chemical Institute did not then accept women, but he did make a concession in her favor. With the condition that she was not to enter the laboratories where male students were working, she was permitted to work with me in the wood shop.

The time was 1907, the place the University of Berlin, and the woman Lise Meitner, later recognized as one of the outstanding physicists of the early twentieth century. The words are Otto Hahn's who was her long-time collaborator (1966, 51). Having worked as an "assistant" before World War I, Meitner was able to join the physics faculty after the war when women were admitted to the professorial ranks. But as Hahn commented, "to many the concept of a 'scientific female' was still somewhat weird" (1966, 66). A newspaper misreported the title of Meitner's first lecture, "Problems of Cosmic Physics," as "Problems of Cosmetic Physics"— either a Freudian slip or an intentional slight.

The situation of women in science has vastly improved since Lise Meitner's time. Nonetheless, gender disparities, although modified in shape and degree, have persisted: many women scientists still tend to work, figuratively, out "in the wood shop." Thus, the gender dimension of science has become the focus of intense research interest.

WHY WOMEN ARE LESS LIKELY TO SUCCEED: TWO MODELS

Why are women scientists, as a group, likely to have less successful careers than men scientists? The various answers that scholars have given to this question fall into two general categories: women are treated differently in science (we call this the *deficit model*), and women act differently in science (we call this the *difference model*).

1

The Deficit Model

According to the deficit model, women as a group receive fewer chances and opportunities in their careers; and for this reason they collectively have worse career outcomes. The model emphasizes structural obstacles—legal, political, and social—that exist (or existed earlier) within the social system of science. It is assumed that women's goals are similar to men's goals, but that barriers to advancement keep women from accomplishing these goals on par with men.

Structural obstacles can be ordered along a formal-informal spectrum. Formal structural obstacles are the most powerful barriers to women's career success. In the past, for example, the admission rules of many colleges and universities denied women access to education and thus severely restricted their career opportunities in the sciences. Outright gender discrimination, which denies women good entry-level jobs, promotions, tenure, and research funding because of their gender can also be considered a formal structural obstacle. Although these obstacles are the hardest for individual women to overcome, they are also the easiest to identify—and remove, if there is a will to do so.

During the 1970s and 80s, formal structural barriers were outlawed in the United States; and gender disparities in the sciences have subsequently decreased. Nevertheless, full gender equity is still elusive. As a result, attention has recently turned to the more subtle, informal barriers that women face within the social system of science. Published research findings generally agree that women scientists are still handicapped by these informal structural obstacles. For example, women have less access to strategic resources, such as social networks, which are essential for career success. Compared with men scientists, women scientists may be more socially isolated from mentors (usually male) during their training and from the network of colleagues during later phases (Epstein 1970; Kaufman 1978). Thus, women tend to remain in the "outer circle" (Zuckerman, Cole, and Bruer 1991): they are not admitted to the influential clique of scientific power brokers, key researchers, and administrators who make important decisions about the future of a research field or an academic discipline. Even without formal discrimination women holding a minority position in a male-dominated field may be subject to the adverse effects of tokenism (Kanter 1977).

Formal and informal structural barriers may directly affect the careers of women scientists, but they may also indirectly affect an even larger number of women by turning them away from a science career. If women perceive that structural obstacles in the social system of science may tarnish the potential rewards of a scientific career, they may choose to avoid a career whose potential costs appear to outweigh potential benefits (Moen 1988; Weitzman 1984).

The Difference Model

The difference model emphasizes deep-rooted differences in the outlook and goals of women and men. According to this model, the obstacles to career achievement lie within women themselves; they are either innate or the result of gender-role socialization and concomitant cultural values.

In the past, many scholars speculated or assumed that gender-specific genetic differences made women less intelligent, creative, and scientifically able. In respect to intelligence, however, which at first glance seems likely to influence scientific success, women scientists score slightly *higher* than men on IQ tests (Cole 1979, 61). And in any case, research shows that scientists' IQ scores are not correlated with scientific accomplishment (Bayer and Folger 1966; Cole and Cole 1973; Folger, Astin, and Bayer 1970). This does not imply that intelligence is unrelated to scientific ability in the general population: scientists as a group certainly possess above-average IQ test results. But *within* the group of scientists, differences in intelligence do not translate into differences in scientific accomplishment.

It has also been claimed that a gender-related genetic factor gives males superior mathematical abilities (Benbow and Stanley 1980; Hoben 1985). This view has been vigorously criticized by those who see early socialization as the cause of the gender differential in mathematical ability (Campbell and Geller 1984; Eccles and Jacobs 1986; Entwisle and Hayduk 1988). In their landmark survey of studies of gender differences, Maccoby and Jacklin (1974) concluded that convincing evidence for a genetically determined gender difference existed in only two areas: the average male is more aggressive and has better visual-spatial ability than the average female. Neither female superiority in measures of verbal ability nor male superiority in measures of mathematical ability appear to have a genetic basis (Maccoby and Jacklin 1974).

There is no general consensus about the existence or extent of genetically determined advantages and obstacles and one may never materialize. It appears safe to say, however, that there is considerable intragender variability and a large overlap between the two gender distributions, at least among the intellectual abilities relevant to scientific work. Thus, average genetic differences between the genders in relevant dimensions (such as mathematical talent) will fall far short of sufficiently explaining an individual's aptitude and career success in science—even if those genetic differences exist. Because the men and women in our sample have already proven their extraordinary competence in science, we can safely assume that they all come from the top echelons of scientific ability as it is distributed among the general population.

From the variety of culturally determined differences mentioned in the literature, three categories can be distinguished. First, women may be more likely than men to be socialized with general orientations and attitudes that reduce the drive toward professional success in any field. Second, particular attitudes about science may define it as a male field and thus encourage males and discourage females to participate. Third, deep-seated epistemological gender differences may make science, as practiced today, not sufficiently compatible with women's ways of thinking.

Traditional gender-specific socialization is based on, and reinforces, a fundamental division of labor by gender: women have primary responsibility for the home and family while men are expected to be breadwinners. This division of gender roles has been considerably weakened in recent times, particularly because of women's increasing participation in the labor force. In spite of emerging egalitarian patterns, however, it has not completely disappeared. Although more women have become breadwinners, gender differences in career patterns remain. One interpretation of these persisting differences posits that weakening traditional role divisions allow women a broader range of culturally acceptable options. Whereas career remains men's main avenue to respectability and success, women can choose career, homemaking, or both as acceptable pursuits (Cole and Fiorentine 1991). Yet women's wider range of acceptable options can also be interpreted as a wider range of responsibilities. In the majority of dual-career couples studied by Hochschild (1989), it was the woman who had to fulfill most of the domestic duties.

Even with the decline of rigid gender-role socialization, social practices still reinforce the image of the aggressive, successful man and the nurturing, supportive woman. From an early age, for example, girls tend to be discouraged from developing a strong motivation for achievement (Eccles 1987; Eccles-Parsons, Adler, and Kaczala 1982; Entwisle and Hayduk 1988; Lipman-Blumen 1972, Stein and Bailey 1973).

While they are socialized to interact in a style that de-emphasizes aggressiveness and competitiveness, those characteristics are encouraged in boys and become embedded in a male interaction style (Tannen 1990).

Chodorow (1974) traced backed to early childhood dynamics women's greater connectedness with others and men's greater independence. In Chodorow's view, processes of individuation and separation from the mother are more central for young boys (who need to form a male identity) than for young girls (who can adapt the mother's female identity). These socialization patterns tend to distance women from precisely the characteristics that the current social system of science rewards and reinforces: ambition, self-confidence, resilience, aggressiveness, and competitiveness.

In addition, cultural beliefs about science and scientists may distance women from the field. Science is commonly perceived as a thoroughly male domain; and scientific textbooks have reinforced this notion (at least until recently) by mentioning and picturing men almost exclusively and by showing the few women who do appear in gender-stereotypical roles (Heikkinen 1978; Kelly 1985). As a result, girls and young women students lack role models of successful women scientists and may be discouraged from pursuing scientific interests that boys and young men are simultaneously encouraged to follow. Furthermore, there is a powerful antiscience theme in popular culture. A common stereotype, the "egghead" or the "nerd," is portrayed as undersocialized and barely functional, a person whose scientific pursuits leave him grotesquely detached from the real world. But like its positive textbook counterpart, this negative image characterizes the scientist as male. As Brush points out, it is "difficult to imagine that the incessant pairing of 'scientist' and 'man' has no effect on young women" (1991, 406). Thus, a young woman with scientific aspirations may face a double marginalization: entering the stigmatized subculture of nerds, and then being an oddity among her fellow nerds because of her gender.

Some scholars see the maleness of contemporary science expressed through not only who the scientists are and how they socially interact but even how they do science. According to this view, current scientific epistemology and methodology are androcentric. Science is said, for instance, to embody a masculine type of objectivity and rationality; women's epistemological style is different—more intuitive, synthetic, and holistic (Belenky et al. 1986; Keller 1983, 1985, 1989; Kerr 1988). If women have a different methodological approach to science and epistemologically different ideas of what constitutes good science, the fundamental incompatibility of this view with an androcentric system of science might handicap them severely. (Keller [1983] portrayed the biologist Barbara McClintock as a scientist with a particularly female style.) But among the various types of women's obstacles we have mentioned, the hypothesis of an androcentric epistemology in current science is one of the most controversial and has encountered vigorous opposition (for example, Haack 1993, Levin 1988).

Just as we should remember that supposed genetic gender differences cannot explain the observed gender differences in science careers, we should heed Weitzman's (1984) warning against painting an oversocialized portrait of women as prisoners of socialization. Gender-role socialization does not completely determine the outlook of women. First, it is overlaid with a variety of other socialization patterns, especially in a country such as the United States, with its multiple ethnic, cultural, and religious traditions and class division. Moreover, some room is always left for individual differences, much more so when traditional gender roles are in flux. In particular, the women in our sample, who successfully completed a doctorate in the sciences and won a competitive postdoctoral fellowship, cannot be viewed as typical products of traditional gender-role socialization.

For reasons of conceptual clarity, we have distinguished between structural obstacles (barriers that exist as a feature of the social system of science) and internal obstacles (barriers that exist in the form of women's attitudes and values). But in reality these interwined categories reinforce each other. On the one hand, the attitude and values of others (parents, teachers, and peers) may translate into structural obstacles. For instance, if teachers are convinced that science is an unfeminine profession, they may tend to give their attention and rewards, such as prizes and scholarships, to boys rather than girls. Their acts then become a structural obstacle for girls. On the other hand, if girls who come up against a series of such structural obstacles finally get the message that they are not wanted in this arena, they may internalize those barriers by revising their outlook, aspirations, and self-confidence. Nevertheless, if we are to understand the complexities of women scientists' career paths, we must examine both models of career achievement—the deficit model, with its focus on structural obstacles, and the difference model, with its focus on internal differences between men and women.

We have mentioned women's distinctive traits (as described in the difference model) as obstacles to their career success in science. From a more general perspective, however, scholars hold a wide range of views on these traits. Some denounce them as internalizations of oppressive societal structures. These traits are regarded as the most insidious form of oppression because internalization makes the victims collaborate in maintaining their own undervalued position. If societal oppression vanishes, proponents believe, the distorted feminine traits that have kept women from achieving success will similarly fade away.

Others, however, see feminine traits as women's inner core of resistance against oppression. Consequently, they laud typically female characteristics and advocate new and different societal structures that build on rather than marginalize some of those characteristics. Instead of urging women scientists to act more like men scientists, for instance, they promote a thorough social and epistemological reform of science that would accommodate supposed female traits.

Historically, these opposing evaluations of gender differences can be linked to distinct phases within the women's movement as it has developed since the late 1960s. Although any large movement will contain diverse shades of opinion, the mainstream of feminism has shifted from a negative to a positive evaluation of gender differences. In her analysis of contemporary feminist thought, Eisenstein noted that in the first phase of the women's movement, most of its protagonists advocated "the replacement of gender polarization with some form of androgyny" (1983, xi). The deficit model of career achievement was predominant and the key difference between women and men appeared to be external: barriers maintained by societal structures kept women from achieving the same kind of career success as men. Among those theorists who moved toward the difference model, internal gender differences were seen in a negative light—as the extension and internalization of structural oppression.

In the second phase, many feminists developed "a woman-centered perspective" (Eisenstein 1983, xi). They focused on the difference model—more precisely, on a difference model in which particularly female traits received a positive evaluation. Harding (1986, 1989) described the same shift within the feminist critique of science, calling it a transition from a reformist to a revolutionary position, "from analyses that offered the possibility of improving the science we have, to calls for a transformation in the very foundations both of science and the cultures that accord it value" (1986, 9). But feminist critics who argue for the existence of typically female traits and characterize them as positive would agree that, in the current social system of science, such traits are likely to put women at a disadvantage.

THE LEAKY PIPELINE: A CHRONOLOGY OF OBSTACLES

Science careers are like a leaky pipeline: at various segments of the pipeline, people drop out but rarely drop in. Unfortunately, the dropouts are disproportionately female. From childhood through later stages of scientific training and professional careers, gender differences shape opportunities, obstacles, and the responses people make to both.

Family Influence

Crucial processes of gender-role socialization take place in the family. Differences in basic outlook—for instance, in achievement orientation and self-confidence—are to a considerable extent formed at an early stage and influence men's and women's later career and life choices (Eccles, Jacobs, and Harold 1990; Eccles-Parsons, Adler, and Kaczala 1982). The mother's employment history appears to have a major impact on the daughter's career orientation. Daughters of mothers who were employed during the daughters' childhood or adolescence showed higher career aspirations than daughters of mothers who had stayed home (Huston-Stein and Higgins-Trenk 1978; Tangri 1972). In addition, the interaction between father and daughter shapes the daughter's achievement motivation. Fathers particularly appear to encourage achievement in first-born daughters or in daughters if they have no sons (Huston-Stein and Higgins-Trenk 1978).

Early Institutional Support

School can instill cultural gender roles that distance girls from academic achievement, particularly in the sciences. Both teachers and peers may contribute to the process (Weitzman 1984, 183–193). To some degree, lingering structural barriers may keep girls from receiving additional or specialized instruction in the sciences—for instance, counselors who direct girls away from advanced-placement mathematics.

College

In college, women tend to experience a variety of pressures that can work against developing or maintaining a career interest in the sciences. In many institutions, young women with scientific aspirations are viewed as odd; peer pressure and the desire to be popular may deter them from taking the first steps in science. In a more structural sense, women may encounter a classroom atmosphere of neglect or outright hostility both from their predominantly male peers and the predominately male faculty (Hall 1982). Women may lack opportunities for mentorship and be confronted with lower faculty expectations (McBay 1987; Moen 1988). Such experiences may cause them to lose confidence in their scientific ability (Widnall 1988). In sum, encounters with structural barriers during the college years, as well as ongoing gender-role socialization, direct many women away from science careers. (Proponents of women's colleges cite these persistent problems as a reason for supporting women's single-sex college education, even though women are no longer formally excluded from colleges or universities.)

Graduate School

Graduate school is another important phase in a scientist's education. Here again, women may face structural obstacles, which even at this relatively late stage may discourage those disposed to science. For example, insufficient financial support for women, relative to men, appears to be a key cause for women's lower participation in graduate studies as well as their lower completion rates (Hornig 1987; Widnall 1988).

In fact, there are deficiencies in both formal and informal support for women. Fewer women graduate students become research assistants (Widnall 1988), and women students have less prominent mentors than male students do (Moen 1988). Both inside and outside the office, there is less contact and cooperation between (usually male) advisors and female students than between advisors and male students (Kjerulff and Blood 1973), although in many cases the women have a particular need for guidance (McBay 1987). Advisors are reported to have lower expectations for female students (Kistiakowsky 1980; Widnall 1988); and they are also reluctant to criticize women, which means that women students get less feedback (Dresselhaus 1986). Many women find it difficult to identify with male advisors (Widnall 1988). In particular, foreign teaching assistants and assistant professors may discourage women (Moen 1988). Thus, women frequently do not learn the "hidden agenda" of skills essential for a successful science career (Widnall 1988, 1744).

At the internal level, many women graduate students also find it difficult to cope with a milieu characterized by hostility and aggressiveness—a "combative style of interaction" (Widnall 1988, 1744). This approach is a corollary of the typically masculine interaction pattern we mentioned earlier (Tannen 1990). Women are more frequently interrupted in discussions, and their contributions are more likely to be ignored (Hall 1982). Because women are not well integrated into the student network, they are often left out of social activities in which faculty and male graduate students informally mingle (Kistiakowsky 1980; Widnall 1988).

To some degree, women graduate students were reported to suffer from an "'imposter' syndrome," a deep sense of inadequacy that is objectively unfounded (Widnall 1988, 1743). In the words of an older woman scientist looking back on her education and career: "All those years, I really thought that there was something wrong with me: I had not worked hard enough; I was not smart enough" (Briscoe 1984, 154). Women graduate students have been reported to have much lower self-confidence than men, even if their grades are comparable or better (Hornig 1987; Widnall 1988).

Professional Career

The professional career appears to be the phase during which some women scientists most clearly experience structural obstacles, usually in the form of discrimination in hiring, promotion, tenure awards, or research funding. Whereas instances of open discrimination are rare (they carry heavy legal penalties), subtle and informal structural barriers may linger. Women scientists are marginal in both the formal and informal scientific communication systems (Moen 1988). They find it harder to collaborate with colleagues (Reskin 1978) and may lack access to resources, positions, and power (Briscoe 1984). Moreover, they tend to face prejudice from the "old boys" (Koshland 1988) and may be excluded from the inner circle of the scientific establishment (Kistiakowsky 1980).

Family Matters

One of the major obstacles for women scientists, on both the structural and internal levels, involves marriage and parenthood. The integration of career and family life is a highly complex issue for women scientists. Many young women consider being married and having children desirable goals for which they are willing to make career sacrifices. On the other hand, they may be forced to play the role of unassisted housewife and mother because of their husbands' career requirements, attitudes, or behaviors.

Women scientists interrupt their career more frequently than men scientists do (Lewis 1986), often because of the responsibilities of raising a family. Although pregnancy and childbirth are biological functions of womanhood, women's traditional responsibility for raising children is not. Rather, this predominately structural barrier is based on deep-seated cultural values. According to a widespread stereotype reported among male professors, female students lack commitment and are prone to leave science in favor of raising a family (Widnall 1988). Yet women scientists who do persist in their careers, even when they have a family, may appear to violate societal role expectations. They may be criticized for neglecting their children (Koshland 1988) or feel guilty about it themselves.

A much higher proportion of women scientists than men scientists are married to another scientist, very often in the same field. Hence, the "two-body problem" of finding two science positions in the same geographical area is an important issue for many women scientists. In dual-career marriages, priority is typically given to the husband's career opportunities (Ferber and Huber 1979; NRC 1981; Rosenfeld 1984). Thus, geographical restriction in women's job choices is one of the structural barriers imposed by marriage (Moen 1988; NRC 1981).

Both intuitively and in light of the preceding discussion, one might assume that marriage and child rearing hamper women's science careers. This assumption, however, is not unequivocally supported by research findings. Some researchers found no negative effect of marriage and motherhood on scientific productivity (Astin 1978; Cole and Zuckerman 1987); but some did (Hargens, McCann, and Reskin 1978; Kistiakowsky 1980; Moen 1988). Later in the book we will examine the interplay of marital and parental status with career path.

THRESHOLDS AND GLASS CEILINGS

Passing through the science pipeline has been conceptualized as a complex dynamic process characterized by feedback loops and self-fulfilling prophecies that accumulate advantages and disadvantages (Cole and Cole 1973; Merton 1973; Zuckerman 1989). Allison and Stewart (1974) showed empirically how small initial differences have a huge effect on later publication productivity. According to the concept of the accumulation of advantages and disadvantages, a sequence of slight difficulties in early sections of the pipeline might lead to larger difficulties at later career phases and to an increased probability of dropping out. Women as a group appear to be handicapped from the start; compared with men, they accumulate fewer advantages and more disadvantages on their way through the science pipeline (Primack and O'Leary 1993).

The people in our sample successfully mastered the earlier phases of the science pipeline up to the doctorate and accumulated their share of advantages, including a prestigious postdoctoral fellowship. In other words, the women in this sample successfully overcame the early obstacles presented by cultural values, family environment, and school. Traditional gender-role socialization may to a certain degree still be in force in society, but it has certainly not kept these women from pursuing a science career up to the end of formal education. One of our key questions was whether our group of women had passed a threshold beyond which their careers paralleled those of their male cohorts or whether they faced a glass ceiling impeding their careers.

When we analyzed our data on the 508 men and 191 women in our larger sample, we identified a number of key disparities between the men and women. (For a detailed description of the sample and tables of key results, see the appendix.) It is important to remember that the gender gap in science has diminished during recent decades. We found, for instance, that attrition and unemployment rates were similar for men and women respondents. We also found no substantial gender differences in academic-rank achievement in the biological sciences, a field where the women former postdoctoral fellows appear to have overcome a threshold beyond which they proceed on relatively equal footing with men. Nonetheless, gender disparities do remain; they are just more subtle. We highlight the disparities found in our sample rather than women's recent gains because we feel this is not yet a time for complacency. In various forms, glass ceilings still exist.

- In contrast with the situation in the biological sciences, women in the physical sciences, mathematics, and engineering hold considerably lower academic ranks, on average, than their male counterparts, controlling for year of doctorate (table 3).
- Women are particularly underrepresented at the top end of academic achievement—that is, in the position of full professor at major universities (tables 4 and 5).
- In all fields, women publish less frequently than men do, on average. But differences in rank achievement persist even after controlling for productivity (tables 6 and 7). Moreover, a pilot study we conducted among biologists indicates that the quality of women's publications, as measured by the number of citations each article receives, is better than the men's, on average (22.4 citations per women's article versus 14.4 citations per men's; Sonnert, in press, b).
- Compared with men, women as a group have a less collaborative research style at later career stages (during the postdoctoral fellowship and later) even though they are more collaborative at an earlier stage (during graduate school). Thus, women are more likely than men to experience collaboration as a junior partner and less

likely to collaborate with colleagues or their own students (table 8). Moreover, a highly collaborative research style during the postdoctoral fellowship appears to be negatively related with later career outcome for women but positively related for men. This discrepancy may indicate that the women postdoctoral fellows who did collaborate were more likely than men to occupy a subordinate position in the collaboration (table 9).

- For women but not for men, family responsibilities are connected with working part time (tables 10 and 11). Although the general status of being married and a mother has little detrimental impact on women's careers in our sample, specific consequences of marriage and motherhood appear more influential. Women were more likely than men to take their postdoctoral fellowship in order to be in the same location as their spouse. This motivation correlates with a less successful career outcome in terms of academic rank (table 12).

Most of these gender disparities indicate that relatively larger or more frequent obstacles to women's science careers persist within the social system of science. In addition, combining marriage and motherhood with the requirements of a scientific career poses problems for many women.

We must reemphasize that the questionnaire phase of our study looked at the relative experiences of matched groups of men and women who set out to pursue a career in research science. For every statement of a general trend, one might find a contrary case in some individual. But this does not change the general trends discerned by studying large groups.

WHO CARES? A QUESTION FOR POLICYMAKERS

Why should our society care about women's underrepresentation in science, and why should we adopt policies designed to increase the number of women scientists? Here, we point out some of the broad social issues raised by the overall scarcity of women in science. At the end of the book, we return to these questions with specific recommendations for policymakers and aspiring scientists, which were drawn from the profiles and the Project Access data.

Two main arguments for increasing the number of women scientists, very diverse in origin, have recently joined forces, uniting technocrats and feminists in a somewhat surprising coalition. The first argument arises from a human-resource perspective and aims at ameliorating a projected shortfall of scientific personnel in the United States. The second argument comes from an equity perspective and is concerned about the continuing underrepresentation of women in important professional fields.

Proponents of the human-resource argument have relied primarily on NSF estimates, which projected a serious shortfall of scientists in the coming decades (NSF 1990). These projections have alarmed those who consider an emaciated science sector a sure recipe for long-term national decline (Griliches 1987). In this situation, policies that increase the participation of hitherto underrepresented groups, such as women and minorities, are seen as ways to make up for the expected decline of candidates from the traditional source—the white male population. Although these shortfall projections enjoyed wide acceptance for a while, they have recently been seriously challenged (*Washington Post*, 9 April 1992, p. A1; Shamos, in press). Thus, the alliance may be short-lived between those worried about the supply of scientists and those who wish to promote women in all fields.

For those concerned with equity, strengthening the representation of women in science is a matter of basic justice. These proponents denounce women's traditional underrepresentation as the result of a long-standing power imbalance between the genders. To redress the imbalance and establish equity between the genders, proponents advocate policies that break the barriers against women's professional and career success and open powerful and prestigious professions that have traditionally been male domains. Science is among these professions—one that, in many specialties, still substantially underrepresents women.

Policymakers might ask at what stage they should intervene to plug the leakage in the pipeline—to keep women from dropping out of science careers. Of course, this is not an either-or issue. Stopping the flow of dropouts at any point of the pipeline is beneficial. Nevertheless, limited resources mean that priorities have been and will continue to be set. Tobias noted that, in the opinion of large segments of the scientific community, early childhood is the best time for intervention (1990, 8–9). This translates into a long-term, indirect approach that emphasizes changing the cultural patterns of socialization. But the main focus of this book is on a much later phase—the post-training professional career—when new policies may be targeted more specifically and results may be more immediate. In the long run it is reasonable and necessary to interest more young girls in science so that we have a more equitable representation of women among future scientists. But we emphasize that the relatively few women who have made it through a leaky pipeline constitute a valuable human resource that is now available to work at its highest potential. Society has already invested heavily in women scientists who have reached the postdoctoral level, and these women themselves have invested an enormous amount of time and energy in science. Obstacles that prevent them from making full use of their skills and talents are particularly wasteful. Moreover, from an equity point of view, these women have the potential to enter leadership positions in science quickly. Thus, as science administrators, policymakers, and role models, they can boost the future representation of women in science.

CHAPTER 2
▼ ▼ ▼

Reaching the Top
of Academe:
Ten Who Succeeded

Few men or women who embark on an academic science career reach what might be considered the top of their profession. Here we present the profiles of ten former postdoctoral fellows who did just that. We hear their actual voices discussing their lives and career paths—some well-established, others nearer the beginning—the fortuitous twists and turns that led to their success, and the obstacles they encountered. We also learn about their scientific working style and share details of their private and family lives.

The profiles are based on extensive interviews, typically lasting between two and three hours each. To protect the anonymity of these women and men, we have given them pseudonyms. In addition, we do not mention the names of other persons or institutions and do not identify the respondents' scientific disciplines. (For more information about interview methodology and presentation style, see the appendix.) Of course, in some cases we longed to include information about specific research projects, scientific disciplines, or other details. Yet because we did not focus on these particularities, our profiles have the advantage of highlighting the generalities of scientists' career paths. Rather than focusing your attention on profiles from your own discipline, all the profiles appear potentially relevant to every reader.

Our analysis in chapters 4 and 5 only begins to touch on the rich variety of attitudes, opinions, and experiences that the twenty profiles in chapters 2 and 3 reveal. As you read these life stories, you will undoubtedly discover specific insights relevant to your own situation.

FIVE WOMEN

Ann

Ann is a successful scientist in her fifties, a leader in her research specialty. She is married for the second time, with no children.

Ann grew up on a farm, a rural life-style that did not predestine her to become a scientist. From an early age, however, she was an outstanding student. "I was smarter than everybody else in my high school or grade school. I could do anything that anybody asked of me, except for drawing—artwork—and writing—penmanship—in school."

As a child, Ann was a loner who had little interaction with other children. "All my cousins were much younger than I, and my sister is six years younger than I am. I grew up by reading books and so I was very good in school. Kids found out that they could tease me very easily—I was very soft-skinned in grade school. And they teased me, and they'd hurt me and I'd cry. Then I learned how to put on a hard shell on the outside." Her parents were generally encouraging, although "usually they never said anything. They let me do what I wanted."

The pivotal event that steered her toward a successful science career was a summer course on the East Coast, which gave her an exciting introduction to science. "I read about a program for high school students in *Seventeen* magazine and wrote off and got an application and applied and managed to get in." The summer school involved twenty-five high school students and a group of college students as well as a meeting of renowned scientists in the discipline. Ann took advantage of the college program and the evening seminars held by the scientists. "They asked certain people to come back the second summer, sort of as second-year students. I think there were six of us that came back. Anyway, I was one of the ones that came back. I think that was very pivotal in my career."

The experience changed her outlook. Previously, she had assumed she would attend a nearby college, but her experience in the summer course led her to apply to more renowned schools. She was accepted at prestigious X University, which offered her a scholarship. In her freshman year, she was able to take advanced science courses owing to her experience at the summer school. She recalled that, her advisor, a woman, tried to discourage her from taking "all that science," especially advanced courses. When Ann presented her plan for a schedule that included advanced science courses, her advisor "looked at my schedule, and she said, 'You can't do that.' And I said, 'Well, why can't I do this?' and she said, 'You just can't take all that science, you just can't do that.' And I said, 'Why not?' She said, 'It's too hard.' Anyway, she finally let me go, but I think it should be different nowadays. When women come into college and want to do science, they're allowed to go ahead. But there need to be counselors at that freshman stage that help you decide can you do it or can't you do it, and encourage you to try."

Because the scholarship did not cover all expenses, Ann found various research jobs, all of them menial. But during her junior year a lecture by a famous researcher became a turning point. Afterward, Ann asked him a question related to the lecture. He did not have a definite answer and asked her if she "would like to try to find it out." This started Ann in a field of research that she is still working in now. Once intending to become a practicing veterinarian, she decided instead to apply to graduate school and pursue a research career.

For graduate school, Ann attended prestigious Y University, where a graduate fellowship partially freed her from teaching obligations. She was also fortunate in having an advisor who emphasized the research training of his students. "He was of the philosophy [that] you came to graduate school to do research, which I think is great, and that you shouldn't take many courses."

For a postdoctoral fellowship, she went back to X University, her undergraduate school. Ann considered the postdoctoral fellowship a great opportunity because it allowed her to get additional training. But her main reason for taking the fellowship at that institution was that her husband, a graduate student in a different field, wanted to go there.

During the postdoctoral fellowship, she encountered a specific difficulty in her research field: although new methodologies made dealing with three-dimensional concepts important, she had serious problems with spatial perception. Recognizing this problem, Ann changed the focus of her research. She calls her weakness in spatial perception a "wiring problem." In her opinion, it might be connected with being left-handed, but she has also observed the same weakness in other female scientists.

After the postdoctoral fellowship, she stayed in the area because of her husband's graduate studies and found a position at a college where she taught introductory courses for two years. But she soon got tired of teaching. "I wanted to do research. I didn't even know about this teaching versus research type of thing. I really hadn't thought about it. I just knew I liked to do basic research."

Fortunately, her old mentor at X University gave her a job in his laboratory and subsequently hired her as an assistant professor. Thus, she became the first woman to receive a professorship in this university department. Although she knew from the start that X University rarely promotes junior faculty to tenure status, she harbored some hopes that she might be one of the few who could beat the system. But she was not. At the time, she regarded this as a setback; but in hindsight she thinks it was an advantage because it forced her out of the shadow of her famous mentor into a completely independent career. "I think if I had stayed there, obviously, since I work in the same general area as [the mentor], I would have been always considered part of his lab, no matter who I was."

Ann "grew up with the idea that as a woman, you get married, you have a family." She got married during graduate school and planned to have children after graduate school. Her mother had given up her job after marriage, and Ann intended to follow her example. "My mother had been a schoolteacher, a high school English and Latin teacher, but she did not teach after she got married, except for substitute teaching. I had figured that this was what I was going to do." The marriage broke up, however, due, she says, to her husband's severe psychological problems. After her divorce, Ann felt that circumstances forced her to revise her plans and focus on her original interest in research. "At that point I was single again, and I had to make it a career, and I had to do what I wanted. I still liked to play in the lab."

She entered her second marriage in her thirties while she was a junior professor at X University. Her new husband was a scientist in the same field. "At that point I consciously decided not to have kids because I felt that it would divert my attention from focusing on my career." Her husband was similarly committed to his career and also did not want children.

Ann admires women who appear to balance successful careers and family lives; but without substantial outside help, such as a resident baby-sitter and housekeeper, this balance seems problematic to her. Even a female colleague who did have a maid to take care of most routine chores, Ann observed, got distracted when problems arose, such as when the children fell sick. She notices that her somewhat unusual life and career choices made "other members of my family [excluding her parents] think I'm sort of weird because I didn't get married and have kids and be like everybody else in the family. You know, the typical type of thing."

When her appointment at X University came to an end, Ann and her husband faced the difficulty of looking for two job openings in the same department. But they did receive dual job offers from two universities. They chose Z University, where they have worked ever since.

The work in Ann's laboratory is not focused on one specific problem; she leaves her co-workers room to pursue their own interests. Sometimes this arrangement frustrates her because she thinks a concentrated effort would ensure faster progress. She feels at times that she should focus more, but her focus tends to expand. This, she thinks, is partly due to the way in which she was brought up in science. Her graduate advisor, for instance, "said that a graduate student should do two different things. So in case something goes wrong with one project, you always have something in the background. And I mean I really did two different things."

Ann's working style is characterized by great carefulness. "You think you have something, and then when you've done it three or four times, you don't get it back, and you really didn't have it. But people publish on those first couple of times [when] it looks like there might be something there. I think there's a lot of junk in the literature because people aren't careful. So I think I'm a careful scientist, and I try to teach my students, my postdocs, to be careful scientists and think about what they're doing and to think about all the angles in it." Ann realizes that at times she might overdo her carefulness to the point of perfectionism. "Sometimes I get an idea, and I'll do the experiment. And then I think that tells me one thing, and then I'll do another experiment. But sometimes, for instance, even though I know the answer, I can see it, I wouldn't publish it. Then I become a perfectionist. That can become a detriment, when you try to get the best possible. Then you look at other things in the literature, and things aren't quite so beautiful, but the answer is still there."

Rather than writing strings of short papers, Ann tends to produce more complete and synthetic research papers that connect particular results with the bigger picture. "I try to relate things back, and this sometimes makes my papers complicated, and people don't understand it. It takes them three or four years. When I give a talk, they say you just put too much in because you're trying to put it all back together." Because "we aren't in the most competitive field in the world," Ann says she can get away with publication habits that do not maximize the number of research papers.

Ann considers it a general trend of female research scientists not to rush into publication but to present results that are both more complete and more thorough. "I think the females tend to work harder, in the sense that they want things to be more complete when they publish than men sometimes do. I think that tends to be more male: go in there and do something and then worry about the controls and all the possibilities of things that might have gone wrong afterwards rather than worrying about them in the beginning."

When considering internal qualities that are advantageous for her work in science, she mentions persistence and inquisitiveness: "wanting to find out—wanting to ask questions." Often she is creative through association. "Sometimes I can't get ideas out of the blue, but when I read something, then it'll start a train of thought that will go far beyond whatever that said." Similarly, very close observation of an object or experiment also tends to reveal new insights to her. "Sometimes when I'm doing the experiments or when I'm observing something, I see something else. It's something I may not have even thought about at the time."

For Ann, good scientific work is a synthesis of previously unconnected facts. "Really, the top-notch scientists are the ones who take certain phenomena and have enough of a background in different areas that they suddenly can put two and two together and then experimentally go in and find out that that really is why it works that way."

Ann considers herself resilient, hardworking, and energetic—she calls herself a workaholic. She traces these traits to her upbringing, "growing up on a farm where there's always something to do."

> I helped with the farm work. I didn't have to work my fingers to the bone, but we had to do things and things had to be done at certain times, and you knew that. It's sort of a discipline, I guess. And even after my father stopped farming, he was never the nine-to-five kind of person. And although my mother never worked, my mother was very active. She was Girl Scout leader, Sunday school teacher, that kind of thing. So I guess we worked a lot. I wish I had had two weeks of vacation in summer. Sometimes we'd go somewhere on Sunday, sometimes not. It wasn't the kind of nine-to-five, five-days-a-week existence that seems to be the general norm now—certainly something I still can't do.

She is more ambitious than her average colleague, male or female, but her ambitions are restricted to scientific achievements. She does not aspire to the kind of power that comes from organizational leadership positions. "I've always wondered why people want to be chairman or something, and I don't know of many women that want to be chairman, except nowadays sometimes this is forced on one because there should be women in that position. I've been asked, too, to apply for chairmanships, and I decided I didn't want to be a chairman. So I just haven't applied and wrote them kindly and thanked them no thank you. It seems to me that there are more men who want to do this and move on up the ladder."

In a way, Ann can understand how building a department could be satisfying, but "then there would be all the problems of people." Though the aspect she likes most about science is "working in the lab," she has held office in various national and international scientific organizations. She hopes that in this way she can do some good for her discipline and her fellow scientists, especially those from the developing world.

In spite of her successful career, Ann is "not completely self-confident because I get sort of down on some things because I blame myself. And I think I probably shouldn't blame myself, but I've done it wrong and therefore that's why things have gone wrong. My husband tells me it's a lack of self-confidence, so it probably is." This lack of self-confidence partly stems from having "too high an expectation of what I need to achieve."

Ann thinks she is clumsy with her hands. She thanks her mentor, her husband, and a technician for helping her with the parts of her research that are difficult for her because of her lack of dexterity. Dealing with people is also a weak point. As we already mentioned, Ann was a loner as a child and was teased a great deal in school. Even now, social chit-chat does not come easy. "I'm not very good at starting conversations, and I'm sure that if I knew the art of conversation, which I don't, I could get into these bull sessions at scientific meetings." Her dislike of alcohol further limits social interaction with other scientists, especially male scientists. "In a sense it's not so bad now, but I would say twenty years ago, if you didn't go out for beer, enjoy this kind of thing, you were sort of looked down on as a little funny. And certainly a lot of women are very good drinkers, but I think there are a lot of women who just don't like it. And going out for drinks with the boys is certainly something that you do. That's sort of a social grace."

She has more problems with women graduate students than with male ones. In her opinion, some of her female students, although they are very bright, do not work as hard as males usually do. She feels that these women are not sufficiently research-minded and might be more interested in teaching.

> I obviously am a workaholic, and some of them don't want to be. So my attitude is: Don't plan on being a woman in science. Do the best work you can do; be a scientist. And sometimes some of the women graduate students, although they're very bright in their studies, as far as learning things, synthesizing it, and putting it on exams, just haven't been taught to work hard in the lab. After a year or two, most of them will turn around, but there are some that don't. And yet they're still very bright people, and they do get Ph.D.'s, and some of them do

very good things teaching or something else, but they just aren't research-minded. And I think that's when the conflict may come. It's obvious, from the research point of view, they aren't so good—and this is hard.

While some female graduate students do not know what to do later on, Ann thinks that men graduate students have fixed their sights on science as a career and really strive to make it a success. In her opinion, the conflict between marriage and family on the one hand and a career in research science on the other still persists for women, regardless of the changes brought about by the women's movement.

When men come to graduate school, you know that's their career. Some of them also drop out because they discover that that's not what they really want to do; but if they have decided that that's really what they want to do, they learn. And it may take them a while to learn the kind of lab work that they want to do, but they get into something and they will really strive for it. At least, all my male graduate students have done this. But I think some of the females still have a real conflict about what are they are going to do when they get out. I've got one now who is a tremendous thinker and so forth. Even though she's worked in the lab five years and she can do things very well, it takes her maybe three times to get one thing really nice so that she can finish it for a thesis, whereas a guy, if he had worked that long on this, would be beyond that point. But the other problem, her real problem, is what does she really want to do after graduate school? (And she's older; she came back to graduate school after several years of working.) Does she want to get married, have a family? Because she should do that, if she's going to do that, right now because she's just over thirty. I think in spite of all women's lib and everything, the conflict [between a science career and family] is still there, whereas that conflict doesn't seem to be there [for men]. A guy can get married, he can have a family, he can even spend time with his family, but somehow it's not as big a decision. For a woman, if the laboratory science doesn't come easily for her, then it's even more of a problem because she has to then decide, well, what does she want to do with it. And I think that's where the rub comes.

Ann has never contemplated leaving science, and she completely identifies with being an academic. Science takes a clear priority over all other aspects of her life; she has no strong outside interests. She usually works twelve to fourteen hours a day, seven days a week, and so does her husband. During their long marriage they have taken only one three-week vacation.

She thinks she has faced an average number of obstacles. "There are two types of women my age. There are women who have stayed in science, and women who have gone out for a while and come back; and I would say they've had the most difficulties because most of them have not come back into good positions. The women who have stayed in science, at least in my own small area, the ones whom I know best, I think we've all had about the same [obstacles]."

Ann thinks she has "made the most of everything, and the setbacks—it really wasn't much of a setback." She says she has experienced no sex discrimination nor any other form of discrimination, but she voices some concern about women's underrepresentation in the very elite group of scientists, those who receive awards and honors for extraordinary achievement. "I suppose the only thing that some of us [women] fear is that maybe we've not gotten as much recognition as the men of our age; but in this day and age if you still have grants, then I guess that's really recognition. But you look at the [small] number of women getting the prizes in the societies and that kind of thing—there's no comparison. I think it takes a woman longer to get into the International Academy, longer to get those kinds of things at the end of your career than it does for the men."

Ann is not an activist in promoting the cause of women in science. "Since my philosophy is, well, a woman shouldn't get anything just because she's a woman and she should do it on the basis of her science or whatever her profession is, therefore I guess I'm not sympathetic toward women doing things as women." She did, however, give moral support to a female colleague who was unfairly threatened with tenure denial. Under the same circumstances, she would probably not have offered this support to a man.

When Ann was the only woman faculty member in a department, she was in high demand for all sorts of committees. "I suppose the women's movement has made it easier, and I think sometimes it's made it harder, because in the beginning, when you're the only woman, and they need a woman to balance their committees and that sort of thing, then you're the woman. You're there, and then it's hard to say no to that type of thing." She is glad that in her current department, where she has several female colleagues, such demands do not exist. "There's never been anything that makes me feel different, whether you're a woman or a man, which is great." Her only reference to her femininity in professional life is her self-chosen dress code. "One thing I always do, I still lecture in skirts—no matter what. When I stand up in front of a class, I think I should look like a female, I guess."

Ann is satisfied with her career and with her life in general. Her idea of the good life is to do what she wants. Conversely, "a bad life would be something where you were forced by circumstances to do something you didn't really like to do, as far as your work." She admires people who face adversity and still make the best of it. She explicitly mentions Stephen Hawking, the brilliant English physicist with a crippling case of Lou Gehrig's disease.

Key points:
- Maintains a single-minded focus on science
- Believes it is impossible to "have it all"
- Is married to another workaholic scientist
- Values the meritocracy of science

Ann belongs to a group of pioneer women scientists who were the first to attain certain advanced positions. (She was the first woman professor in a prestigious department.) Among her most striking characteristics are a single-minded devotion to science, a belief in the necessity of tough choices and sacrifice, and a basic trust in the meritocratic nature of science.

Overall, her career path was relatively smooth. She never stopped working as a scientist or even seriously contemplated it. Hers is a successful example of how to attract talented women from unpromising backgrounds. Several fellowships facilitated her science career, and she received significant support at two important points (from the summer science program and from the senior scientist who became her mentor and got her a professorship at X University). For Ann the system did work. Her mentors were men who treated her well and advanced her career. She says she has not encountered any gender discrimination and does not espouse feminist activism. Her good fortune has led to a deeply meritocratic, gender-blind outlook.

Her crucial decision to funnel all her energy into her science career was almost forced upon her by circumstance. After her divorce she revised her expectation of a family life with children and embarked without reservation on a career in research science, which had always been her wish. The general lesson she took from this experience was that tough choices are necessary. It is impossible to have it all, and women must be prepared to make sacrifices for their career. Interestingly, she is impatient with those female graduate students who, in her opinion, do not understand the conflict between family and career and the necessity of formulating firm priorities. One wonders how much she recognizes herself in these young women; for at their age she, too, still planned to start a family. Ann was fortunate to have found compatibility with her second husband. They are happy together while maintaining a workaholic lifestyle to which many spouses would object.

Barbara

Barbara is a successful scientist in her late forties, a recognized leader in her field of research. She is married with one child.

From an early age Barbara was heading toward scientific pursuits. "The reason I went into science: I was always very interested in science, and I was always strongly encouraged by my father. And I think that's probably very important in a lot of women having careers per se, and especially having careers in science. In a certain sense, [my father] was sort of a frustrated scientist who never became a scientist, and I think there was a little bit of transference there."

Barbara attended X College in the Midwest, where she majored in a science and took advantage of a co-op work-study program. "There are jobs all over the country in various areas, and I happened to end up [at renowned Y University] and that was very, very exciting. And it was clear that I was very interested in [a particular science]." But the work-intensive life-style of the researchers at this university put her off. "I saw the graduate students and the postdocs working very, very hard in the lab—nights, weekends, etcetera. And I started thinking, gee, how can a woman have both a family and do this? It must be impossible, and therefore I shouldn't really do this even though I'm interested in it. I should go to medical school, because you can control these careers more."

Therefore, she applied to medical school instead of graduate school. In the summer before she planned to begin her medical studies, she had a research job with a male scientist who became a mentor. At this time, it became clear to her that she preferred research science to medicine. "By August 1, I decided that I really didn't want to go to medical school, didn't like sick people anyhow, and I really should be going to graduate school. And [the mentor] encouraged me even at that point to apply." "At the last minute," she applied for graduate school at prestigious Z University and was accepted. Barbara regards her experience with this mentor during the summer job and the subsequent change of plans as an extremely important turning point in her career.

In the graduate program, her male thesis supervisor was a very supportive mentor. This supervisor had originally been her second choice, and she worked with him because her first choice had been reluctant to take her on. "The person that I really wanted to work with basically told me that he didn't take women, and what would I do if I got married and had children. And it was such a disillusioning interview that I went to my second choice who, in fact, had never had a woman graduate student before, had turned down all previous ones, and for some reason he took me. And so I was the first female graduate student in his lab, and he was very wonderful in a lot of ways, and has always been very helpful and supportive to me."

For her postdoctoral fellowship she went abroad, following her husband, a scientist in another branch of the same discipline. Her graduate supervisor used his contacts to secure a place for her at the foreign institution. At first, she had no space in this laboratory, but eventually a young staff member "offered me a little bit of bench space in his lab. He was then very influential in terms of what I did and served very much as a scientific advisor, although he never put his name on any papers."

After returning to the U.S., Barbara's husband briefly worked at a prestigious American university, and Barbara planned to do research in a string of postdoctoral or research associate positions. "At the time that I was a graduate student there simply weren't any women on the faculties, and so I had never expected to join a faculty, and I had never thought of myself that way. I had just expected to continue to work in someone's lab." But while she had been abroad, the women's movement had gathered momentum, "and all of the sudden there was a lot of pressure for all universities to hire women. . . . And so when we came back, unaware of what had been going on, all of a sudden there were all sorts of places that were interested." Several institutions offered positions both to herself and her husband. The couple chose renowned W University, which had made the best offer, and have been there ever since. "I don't think I'd have a professional life if it hadn't been for the women's movement."

Barbara's career aspirations were very modest at the beginning because of the scarcity of women faculty in her field. Later, as a faculty member herself, she initially presumed "that maybe I would have one or two graduate students who would be female, because there would be no way that a male would ever want to set foot in a female's lab. In fact, the first two or three students I had were males, which just totally floored me. I hoped that people would think that I did a good job in terms of what I was doing. But I never expected to succeed to any great extent."

Support came from her mentors and, most of all, her husband. "My husband, of course, has always been very supportive, which is wonderful." Although she had no great expectations, she took advantage of opportunities when they arose. "Once something was broached or offered, I've always wanted to take on the challenge." She feels that she made more of the opportunities and advantages than would have been realistic to expect.

Good luck contributed a great deal to the advancement of her career. "In terms of science, and what I've been doing for the last ten years, it was a very serendipitous happening. It clearly was a matter of being in the right place at the right time with the right sort of connections to put things together so that something significant happened subsequently."

In terms of positive internal qualities that might have had an impact on her career, Barbara considers herself to be resilient, hardworking, and energetic—traits she attributes to her early upbringing. At the beginning of her career, she was much less self-confident than she is now, but the success she enjoyed in her career increased her confidence. Now Barbara considers herself somewhat more ambitious than the average scientist.

In general, she does not think she encountered great obstacles or setbacks. She believes she has met with fewer difficulties than comparable scientists (both male and female). "In fact, if you look back on [the setbacks] you can rationalize that they turned out for the best." But she recalls two cases of sex discrimination. The first, and most blatant, was her rejection in graduate school by the professor who would not have a woman as his advisee. The second was more recent, involving dealings with people in the university hierarchy. Men "face the obstacle of numbers. Because of the fact that there are fewer women in the field, a woman is more noticeable, which can be either positive or negative, and a man doesn't have that advantage—or disadvantage."

With respect to internal traits that may have impeded her career, Barbara says, "I'm not as smart as I'd like to be. I can't do things as fast as I'd like to do them. I can't remember as much as I should remember. I can't speak extemporaneously well enough. I'm not funny, can't make jokes easily."

In her attitude toward her work, Barbara is "very goal-oriented. I'm a perfectionist; I like to finish things off more than start things." She considers her perfectionism a trait shared by many women scientists. She observes that women scientists tend to choose proven methods in their work to shield themselves from criticism as much as possible. "One has to choose methods that are going to give absolutely solid answers, that are going to be unassailable and unequivocal in terms of their proving to the scientific public that whatever you conclude is absolutely correct. In other words, make everything completely objective, so that there's no room for subjective judgment, because there's the underlying fear that that might work against you."

Barbara tends to select research problems that are completely her own. "I very much dislike working on problems that I know other people are working on." Rather than compete with other research groups in a race toward the solution of the same problem, she carves out a niche for herself. "This is also something that I've noticed in my excellent female students, so I think there is some sex connection to this; and that is that in choosing a subject, there has been a deliberate and very strong desire to choose something that can be completely one's own. And this is clearly true with me, in terms of what I've chosen, even if it's high risk."

What she likes best about science is "finding out something new that nobody ever knew before. . . . The whole process of being involved and finding out things and the excitement of discovery is absolutely tremendous." She characterizes top-quality work as work "that's important, that has impact on thinking about other problems."

Although many scientists might envy Barbara's long bibliography, she feels caught up against her better instincts in the publication numbers game. She says, "there's probably more [publications] than there should be. If we did more important things all the time, there would be fewer and more significant publications."

She acknowledges that in the "very social endeavor" of science, power relationships are important. Her own power, which derives from her reputation, is greater "than I feel capable of handling truly well." Barbara clearly enjoys the social aspects of laboratory work. "Somehow I've done fairly well with people in my lab in terms of making them happy and making good things happen in the lab because of the fact that they feel that it's a positive environment." For her, "the most fun part" of science is having stimulating students and postdocs in her lab.

In regard to interactions with her predominantly male colleagues, she feels her gender has been an obstacle only in certain limited respects. A woman's "contacts with one's professional peers, I think, are probably very different from what men experience, because they talk to each other in a way that is slightly different, in terms of sharing problems and stuff like that, from what one's able to do if you're of the opposite sex. And if you don't have people to talk to about these things, you have to be fiercely independent." Only very recently has Barbara had female colleagues with whom she can talk. "Semiprofessional things, how to deal with problems, whether they're problems with people you're interacting with, or to some extent even scientific problems, how you interact with your department, how you interact with your university—you don't discuss those things the same way with somebody of the opposite sex as you do with somebody of the same sex, and so that clearly makes a difference."

Barbara completely identifies with her profession as a scientist, "and I do very little else," but somehow she wishes she could spend more time in other activities. A few people whom she admires are able to do that, but she feels she is not smart enough to dissipate any of her energy in activities other than science. She estimates that she spends between 60 and 70 percent of her waking hours doing science. She considers herself "politically unaware, unengaged," although she donates money to social causes.

She does feel a tension in handling the various roles she plays in her life: being a professional scientist, a wife, and a mother. On the other hand, her marriage is also the source of very strong support in her work. In general, Barbara thinks that, apart from a husband's emotional and scientific support, being married also improves a woman's social interactions at work. "I know this from some of my unmarried female scientific colleagues; I think it helps a lot to be married. To have someone there, especially if that's someone who is supportive and is helpful. A lot of unmarried women in my field do run into problems with men, basically because they're considered fair game for anybody because they're not married. And if you're married you're protected." A negative aspect of being married is restricted geographic mobility. If it had not been for her husband, she would probably have moved to another region.

Barbara and her husband have one child. Because of the child, "I work less nights and weekends than I used to." Career considerations played a part in deciding not to have more children. Barbara is very satisfied with her life. With minor exceptions, her idea of a good life corresponds to her actual life. The only thing she thinks she should have done differently is that "maybe I should have had two children instead of one."

Key points:
- Takes advantage of opportunities
- Has benefited from affirmative action
- Employed in same location as scientist husband

Opportunism in its best sense—taking advantage of opportunities—was a key to Barbara's career success. Although always hard working and excited by scientific discovery, Barbara had very low career ambitions at the outset. She made the most of the chances that presented themselves and grew more ambitious and self-confident as she rose in the scientific hierarchy.

Barbara belongs to a cohort of women scientists who went through their crucial early career phases during a period auspicious for women's advancement. She explicitly acknowledges that she benefited from universities' efforts to recruit women.

Barbara is acutely aware of gender differences in various aspects of science. Although she enjoys the social interactions in connection with her scientific work, she takes note of how the tone and style of collegial interaction differs depending on the gender of the participants. She also talks about gender differences in methodology and problem selection.

Her marriage to a scientist in the same field is a two-scientist success story. The crucial element of their success was the offer of two good jobs in a good place. Barbara seems to have reaped the benefits of marriage without having suffered the potential disadvantages. She comes close to "having it all"—successful career, husband, family—although she regrets not having had another child.

Christine

Christine is a successful scientist, about fifty years old, who works at a renowned research university. She has never been married.

Christine comes from a scientifically inclined family. Her grandfather was a famous scientist, two of his four sons became scientists, and his daughter (Christine's mother) also had a great interest in science and worked as a research assistant. Christine's parents did not actively push her into or away from science; they were generally supportive of any career choice. "I never had the type of advice that, oh, girls don't do that sort of thing. Any kind of biased upbringing just never occurred to my parents. My brothers and I had very similar upbringing, and we were encouraged to pursue whatever we were interested in." While growing up, she spent a good deal of time with her grandfather the scientist, whom she calls "an inspirational person."

Although Christine mentions that a high school mathematics teacher, whom she liked very much, became a mentor, the most important impetus for her later career came from various work experiences during high school. Through her mother, who was a research assistant at a prestigious university, Christine obtained a summer job. "I was doing some secretarial work, filling in for a person on leave, and also some data analysis work. I met several of the graduate students as well as the scientists themselves, and I really liked them as people. I thought I would like to spend my career with this type of person." Christine had several summer jobs in both industrial and academic research settings. These experiences steered her toward an academic or "pure" science career as opposed to applied industrial research because she felt that the academic atmosphere was "most congenial."

To get a liberal arts education, Christine enrolled in X College, where she soon decided to major in a science. "There were about a dozen majors [in that science], and I was the only woman in my class. I was living in an all-girls' dorm—at that time there weren't any coed dorms anyway—and so I had plenty of other female companionship. Most of my female friends were not in the sciences, though my roommate was a premed student. I had plenty of encouragement and I remember some very good teachers, but by then I was pretty much on track."

Christine went to Y University, a renowned research university, for graduate study. The pace there was different from what she was used to. "It was a lot harder than it had been as an undergraduate, and all of a sudden I had to take it a lot more seriously." She failed exams and had to take them again. The rigors of her program were her only difficulties; she did not encounter any gender-based problems. "I do not recall encountering any barriers in the way of discrimination or discouragement. Nor was I ever made to feel odd, or not one of the kids, just because of there being fewer women in [this science]. I never felt particularly isolated, because I always had found it pretty easy to make friends with both men and women, and I had always plenty of female friends outside my field of specialization." Christine also acknowledges supportive advisors at Y University.

After graduate school, Christine had two postdoctoral fellowships. She went abroad for her first fellowship. "I was continuing mainly along the same lines as my Ph.D. thesis, and I had the good fortune to find a wonderful collaborator with whom I still am very good friends, although we don't work together so much any more." Then, for lack of other jobs, she took another postdoctoral fellowship at an American university. She was not as interested in the specific research field of that fellowship, but she learned a lot.

By the early 1970s, Christine felt "the job market suddenly started improving, and I had a couple of faculty offers to choose from, including this one here, and a few research job offers. I think, also, that affirmative action was being paid a lot of attention then. And once people knew I was available, I got several calls asking, 'Would you be interested in considering a job at so-and-so?' At that stage, being a woman may even have helped; it certainly didn't hinder my getting a job." She joined the faculty of Y University and has been there ever since.

Christine says she has encountered no major obstacles or setbacks in her career—only "minor disappointments." During her education, she never had a serious problem with funding. In college, she held a scholarship from a private foundation and, in graduate school, an NSF fellowship followed by a research assistantship. She also received NSF funding for part of her postdoctoral fellowship abroad. When minor difficulties have arisen, she has typically turned to good friends. Interestingly, mentors have not played much of a role. "I'd almost outgrown the need for mentorship—not that anyone really does, I guess—but when I came here as an assistant professor and was working my way up, I didn't have a mentor even then. My former Ph.D. thesis advisor, who is a senior scientist in our group here, never really served as a mentor. I think he would have if I had needed him, but I preferred to work independently."

When Christine started out in science, she aspired to an academic career. "That's the kind of environment in which I pictured myself, working with students and teaching. And as for science, I hoped I would make some kind of significant discovery or some major contribution to research." Everybody in her environment supported these aspirations. "When I was in high school I was not a particularly social person; I had friends, but they were all slightly odd people with unusual aspirations. But later on, when you're in an academic environment anyway, and more than half of your college class is going on to graduate school in some field, [an academic science career] was a perfectly reasonable thing for me to aspire to."

Christine has fulfilled most of her original aspirations and is satisfied with the course of her career and her achievements. She has never seriously contemplated abandoning science, although ever-increasing work loads and responsibilities sometimes make her think about concentrating on teaching and abandoning research. She feels that she has made the most of her advantages and opportunities, but she also says, "I always feel that I could do more." She considers herself about as ambitious as her average colleague.

As one of the traits that made her particularly suitable for her work, Christine mentions that she has "always been pretty good at relating to people, and especially students." She adds, however, that in classroom situations she has sometimes not been as effective a teacher as she would have liked. Christine also thinks of herself as "a conscientious person who manages to get things done, to finish things."

She acknowledges the role of good luck in her science career: she was "at the right place at the right time" to get her faculty job at Y University. Furthermore, she feels that she has "shown good taste in choosing research projects" that have led to a substantial advancement of knowledge in her field. She is self-confident, partly because of her upbringing, partly because she is successful at what she does. She also has a strong work ethic and motivation to achieve. "My siblings and myself were certainly encouraged by our parents to work hard in school and get as good grades as we could, and do other things such as music lessons or sports or whatever else we were interested in. I have tried to fulfil those expectations of my parents, and also my own expectations."

The trend in her field to do research in larger and larger collaborations might restrict her in the future because she is "not a very good joiner. I enjoy mostly working by myself or with a small number of scientists and students." Christine does not participate in the inflation of publication authorships brought about by large-scale collaboration. "With all the collaborative effort that goes on these days, some people have their names on lots of papers that they haven't really contributed to. I have avoided this, and I think that all the papers that you'll see on my list of publications, with a very few exceptions, are ones that I've made a central contribution to."

The aspects of science that she likes most are "the sense of discovery" and social interaction with other scientists. Her main criterion for really good scientific work is that it considerably advances knowledge and puts the new knowledge in a larger context or connects it with the already known. Her standards for scientific quality may be slightly higher than the overall standards in her field. "I find myself being pretty critical of people's work. I'm not saying that it's bad, but saying that it's uninteresting. That's almost as bad."

These criteria guided her own selection of research problems. "The subjects that I've chosen have all been fundamental in some way. To me they have been of central importance to the field in which I'm working, rather than just adding on a bit of knowledge or applying a proven technique to yet another example. I've tried to do things that I think have really advanced and consolidated our knowledge. I've also tried to pick problems that were accessible to a relatively small group of people." Furthermore, she has paid attention to her students' needs. "The education of my graduate students has always been important to me, and I've tried to choose a problem that a student could take on as a Ph.D. thesis, and not just as a 'cog in the wheel,' but with some mastery over the whole thing."

Christine thinks that being female does not influence the way she does science in any significant way, and she does not think she has interacted differently with men and women colleagues. She cannot tell if there are any gender differences in the ways in which scientists in her field work.

Christine believes the women's movement has had little influence on her life, although affirmative action might have played a role in her faculty appointment. "Not that I don't support [the women's movement], or feel that it's not a good idea, but I don't think that it has really helped me in any way to get to where I am. I think I just got there independently of the women's movement."

Through her success as a scientist, Christine has acquired a certain amount of power. She sees herself as a conscientious decision maker and tries to exercise her power in a constructive and objective way. "My opinion is sought on committees and on peer review boards and editorial boards. I certainly have made decisions about other people's work, have exercised power, if you want to call it that."

Christine believes that good scientific work does not necessarily require devoting oneself entirely to one's profession. She complains that her job is increasingly taking over too much of her life. "People think that until you get tenure you have to work all the time, and then once you get tenure and you're a full professor you can relax a bit. For me, it's been almost exactly the opposite." Ideally, she would like her science career and private life to have about equal weight, but at the moment the career absorbs two-thirds to three-quarters of her time. Because she is single, she does not feel a tension between career and family; but she does feel a tension between her career and her other interests, which include medieval music, international cuisine, detective fiction, and landscape painting. Christine does not consider herself especially politically aware or engaged. She and most of her colleagues are "aware of what's going on, but we're not really active."

Career considerations did not play a role in the fact that Christine never married; staying single was never a conscious decision, just "the absence of the right person at the right time." She does not feel that "being a single person singled [her] out in any unfavorable way" in her career path. On the other hand, being unattached may have given her the geographic flexibility that she appreciates. "My geographical location has always been relatively important to me. I haven't had to compromise yet." Being childless is not something Christine regrets. "I don't feel unfulfilled because I don't have children. I think I got shortchanged on maternal genes or something."

Her idea of a good life is one "that makes some difference to mankind as a whole, so that after you die there's something left behind. It could be children, it could be students that you have educated, it could be some scientific knowledge that you've helped to discover, it could be a work of art, of composition, or the like." It also entails a wide appreciation of nature and culture, "having time to live as a whole human being rather than just totally devoting oneself to a profession."

Christine is only moderately satisfied with her life in general. One thing that she dislikes in the atmosphere of her university is that it is "too technologically oriented, too factory-like." She feels that an environment more attuned to the liberal arts would be more congenial. Furthermore, "I am not satisfied with my current interpersonal relationships. That could certainly be better."

Key points:
- Has always followed a straight career path
- Displays great independence and self-confidence
- Claims a gender-blind outlook
- Has interests outside science

Christine has had such a smooth career path that her success almost seems predestined or inevitable. She has always self-confidently followed her goal and has not encountered any serious obstacles or setbacks in her career. The independence with which she has pursued her career is striking. Early in college, she was already "set in her tracks." Although she acknowledges the help and support of other scientists at various career stages, she neither had nor wanted to have mentors in the typical sense. Although she enjoys contact with people, she is "not a joiner" of large research teams in her increasingly collaborative field, a preference that might restrict her research options in the long run.

Like Ann, Christine is a senior woman scientist with a gender-blind outlook. She does not think gender plays a great role in science. Although she is not clear about the extent to which affirmative action helped her, she is convinced that she would have ended up being a professor in her chosen field under many different sets of circumstances. In some ways, Christine and Ann resemble those older women scientists who have followed "'the traditional male' model" of a science career (Etzkowitz et al. 1994).

Christine has a wide range of interests outside of science and—unlike Ann and Barbara—does not completely identify herself with her profession. She would like to live as a whole human being and resents that work encroaches on her time for her other interests. She appears to represent the dying breed of scholars who aspire to the liberal arts or humanistic ideal of the well-rounded, educated person.

Deborah

Deborah is a successful scientist in her late thirties. She works at a renowned research university, where she has moved speedily through the academic ranks. She is married with two children.

As a child, Deborah had "just sheer drive" and a "general thirst for knowledge." She took great pleasure in arithmetic and memorization. Raised in a churchgoing family, she remembers being "particularly good at memorizing Bible verses." She excelled in school; and when she was in second grade, her parents bought her a *World Book* encyclopedia. "I would pick out a volume—I remember I would often pick 'H' because it had horses in it—but once I was in 'H' I would read about Hindus, I would read about whatever." She was an exploratory reader who would pick up one of the *Classic Comics* as well as the encyclopedia. "And that somehow fed into getting interested in more advanced stuff. It's not that the actual material I was reading was significant, but it gave me a sense of connectedness, later, with things that really were advanced."

Because Deborah's father was an engineer, she grew up with drafting tools and learned to use the slide rule by the time she was in junior high school. Thus, her early interest in science "was a combination of my being curious and ambitious, and there being things available like *World Book* encyclopedias and slide rules, etcetera. ' Furthermore, the idea that women work was ingrained from early on. "My mother worked, her sister worked, my grandmother worked. They'd all been schoolteachers. And so it was just kind of accepted." She believes that "in more traditionally middle-class families [they] have had a couple generations where women didn't work and so they think that's the norm. But if you're from a rural area, and you know women work all the time, it doesn't seem as unusual to be working full time."

Deborah is full of praise for her public-school science teachers.

In particular, she considers a female science teacher in her senior year "probably just critical for my success later." From the fifth grade on, she took accelerated mathematics and science. She regards her solid training in mathematics as particularly helpful because it gave her a "certain fearlessness about math."

Deborah recalls a visit to the laboratory of a friend's mother who was a part-time scientist. "She wasn't a successful professor or anything, but she was a woman who was a scientist, and maybe that had an effect. I think it certainly gave me the idea women are scientists, which maybe I would have come up with anyway, but maybe not."

Relatively early in high school, her plan to study a science had already crystallized. "Probably a lot of the decisions had been made before I was midway through high school, because I already knew I wanted to go to a place like [X University], which is where I got my degree from and where you don't even apply unless you know you want to be in a science." When Deborah's aspirations became obvious, her parents were "sort of bewildered. . . . I think my being very aggressive put them off." But now they are proud and interested in her achievements.

Deborah recalls her father telling her that the family could not afford a private college for both her brother and herself. Because her brother would be a breadwinner, his education at a private college would take precedence; and Deborah would have to get a scholarship or go to a public university. Thus, from her parents she "had some discouragement, but in a way it was handy to have something to rebel against in such a constructive way, [that is, by] deciding to get a scholarship." She did receive a scholarship and entered X University. Deborah was happy to go to this university because her high school boyfriend was already there, but she would have gone anyway because "I had already decided that's what I wanted to do."

The X University environment helped Deborah escape the social ostracism that she had experienced during her school years. She recalls that she was "rather lonely as a teenager" even though she was extroverted. She was "big, very athletic, talked a lot, not very popular. . . . My achievements probably helped make sure I didn't have many friends when I was in high school." She also did not have many boyfriends. "I knew for sure because I was so ambitious and doing so well, boys didn't like me, but instead of shutting up and becoming withdrawn, I just kept doing it and felt miserable. The drive was stronger than the need for approval, so I just felt wretched all the time, but it didn't shut me up." At X University, by contrast, "nobody's going to scorn you because they think you're too smart," and she formed a number of friendships there.

Deborah's college experience was crucial for her further career path. There were no institutional barriers; "the barriers to me were all internal, my sense of not belonging, my sense of anxiety at failure." Part of her problem in college was "the realization that there were a lot of people out there that were a lot smarter than I was, which if you are an undergraduate at a place like [X University] is inevitable." A crucial turning point came in her senior year when she was asked to be a teaching assistant. "It made me realize that despite the fact that I wasn't what I considered to be as brilliant as other people I might succeed anyway, because other things were important too." The teaching job allowed Deborah to bring one of her strong points into play, the "ability to explain science."

After college Deborah spent "a year and a half of major floundering around." She applied to medical school and was accepted but did not go because of a personal crisis. She broke up with her boyfriend and had little direction for a while. With her new boyfriend (who was to become her husband), she moved to another university and took a job as a part-time technician and later as a teaching assistant. Because she enjoyed these experiences, she chose a science career over a medical career.

For graduate school at prestigious Y University, Deborah was awarded an NSF predoctoral fellowship, which she took as a "tremendous encouragement." She also received valuable guidance about career planning and strategy from a slightly older friend who was in the job market at that time. From him she learned the importance of carefully planning and preparing one's career moves and of making oneself known in the scientific community.

After receiving her Ph.D., she did a postdoctoral fellowship. Although her male postdoctoral advisor was generous and nice to her, Deborah was "sort of a loner" in the laboratory and at first felt that she did not really belong. Then her advisor went to a conference with her and let her give part of the talk. That opportunity allowed Deborah to show her talent for clear, cogent presentations and resulted in several on-the-spot job offers. "That gave me a huge boost, and I think it was probably like that final booster stage in rockets. That was what put me in orbit. It's really been very strongly forward motion ever since then."

When she was looking for a position after the fellowship, she toured several universities and gave talks. "Even if you pay for it with your own money, [visiting campuses] is an investment, because you might hear of things, people know who you are, and in fact that's how I got this job" at prestigious Z University, where she has been ever since.

Deborah's career "more than fulfilled" her original aspirations; but on the way toward becoming an extraordinarily successful academic, she had to overcome profound self-doubts. In graduate school she was full of insecurities. She wanted to be a professor but seriously doubted whether she could achieve that goal. In spite of her lack of self-confidence, she persevered. "I went through times that I just couldn't see myself doing this, and yet I kept going." A key element in her battle with self-doubt was a survey conducted when she was a freshman at X University. Two-thirds of the freshman class, almost all of whom were male, felt that they had been accepted by mistake and that someone was going to find them out. From this survey, Deborah concluded that "just having the thought you didn't belong was not something that meant you didn't belong. Plenty of people had that thought and then ignored it. And I really enunciated that insight in almost those words to myself many times as a graduate student, because I knew I had the feeling of not belonging, and I knew it was okay not to take that feeling seriously."

Now she considers herself fundamentally self-confident. "Within my immediate field, I'm probably the best there is." Her self-confidence developed partly because of positive experiences, partly because of strengths that she has always had. Deborah does not consider herself a "natural at a lot of aspects of experimental science," but she can call on the inner resource of a basic optimism. This is the "confidence that you can get up tomorrow, and it's a new day. Even if you made a just awful blunder, it's okay, you can go on." On the other hand, she still reports some lingering feelings of not belonging.

Among her major assets Deborah counts "some very central sincerity" about her personal and scientific flaws and "the ability to live with self-criticism in a creative way." For her, recognizing, analyzing, and dealing with her flaws are part of "a personality growth process." Deborah also notes that she is very driven and ambitious—more so than most of her colleagues. She considers herself resilient but thinks her resilience has not "really been tested in ways other people's might be." Deborah is also a hard worker. "I find work very appealing, and there'll be many a night when I come back to work, just because I don't want to be away from my lab, even if I don't have a specific thing I want to do. I want to be here, be part of the action. It's that as much as just the sheer love of the process."

An internal weakness is being "afraid of people disapproving of me." Her status as a social misfit in high school created "feelings of loneliness and misery." When she became an assistant professor, she realized that it is impossible to be liked by everybody. Before that discovery "I secretly believed that if I was just a perfect enough, nice enough person, everybody would approve of me and like me all the time."

Deborah recounts several relatively minor instances in her career when she wasted an opportunity or thinks she should have done better or done something different. But she also believes that she has met smaller difficulties and obstacles than others have. She does not think she has been subjected to any kind of discrimination. Her career was helped by "all kinds of good luck."

One obstacle she mentions is that she almost did not get a grant renewed. But it was renewed eventually, and she learned how to write better grant proposals. Occasionally, papers are rejected and she gets depressed, "but the depression always [gives] way to determination, to irritated determination to show them and put in a better one."

Deborah says she is very creative. Ideas come easily to her, but she considers it one of her weaknesses that she is not critical enough in winnowing out the really good ones. Her working style is "saltatory. I make a lot of jumps." Phases in which she makes rapid, insightful advances alternate with phases "where I'm sort of in maintenance mode." She thinks she may be a little less focused than the average scientist in her field. What she likes best about science are "surprises. People think that it must be really horrible in science when the idea that you have turns out not to be true, but I find the opposite almost—because when what you thought was going to happen isn't true, you're surprised. And I find that really great. I love it!" Really good scientific work is characterized by "honesty, self-criticism, technical fearlessness, and imagination." In terms of publication habits, Deborah notes that she and her collaborators "put more together for a single paper than some labs do."

Being female affects her choice of subject "less than it seems to affect some women. I'm not afraid of competition, and I feel very aggressive about my subject matter." Deborah has observed that other women in her field tend to choose research problems where there is not much competition.

Gender, however, definitely influences her professional conduct. She consciously behaves in ways that avoid any possibility of sexual misinterpretation. "The first few years when I was a postdoc and going to meetings, I was out there partying with everybody else. I somehow became very aware of that as something I didn't want to do, because it looks one way in a woman, and it looks like something else in a man. So I'm really reclusive almost at meetings and, increasingly as I get older, have a real built-in sense of what decorum is. Of course, once I get old enough, it won't matter anymore; nobody will suspect me of fooling around. But I don't, and I don't even want anybody to think that, so I'm very conservative about my professional behavior." In her interactions with her students and postdoctoral fellows, Deborah observed, "the currency of conversation tends to be slightly different" from how her male colleagues interact with their co-workers. Deborah emphasizes a more personal interaction style but does not engage in sports activities with her co-workers, as a male colleague does.

Interestingly, when asked about power in science, she talked about how the researcher forces the subject matter to give up the information he or she is seeking. When the question was focused on the more usual interpretation of power as related to the politics of science, Deborah acknowledged that she commands "more than medium" power compared with her cohorts, especially after winning a prestigious award, but she is not eager to use it. She has "a lot of leverage, or influence. Anyway, leverage implies that you want to move the lever—and I don't necessarily."

Deborah has not been active in the women's movement because she is "not a joiner." But, she realizes the importance of role models for many female students and therefore attends the women's programs at conferences. Politically, she considers herself more apathetic than the average person, although she is becoming more determined to do something to aid minority students. She actively practices her religion, "and I don't think there's any other person under the age of fifty in this department who belongs to a church."

Deborah says she attributes about equal priority to her science career and her private life. She is the only salary earner; her husband is a self-employed professional with irregular income. Being the primary wage earner reinforced her determination to pursue career success. While she acknowledges that considerable time pressures result from having both a science career and a family, the marriage also "made me more secure; it let me devote myself to my work in ways I might not otherwise have, because my attention would have been diverted to finding a mate, or finding a companion, and being married helped me be settled."

Deborah has two children, "but I've never even looked sideways at the thought of not pursuing what I'm doing now." Nonetheless, she acknowledges that parenthood has somewhat encroached on her scientific work. Now she cannot spend as much time in the lab at night as she used to do. Also, "the years when I've had my children and immediately thereafter, I was kind of passive. I think a lot of it was just that I was so tired." Besides this "effect on my energy level, [having children] also had a slight, but for me detectable, mental effect that I've talked about with other women who had babies. They felt that in terms of their ability to focus and be really creative, it took about a year for everything to kick back in. I think that was true for me."

Deborah's idea of the good life involves comfort, good bonds with other people, and the strength to move toward the "things that are important beyond yourself." As to the last aspect, she acknowledges a deficit. She says she is "rather self-absorbed" but has made progress toward being less selfish.

Key points:
- Overcame internal self-doubts
- Is aware of the politics of science
- Made herself known in the scientific community
- Acknowledges the pluses and minuses of combining family and career

Overcoming *internal* obstacles is the dominant theme in Deborah's success story. Although her career outwardly appeared to follow a smooth path after she began graduate school, she fought tough inner battles to overcome her self-doubts. Deborah is one of the most psychologically minded scientists in our group—at least in the interview she shared more of her inner struggles than most of the other scientists did. She still intensively monitors her own personality and makes a conscious effort to improve perceived flaws and achieve personal growth. Sincerity about oneself and self-criticism are central concepts for her. They also color her characterization of good science, where she first of all mentions honesty and self-criticism.

The crucial element of Deborah's success is how she has pitted one part of her personality against another. Tenacity and stubbornness have enabled her to control her feelings of inferiority and develop self-confidence. Although she still thinks that other scientists are more intelligent, she has achieved success through hard work and determination. In the face of adversity, she typically redoubles her efforts until it is overcome.

Deborah's case illustrates how combining a family and a science career can have both negative and positive aspects. Although the compounded demands of work and family stretch her time and energy thin, she also notes that her marriage has provided the necessary stability and support that allowed her to do science in the first place.

Elizabeth

Elizabeth works on the research staff of a prestigious research university. She is in her early forties, is married for the second time, and has one child.

Elizabeth's interest in science reaches back to her childhood. "My father was a farmer, although he had, as a young man, taught mathematics and physics. So he did have some training, but he did not really emphasize science at all to me. It is just something I was naturally interested in for some reason that I do not fully understand. And we had books available at home for me to read, so I did a lot of reading on my own."

School was a total disaster in terms of science education. "I would have to say that elementary school and high school were a dead loss. If anything, the [science] education in my high school was a negative rather than a positive [influence]." For instance, Elizabeth mentions a science teacher who had training not in science but in physical education. Not only was the quality of teaching bad, "but also people were not interested. It was a farming area, and all the boys were interested in farming."

Intending to major in a science, she entered X College, a women's college, where she found it difficult to keep up with the science courses owing to her lack of preparation. She decided to switch to a major in the humanities after her second year, but the friendship and encouragement of a science professor, "an inspiring lady," eventually convinced her to return to the science that she had originally chosen. "Now, whether that would have happened at a coed college where I think women tend to get less attention, I am not sure."

Because switching concentrations in college prevented Elizabeth from accumulating a solid-enough background in the sciences, she was not accepted into any prestigious graduate school. Instead, she completed a master's program in her science at a lesser-known university. She chose this particular university because she was already married by that time and her husband went to a medical school in the same city. During the master's program she remedied the weaknesses in her science background and decided to go on for a doctorate.

It was there that I determined that I really did want to go and make a career out of [this science]. I guess I had not really decided that when I was in college. Although I did really appreciate the environment of the girls' college encouraging women, I do not think they give you a very good sense of what you can actually do with an education. At the time, I never had the sense when I graduated from [X College] that I could go out and become a professor or a professional [scientist], but after getting a master's degree, I realized that this was fully within my reach, so I determined to go on.

Upon entering prestigious Y University for graduate study, she sensed that women were not really considered research-career material. "I think it was expected that women do not stay on in research science. That was a very definite impression that I got from the faculty there. In fact, when I went in, I was not awarded the fellowship, which most of the people were. I was told a year or two later that it was because it was thought it would be wasted money because women, in fact, do not go on to have a career in science."

Her first years of graduate school were "a little bit discouraging, but when I went on, the person I eventually chose for my advisor was very sympathetic, and he was not sure what to expect. I do not think he had ever had any female graduate students before, but he was very sympathetic and very supportive. I cannot say it determined my future, but he supported me in my choices."

When Elizabeth received her doctorate, there were no positions for her locally; but she received several offers from institutions further away. Her husband was already established as a professor and did not want to move. Finally, Elizabeth accepted a postdoctoral fellowship at very prestigious Z University, thousands of miles away. By the time her husband also moved to the area, the marriage had deteriorated and they were divorced.

Elizabeth is now married to a senior colleague at Z University. She still holds a nonprofessorial research appointment there. Because of the recent birth of her first child, she currently works part time. Initially, she found the atmosphere at Z University "pretty encouraging and pretty supportive," but she had to revise this judgment. She now complains about "an extremely nonsupportive atmosphere where people tend to be in cutthroat competition. And in particular, I would say that women who tend to be softer spoken than men usually get beat on more than the men do or maybe ignored more." On the other hand, the few women there fight among themselves; Elizabeth is currently involved in a feud with another woman scientist.

Although Elizabeth would like to leave, she cannot because it would be too difficult to find positions for both herself and her husband. If she were not married, she probably would have left already. Her husband is especially immobile geographically because he has spent a great deal of time and energy setting up a particular research environment and would have to start all over again at a different place. Coming to Z University was an opportunity, but "I think in retrospect that I should also have left it. In order to progress, I would have been much better off having been a postdoc at [Z University] and then gone on somewhere and advanced my career."

At the beginning of Elizabeth's science career, her goals were modest. "When I was getting a master's degree, I did not really have enormously high aspirations. I thought at that time that I probably wanted to be a professor, but whether that would be in a junior college or a college somewhere I did not really know." While working on her doctoral thesis, she developed the "belief that I could actually make a contribution in research." She did not yet achieve her aim of becoming a professor. "However, I did end up at [Z University], which is just about the best place to be. I suppose I did not really expect to end up here. So in one sense, I overachieved, and in another sense underachieved." In terms of research, "I certainly am doing what I expected to do. That was to enter basically a new field, which we helped to develop while I was at [Y University] as a student. We were one of the first groups of people to work [in that field]."

Elizabeth is not entirely satisfied with the course and the achievements of her career so far. She thinks her career may have been slightly more difficult than that of her average colleague. Sometimes, Elizabeth has fleeting moments of self-doubt. Occasional thoughts of abandoning science are never serious. She has not decided "whether I want to be content in my present position or whether I want to press for something else. . . . I had the ambition and the drive, and now I am not quite so ambitious and driven." She blames this change on the antagonistic atmosphere, especially toward women, that prevails at her institution. Her self-confidence has also fluctuated, from initially low to high in the later stages of graduate school, "and right now, I am in a not-self-confident stage."

During her first marriage, Elizabeth "went to whatever city my husband decided to go," but the moves were also beneficial for her career. Now, however, she feels somewhat stuck in a nonprofessorial position at a prestigious but uncongenial institution because of her second husband's career. In her present situation, "professional life gets very mixed up with personal life, and it is hard to sort things out. In a way it is helpful, but in a way it is also not helpful to be married to somebody who is closely related to you in your field. It is helpful in the sense that you can discuss your work and get feedback on it, positive or negative, as the case may be—and in a lot of cases it is positive." On the other hand, her husband rarely takes care of their baby; and because she knows his work so closely she finds it difficult to ask him to take more responsibility at home. "Actually, if I did not know what he was doing, I would feel freer to make demands on his time, probably. I feel less free because I see what he is doing and know exactly how busy he is."

Elizabeth recounts a phase of about a year or two between two research projects "where I really felt at loose ends, where I did not have much to do." The very opposite is true currently. "Right now, I have a ten-month-old baby, so I am working half time. And I find that is a strain getting everything done in half time." Nonetheless, raising her daughter is a source of great joy. "I have to say I am extremely happy having a daughter." With the birth of her baby, "the science career took second place and will continue to take second place for the next few years certainly."

Elizabeth thinks that a major obstacle for her science career was her poor science education, "which carried on through my career for years and really set me back a full four years." Another obstacle occurred at the start of graduate school, when she says she was discriminated against by not getting a fellowship. She also suspects that being female had something to do with the fact that she was not considered for a faculty position at Z University after she had been a postdoctoral fellow there. Male postdoctoral fellows frequently received such consideration. Elizabeth recalls an incident of sexual harassment by a postdoctoral fellow who "made real serious sexual advances which were not welcomed" while she was a graduate student.

As an internal career obstacle, Elizabeth mentions, "I do not like to manage. I do not like to direct other people." She thinks that this may be one of the key reasons for why she did not advance speedily in her career. "I might not make a good professor, because I could not tell other people what to do."

Elizabeth does not believe she is energetic. She regards herself as moderately hardworking and does not think "that work is the only thing there is to do in this world. I think you have to take time to enjoy yourself, too. Now my husband is one of the extremely hardworking types who does not think that there is anything besides work. So that is all he does." In her opinion, good scientific work does not require complete identification with one's profession.

One helpful internal quality is that she is "fairly stubborn. I think you have to be stubborn." She also considers herself resilient.

Elizabeth's research has been "rather disjointed. I work on one thing for a while and then I have to switch gears and work on another thing. So as a result I have not managed to gather a real coherent theme to my research, except that it has all been concentrated in this area." What she likes most about science is "putting together the pieces of the puzzle." Really good scientific work should be creative and responsible, "not a crackpot or harebrained idea." She thinks that her own quality standards are slightly higher than those of most people in her field. She rates her personal power as a scientist in the community of scientists as "not very high."

As to differences gender might make in the way she does science, Elizabeth considers herself less assertive than males, "and I think that is pretty common." She used to feel intimidated by male colleagues but not any longer. "When I first went to graduate school, I was very intimidated by the males because I had come from a women's college where there were no males. So I somehow thought this was a superior sex, and it was only after a few years that I realized that they were not a superior sex, and I gained some self-confidence."

Elizabeth has never been active in the women's movement, but she reads a great number of magazines and books about related issues. She considers herself fairly aware politically and donates money to political candidates as well as to social causes.

"I think having a good life and being a good scientist is mutually exclusive. I think that if you have a good life, you have time to get involved in the things that I said that I am not particularly involved in—that is, social activities, trying to help out in the social needs of the community or of the world. I think it is having time to enjoy some of the beautiful things, like music, that I do not really get a chance to do." Nevertheless, she says she is fairly satisfied with her life.

Key points:
- Benefited from education at a women's college
- Accepted lesser job to remain in same location as husband
- Currently working part time because of young child

There is a distinct difference between Elizabeth and the other four women in this group of successful scientists. Whereas the other four women were outstanding on all three dimensions of success—academic rank, institutional prestige, and productivity—Elizabeth ranked high in only two dimensions: her solid publication record and her affiliation with a renowned university. She has not moved up through the academic ranks.

Her career has been decisively shaped by her two marriages, and she has experienced the location dilemma of the academic dual-career couple not once but twice. The first time, she opted for geographic separation and the marriage fell apart. In the replay of the same basic conflict in her current marriage, she has stayed put and feels trapped in a dead-end job.

Thus, in contrast with the careers of the other four successful women scientists, Elizabeth's career, despite her research productivity, is in limbo. It might take different directions in the future because she is still relatively young. She has presently shifted her priorities to raising her daughter and has correspondingly reduced her career ambitions. The yet-undecided question is whether she will permanently emphasize family life and resign herself to the lower status of nonprofessorial research positions or make a decisive attempt to advance her career in spite of possible family complications.

FIVE MEN

Allan

Allan is a successful scientist at a prestigious university. Now in his fifties, he is married for the second time. He has four children from his first marriage and none from the second.

Allan's interest in science developed early. "I guess I got interested in mathematics and science in my high school years, probably simply because it was relatively easy for me. I enjoyed doing it. The first subject I can remember that really turned me on was geometry. I liked the formalism of proofs and things of that sort." Allan set his sights on a career in engineering, which carried some prestige in his working-class family. "My father had had a series of jobs like bus driver, clerk, things like that. During high school, the idea of engineering arose as a career, probably as a result of a high school career day. I didn't really consider basic science, like chemistry or physics, at that time because I didn't really know people did that as a career. Coming from a family background where no one had ever been to college, even the idea of being an engineer had some sort of status." Allan thinks that this cultural distance from basic science careers, in his case due to social class, is also experienced by members of ethnic minorities. "That may be the same kind of thing that drives a lot of the minority people nowadays into law, medicine, and fields that they know, that they can relate to. I could somehow relate to engineering, but not to basic science."

Allan's father died when Allan was in his early teens. Although Allan's goal was to attend a university with a strong engineering department, his mother sent him to X College, which was associated with her church. She did it "for religious reasons, with the hope that I would become a minister, at the very least a missionary." At X College, Allan found two "very good teachers" in science. "So I was quite fortunate in that regard; I did not end up becoming a minister. You might say I'm a scientific missionary, but it was really the influence of the two teachers at this four-year college that pulled me into [this science]. And I'm quite grateful for the lucky coincidences that put me there, in the presence of two people who were very interested in the subject and good teachers." In his junior year Allan was a laboratory worker, and in his senior year he became a teaching assistant.

Allan intended to go to graduate school in this science immediately after college, but financial problems got in the way. "I had gotten married when I was a senior in college, and my wife had promptly gotten pregnant, and our car broke down, and so we were destitute. And I took two years off and worked to get a little bit financially back on my feet." Then he entered graduate school at Y University, which he picked for its scenic environment. His studies were supported by an NSF predoctoral fellowship. At this school "again, I kind of stumbled into a fortunate atmosphere." Allan became acquainted with a professor and chose a research project in this professor's field. "That more or less directly led to the rest of my career."

The single most influential person in his career was his postdoctoral advisor, who came from prestigious Z University to Allan's graduate school to teach a summer course. Allan took the course and was subsequently recruited by this professor to do a postdoctoral fellowship with him at Z University. This position implied a change of career plans. "I had intended to just finish my Ph.D., that would be enough, go ahead and get a job, probably in industry. By this time I knew the difference between engineering and basic science. I was going to just do a research career in industry." Allan's postdoctoral advisor had a crucial impact, both in terms of science and of career advancement. "It was from him that I really learned my approach to science. And I think directly through his influence, I was able to get the job I have here" at W University, where he still works. He had contacted only two other schools, interviewing at one of them and W University. Thus, his job search "was a very easy experience."

His start at W University was marked by "an overwhelming amount of naïveté." He was not aware that junior professors at this university were rarely promoted to tenure status. He soon discovered it, of course, but "it never was something that I brooded about." Allan says he just had "an unwarranted amount of self-confidence," and he indeed received a promotion in his department. One strong influence was a close female colleague, who educated him about the sociology and politics in his science. "After those two people [this female colleague and his postdoctoral advisor], there really haven't been many people who have influenced me very much since that time. I'm kind of by nature a lone wolf, I guess, and have not ever formed a lot of close friends, but I've had a lot of professional friends from all the meetings and traveling around." A foremost scientist in Allan's field, whose writings he has studied intensely, has been a role model for his scientific research, although Allan hardly knows this scientist personally.

Allan has enjoyed a very successful career since starting at W University. The most difficult period in his career occurred during what he calls his midlife crisis in his late thirties, when he and his wife of fifteen years divorced. Allan attributes the failure of his first marriage largely to his rigorous work schedule (at least ten hours a day). It does not make for "a real healthy family situation when you've got a wife at home with four little kids, taking care of all the dirty diapers, and I'm up here trying to get tenure." For five years after the divorce, Allan was single "and actually a single bachelor father, because the four children stayed with me and my wife married someone else whom she met. We continued to be on good terms, but I voluntarily accepted the job of being single parent for a while." During this period, Allan could not find much time for research. He did not completely drop out of science, however, but continued to teach. Allan considers these five years "a dip" in his career and publication productivity.

Allan eventually married again. His second wife is a researcher in the same field. At this point, his former wife assumed responsibility for raising the children, and Allan returned to devoting most of his energy to science. His professional life now has clear priority over his private life. Because his wife is also a scientist, "her life-style really matches my life-style. It's okay if I work ten hours a day. I'm married to someone now who also likes to work ten hours a day, so it's not a problem." Allan believes that marrying a person who is interested in and supportive of his work has been a great bonus for his career. He does not feel any tensions between the various roles in his life. Although Allan is a self-described workaholic, he does not think good scientific work requires complete identification with one's profession. "I have hobbies, and I have definite times that I get away from my thoughts about [my science]."

When Allan started out in science, he had "little in the way of aspirations other than to have a job that paid well and had some status associated with it." Now he considers himself more ambitious than the average male colleague. The few women scientists in his field whom he knows "strike me as pretty ambitious, more than average." Allan's ambitions have largely been satisfied by the course of his career, and he feels he "could not have accomplished much more than I have. I'm an overachiever probably." He is even somewhat surprised at his successful career: "So much fun, and you get paid for it, too."

In Allan's opinion, good luck played a large part in his career success. One of the most fortunate things was meeting talented students with whom he collaborated. For instance, he and an extremely gifted graduate student "have clicked, we've really interacted well. I think we've stimulated each other to think of things that neither one of us would have thought of alone." He also considers his fellowships at various points a career advantage but does not think they substantially shaped his career. The most important internal quality that has helped his career is patience.

On the negative side, Allan mentions a tendency to procrastinate and not to keep up with the literature. "Given the opportunity to sort of play or think about something that's just fun rather than doing something that's a little bit harder, like studying, doing your homework, I will often opt for the former."

Considering his excellent career, it is astonishing that he is not full of self-confidence. "I have a lot of self-doubts and I kind of torture myself probably more than I should with guilt. I set probably unreasonable standards for myself. . . . I'm always afraid that even though we may have just been through a period of great productivity, that we're going to go into a slump, and everybody's going to quit asking me to come around to give talks and write reviews. People are going to start getting tired of [my current research results]. That's kind of passé now. And I need something else to bring out there, something new. We need to do something different." This lack of self-confidence sharply contrasts with the "unwarranted amount of self-confidence" that he possessed when starting out as an assistant professor at W University.

Sometimes during his midlife crisis Allan felt he did not belong in his chosen field and considered abandoning science. In the end, however, he decided that he really liked what he was doing. In situations of self-doubt, it helped that he was "pretty resilient." His mother was a role model of resilience when his father died, and she raised three children by herself. He works hard, although he thinks he is not as energetic as he used to be owing to his advancing age. He traces being a hard worker to his humble origins. "Children of the blue-collar caste are often overachievers. And I think I'm one of those. One of my colleagues' wives once said that the future of the United States is in the hands of the sons of the truck drivers. And that's exactly the way I feel."

Allan thinks there might have been some social-geographic discrimination against him in the large urban center where he was a postdoctoral fellow. "I felt like the [locals] viewed me as something of a hick," and thus he went to extremes of buying fashionable clothes and disguising his strong regional accent. He does not think, however, that this culture clash negatively affected his career.

Allan has come to understand the division of labor in science, which he considers crucial for his success. "The most important lucky breaks that I've had have really had to do with some students who have elected to do their work with me. In science these days, you can be brilliant and think of brilliant things, but it doesn't do you any good if you don't have some students or postdocs who are going to be able to go in the laboratory and do the work." His role is to conceive the research projects and to secure the funding, "to sit in here and scratch my head and try to think out what experiments to do. . . . I haven't gone in the lab and done an experiment for fifteen years." At the moment, he runs a laboratory with about twenty collaborators. Securing financial support in terms of grant money was a problem during the time he was a single parent and during a more recent period as department chairman.

In terms of publication output, "there are things that I've published that I would just as soon not have." This happens when students of his do not "produce something of real exciting caliber and yet they still want to publish it, and I think they're probably entitled to have it published, and they still want to publish it with the mentor because they derive some reward for having published with someone with an established reputation." Allan thinks that his personal influence and power as a scientist is "greater than I feel I'm entitled to have, actually."

Allan selects problems that have "some kind of subjective aesthetic appeal" in his scientific work. Another motivation in his problem selection "is the desire that people recognize and acknowledge what we've done." Therefore, he does not do research on "arcane" topics that most other scientists would ignore but tries to pick topics that command a great deal of interest in the scientific community.

Compared with the normal working styles in his field, Allan considers his style more innovative and intuitive. Good scientific work, in his opinion, "teaches people something they didn't know" and influences a large number of researchers over a long period of time. What he likes most about science is "solving one of these puzzles. It's like seeing your way through the maze, realizing that you probably figured out the way to do it. That's one high. But the real high is when you can get the experiments done and actually demonstrate that it works."

When asked about gender differences in scientific style, Allan could not say whether a woman would have approached his research differently. But he thinks that a woman might not have received all the excellent students that colleagues referred to him because she might have been less well known in the predominately male circle of leading scientists in his field. He also sees a gender segregation in specialties within his discipline. Some specialties have a fair number of women, but his own specialty does not. According to Allan, his specialty requires "intuitive leaps," not methodical procedure, and he thinks that women are less inclined to take those intuitive leaps. "Perhaps there's something there that you don't find very much in a normal woman's psyche." Allan likens the method in his field to a chess game: no one could systematically consider all possible move sequences because their number rapidly grows into the billions, so one has to rely on hunches. "The most successful people are the ones that somehow—and we still don't understand how, and those of us who do this spend a lot of time trying to figure out how it is we do it—can sense that one direction is going to be more productive. And you're trying to design a project so that when you're done, and you've done the experiments and you've shown that it worked, people will say, 'My God, I would never have thought of that in a thousand years,' and learn something from it." Allan cites the fact that there are fewer female chess masters than male chess masters as further support for his view that women are not as comfortable as men with the required intuitive leaps.

In his interactions with colleagues, Allan deals with females in the same way as males. He is "sensitive to the fact the women have a hard time competing in science because they haven't gotten to a critical mass in a lot of fields yet. And I'm sensitive about that because, for one thing, my wife's a woman scientist, and I sympathize with the problems that women have to go through, living in an almost totally male environment sometimes." Allan mentions that the women he knows in his field are "being terribly imposed upon" by all sorts of committee work, a specifically female obstacle in his opinion. "There is such a demand on their talents to be members of all sorts of things—review bodies, study sections, NSF advisory reviews. There is so much of a mandate to involve women in various activities, and there are so few of them." These appointments, honorific as they may be, tend to distract the women from their research. Allan also notes a case of "reverse discrimination," in which a certain woman scientist received more acknowledgment than her work deserved. But he adds that there may be women who are as good as this woman scientist but have never achieved any recognition because of discrimination.

Allan's idea of a good life is to be happy with one's position in life. "Anyone who has the blessing of enjoying what they do has a good life." He is satisfied with his life in general. "I feel very fortunate to have had the kind of life I've had to this point through being involved in [my science]."

Key points:
- Benefited from relations with mentor
- Focuses on hot topics
- Maintained career while being a single parent
- Uses collaboration as valuable resource
- Struggles with decreasing self-confidence in face of increasing success

Allan exemplifies another American Dream success story. Rising from an inauspicious background, he became one of the leading scientists in his field. He stumbled into his career by taking advantage of a series of lucky coincidences. At several junctures, mentors were crucial in setting him on track for his eventual career: inspiring teachers in college, a professor in graduate school, and his postdoctoral advisor. His major career obstacle was rooted in his family life (being a single parent), a difficulty that appears more typical for women than men.

Contrary to the popular stereotype that women are more intuitive than men, Allan believes that a deep-seated lack of intuition in women makes them less suitable for research in his field. One wonders to what degree such a belief, held by a senior and influential scientist in the field, sends discouraging signals to women scientists and curbs their intuition or even turns them away from this particular specialty.

One of the most intriguing aspects of this biography is that self-confidence apparently decreased with increasing success. Although Allan abounded with naive self-confidence when he started his assistant professorship, he is now tormented by the thought that he may not be able to repeat the outstanding advances he has made and will slip from his prominent position in the international science community. According to Vijh (1987), this fear is part of the psychological makeup of many scientists. Its underlying cause is the recognition that creativity and intuition cannot be forced or controlled. Allan relies on intuition to a particularly high degree. His humble origins taught him resilience and hard work, but these characteristics are not sufficient to overcome a creativity block. Thus Allan, like many scientists and members of other creative professions, fears that the next great idea will never materialize and that he cannot do anything about it. Additionally, the more elevated one's position in the science hierarchy, the more prone one may be to a conspicuous decline if the wellspring of brilliant ideas runs dry.

Allan thrives on the division of labor between himself and his students and postdoctoral fellows: he generates the ideas, and they put them to use in the laboratory. Whereas many other scientists yearn to do actual experimental work, he is content to leave the experiments to others. Because he values recognition in the scientific community, he focuses on hot research topics and appears to be unafraid of competition. This is contrary to the noted tendency in some women scientists to carve out a less competitive niche for themselves.

Brad

Brad is a tenured professor at a prestigious university. He is in his mid-thirties, married with two children.

Brad was the third of seven children. The family moved frequently when he was a child. His father was a physician who had also worked as a medical researcher. His mother had wanted to go to medical school like his father; but although she was the valedictorian in her college class, she was rejected by all medical schools because she had a child. Brad's mother probably "had a bigger influence on my desire to study science than my father did."

"I always liked to take things apart, I guess. When I was two, apparently there was a real ruckus because my neighbor would not let me take apart her stereo." From early on, he found "you can do things and make the world work." By the age of six or seven, Brad was soldering electronic gadgets together. He had always been interested in science, but a serious, focused interest developed in ninth grade when he entered an experimental science program. "Three excellent teachers let me know at a very early age what science was like and what it was all about." They had a profound impact on his later career path.

All seven children "in our family went to college, at the minimum, and that was just kind of the natural thing to do." Brad attended prestigious X University, where he discovered that he was "badly underprepared," especially in mathematics. He failed the mathematics exams in the introductory classes but caught up quickly; "and by the third term of the math, I had the highest score in the class."

> The thing that saved it was that [X University] had put the whole freshman class on pass-fail. They realized there was a big diversity in training of the incoming class. And by doing it pass-fail, they gave people a chance to catch up. If that hadn't been the case and if I had been under pressure to earn some sort of respectable grade the first year, I probably would have dropped out and gone somewhere else; but the fact that [X University] was clearly more interested in seeing whether I could learn than trying to put me through a rat race of some sort, that was probably a very big factor.

During a summer job, Brad developed a scientific interest that was shared by his undergraduate advisor. Brad started to work with the advisor on the problem, which turned out to be very important and "eventually became the major piece of my Ph.D. thesis and about two-thirds of my publications so far." In his senior year at X University, he received a fellowship that allowed him to spend a year abroad after graduation.

That year he also applied to graduate schools and was accepted by five prestigious universities. He chose Y University because it offered to count his fellowship abroad as the first year of graduate school and to supplement the fellowship with their own funds. Brad also held an NSF graduate fellowship.

Early in graduate school, Brad presented a talk at an international conference that garnered widespread attention. This event instantly made him a sought-after expert, and he was invited to collaborate with researchers in various countries.

After completing his doctorate, Brad remained at Y University, spending two years as a postdoctoral fellow. He then joined X University as an assistant professor and took over the laboratory where he had worked as an undergraduate. His work has pioneered an entirely new field of research. He has received tenure and is currently an associate professor.

Brad is satisfied with the course of his career. "Not for a second" has he contemplated abandoning science. He thinks good scientific work requires complete identification with one's profession. He rates the degree of his ambitions "about average. I don't plan to build a kingdom in the sky, and some of my colleagues would like to do that. I want to do my science."

Although from the beginning there was no doubt that Brad wanted to be a research scientist, he had no fixed focus on particular research problems. "I think my actual course has been taking the path that is easiest and most interesting in some combination of the two. I don't know if I had a clear goal as to what I wanted to do in graduate school, for example, when I went [there]. I knew I had things that I was interested in and I wanted to work on, but I didn't really have a sense of having a very clear direction. On the other hand, I didn't worry about it."

Brad attributes a great deal of his career success to "a bit of blind luck. I found myself at the right place in the right time. . . . You can be very competent, but if you don't have any luck, you don't get anywhere." Brad also considers himself fortunate in securing grant support. He suspects he may have benefited from a sort of geographic affirmative action by the agency that awarded his fellowships because he kept his residency in a smaller state rather than in the larger state to which he had moved for college.

Brad mentions an internal quality that makes him well suited to his work: "I have a lot of crazy ideas. But somehow I seem to be able to sort the crazy ones from the not so crazy ones. A lot of our undergraduates that we teach get lots of crazy ideas, but the ability to tell the crazy ones from the not so crazy ones is probably the worst problem."

As a major obstacle in his career, Brad describes a confrontation with a former department chairman. He recounts that the chairman's actions during that controversy "shattered my naïveté about academics." He went the "route of consensus," consulting with many of his colleagues; and after a year the conflict was resolved in his favor. "The whole episode strengthened my resolve, shook me out of a bit of pacifism to a bit more activism in terms of directions I think this department should go in." His stubbornness increased. "I guess I'm not easily pushed in terms of what I want to do. I'll do something if I want to do it and if I'm interested in it." He considers himself fairly self-assured. "Having weathered a rather major storm," he also feels more resilient than before.

As an internal obstacle, Brad mentions a lack of efficiency. "I'm not as efficient as I could be. I mean if you look at my office, you see it's a disaster area." But efficiency seems to improve with experience. "I worked harder as a graduate student than I do today. But I think I'm more efficient now than I was as a graduate student."

He characterizes his working style as "erratic. Scientific method is nice, but I don't know anybody who uses it. That's not what drives experiments. You interpret the results and you think about it, but the scientific method leaves no room for inspiration." The aspect of science he likes best is discovery. Breakthrough ideas might happen anywhere, anytime. "You may get good ideas while on a surfboard on the beach. In fact, one of my best ideas came from a surfboard on the beach, when I was learning how to surf in Hawaii. I was sitting there paddling and it suddenly occurred to me to do a certain experiment that worked very well. The moral of that story is that the government should fund scientists to go to interesting places."

Really good scientific work is characterized by the "spark of creativity." It provides "a new dimension, open[s] a new field. I would be less sympathetic to somebody working in a field that has already been developed for a hundred years, and just digging the pit of knowledge another foot deeper. I'm much more interested in somebody who starts digging a new pit and opening a whole new area of human endeavor." His quality standards are "probably harsher" than the current overall standards. "Bad science is science which for one reason or another is not reproducible, does not stand the test of independent replication."

Brad's definition of power in science is unusual. Instead of concentrating on the power relations within science, as the former fellows we interviewed usually did, he talked about the relation between science and the government. He notes that in other countries, such as Japan and France, scientists and intellectuals inform the government and enter government positions to a higher degree than they do in the United States. In his opinion, the quality of government in these countries benefits from the involvement of scientists, whereas American government suffers from a gulf between science and policy-making.

In the same year when he was hired as an assistant professor, he married a woman whom he had met at an international conference. His wife works as an associate research engineer. They have two children. Brad says he has merged his private and professional lives to an extraordinary degree, but occasionally he does feel some tension between the various roles in his life. "If there's a paper that I'm trying to write, or an experiment that I want to do, and it's a choice between doing that or going out and teaching your son how to ride a bicycle, yes, there's a tension." His marriage had a very beneficial impact on his career, "just in terms of mental stability." It also prompted him to be more cautious in terms of his personal safety. "Having a family changes those perspectives a little bit."

Brad considers himself politically aware but not politically engaged, although he has been a founding member of an organization that battled successfully against a state's creationism law. "That's 1 percent or less of my time, really, but lending my support and advice for something like that, I like to do."

What he values most, Brad says, is honesty and truth. "And that is fundamental to the science, as well as to personal interactions." His idea of the good life is one "in which a person has the freedom to use his ability to the fullest extent possible and is not constrained by the environment to prevent it." An example of a bad life would be working "under a European style of professorial rule, where there's the chief professor of the laboratory, and he directs everybody beneath him what to do. That would be my hell." Brad is very happy with his life.

Key points:
- Has pioneered work in new field
- Took advantage of his early success in graduate school
- Is successful in departmental politics

Brad is very much a "natural" scientist—and something of a scientific wunderkind. He came from a scientifically inclined family and since childhood has had both scientific curiosity and a basic optimism that he would eventually succeed in satisfying his curiosity. At an early stage in his career, during graduate study, his work catapulted him to international prominence. He took advantage of this early renown and began to act like a full-fledged academic scientist. His perspective is extremely science-internal. Firmly rooted within the world of science, he looks at it from the inside, whereas many other scientists, especially women, also look at it from the outside—as one option among alternatives. For Brad, being a scientist was never an option; it was a premise. He naturally belongs to science, although not necessarily to any of its conventional subdivisions.

Brad is an example of the innovative, maverick scientist whose scientific style is erratic and spontaneous. Following his creative inquisitiveness, he transcended traditional boundaries between the fields and created a new field. Not surprisingly, he encountered problems within the social system of science. Not all scientists appreciate or accommodate maverick research that does not fit neatly within one of the traditional disciplines of science. But he had enough political savvy to weather successfully a major controversy in his department.

Charles

Charles is a successful scientist in his early forties. He is married, and one of his wife's two children from a former marriage lived with them for a while.

Charles "had some conscious sense that I wanted to do scientific research on [a particular subject] from the time that I was probably thirteen or fourteen years old." His father was a pharmacist. "I think initially he might have liked the idea of my becoming a physician, but I think he figured out pretty quickly that that wasn't the kind of thing I wanted to do. I didn't want to have to deal with people's problems." His parents were very supportive when his inclination to be a scientist became clear.

A high school teacher in science was crucial in steering Charles toward a science career "inasmuch as she probably recognized that I had a penchant for science." This teacher encouraged him to apply to an NSF-sponsored summer program where he worked with a scientist who "became a model for me. . . . Not only did I admire him as a scientist, but I admired him a lot as a person." Charles went back to that summer program for three additional summers.

During his college years at prestigious X University, he "spent a lot of time working in a laboratory." Although he has since shifted away from this particular kind of research, it was a good experience and "kind of solidified my direction."

For graduate school, Charles went to renowned Y University. His graduate advisor had "a real devotion to research science and a kind of single-mindedness about it that gave him over completely to research. And he had made a decision not to do much else—that is, a lot of the other things that I have found that academics normally do, like going to meetings, and having lots of students, and serving on grant review committees and such, and getting involved in departmental politics. I thought that [the advisor's working style] was the ideal way for a research scientist to live."

Charles finished graduate school during the Vietnam War and was classified as a conscientious objector. While he did two years of alternative service, he "would come into the lab evenings and try and keep my hand in things." The scientist with whom he worked at that time introduced him to a research topic that is still part of his research program.

After his alternative service, Charles went abroad on a postdoctoral fellowship, where he learned a technique that became very important in his field. "So I was quite lucky, actually, to get involved with [my postdoctoral advisor] and learn [the technique] near the beginnings of its development."

Charles returned to Y University as a research associate and later became an assistant professor. He then moved to Z University, where he progressed through the academic ranks and is currently a full professor. When he came to Z University, the chairman was "a kind of father figure" who had a "real love for basic research" and thus was influential in hiring Charles.

Charles feels he has made the most of his opportunities. "In general, I've done what I've wanted to do with the opportunities I've had. I don't have any regrets or wishes that things had gone otherwise." Charles thinks good luck played a large role in his professional success. "I'm a firm believer in luck. All the things that are significant that occur in one's research career result from some kind of lucky break on the one hand and, on the other hand, from what the individual is able to do with it."

Satisfied with the course and the achievements of his scientific career, he thinks he faced fewer obstacles than his average colleague. He rates his scientific ability and technical skills as above average. His ambitions are now about as high as those of his average male colleague and higher than those of his female colleagues. "The men that I've interacted with tend to be a lot more ambitious" than the women in the competitive aspects of a career. At first Charles knew and cared little about the politics of science, but he became more appreciative during the course of his career.

> When I started out, really all I wanted to do was to do good science. I'm not sure that very many young scientists at the time—and certainly not me, although I may have been naive—had any clear picture of the politics and hierarchies involved in science. And without that kind of picture, it's a little bit difficult to develop ambitions beyond just doing good research and being recognized as somebody who does that. Like most others in the field, as I became more sophisticated or was involved in more of the realities of academic science—issues like promotions, awards, appointment to committees, whatever—I became more realistic. To be promoted became an issue; to be recognized, to be appointed to editorial boards, those kinds of things all became things that I wanted to achieve.

Charles is resilient because he has a "basic optimism that whatever it is that I have to do, I can do. [I have] the sense that I have been lucky when it has really counted. And it's almost as though there's something out there that's watching out for me, so I don't have any reason to think that things are going to change or there's any reason to quit." He describes himself as hardworking and energetic, especially when he embarks on new projects. The ethics of working hard have been instilled in him by his parents. He feels self-confident "in professional and scientific settings, not so much in a social setting." His professional self-confidence springs from "lots of reinforcement and success." His uneasiness in interacting socially has "been part of me from a very early time. I was a very shy and introverted kind of person for most of my growing up. Through most of my graduate career, and a good part of my postdoctoral career, I, for a couple of personal reasons, wasn't particularly happy with my social interactions, and my way of dealing with that was to bury myself in the lab." Thus, his personal unhappiness translated into the single-minded pursuit of science. He was a self-styled workaholic.

During his second year at Z University, Charles took a leave for three months to reconsider his priorities. He decided to come back to his academic career, although at times he regrets his straight career path. "There certainly have been times when I have wished that I had, for example, taken time off between college and graduate school or things that a lot of students seem to be more likely to do now, than when I was going through, but I just went through straight."

Although he never felt that he did not belong in his chosen field, he constantly contemplates abandoning science. At first his restlessness was caused by frustration and lack of patience, but increasingly "it has to do with the issue of wanting something new to do." Charles likes to get involved in new challenges and gets bored easily once the novelty wears off. He considers his lack of patience a personality trait that is detrimental to his scientific work. "I tend to be a person who really enjoys doing new things. I'm not all that keen always on taking things all the way to their final conclusions, because I tend to get bored with them." Charles does not think it is necessary to identify completely with the science profession to make significant contributions, but he also mentions that people who become eminent scientists tend to do so.

Charles thinks that being male has influenced his way of doing science. "I tend to be very linear in the way I think about things. And by and large I think that tends to be useful in doing science, although as I get older, I have developed a little more global way of seeing things." Furthermore, in his opinion, men benefit from the cultural reinforcement of useful personality traits. "It's easier [for men] to develop self-confidence, and people reward you for doing the kinds of things that you'll be doing as a professional in a career. Self-confidence is really important in any kind of career, and certainly in science, and I've seen it as a problem for a number of the female students and postdocs I've had in the lab. It's not that they're any less capable or any less bright but they just haven't had the benefit of growing up with that self-confidence."

In general, Charles thinks that male scientists "tend to drive themselves harder." Women scientists who have established themselves in his field have "a greater tendency to become over-extended because they seem like they want to take care of everybody and everything." Charles observes that women scientists have sought his help with their problems more often than men have. "I've had more experience with women crying in my office because of some difficulties they were having, not necessarily with me, but because of something happening on the job and they came to talk to me about the problem. I don't see that happening too much with men. At least in my experience, [women] are more apt to come in and air their problems, and look for help."

Among the criteria for selecting the scientific problems his laboratory works on is "a healthy sense of obligation, that if I'm being supported by taxpayers' monies, then we ought to at least think that we're working on something that's going to benefit the public at some point in the future." In recent years, publishing a large number of papers has lost some of its overriding importance. "My priorities have changed from running a productive lab in the sense of putting out lots of papers in high-profile journals, to a lab where students and postdocs are getting trained well. Now those are not mutually exclusive ways of running the lab, but my priorities tend to be now more invested in the students and postdocs." He notes an increasing "interest and enjoyment of really interacting with people."

Really good scientific work "poses problems that will engender lots of research in the future. So it's not necessarily answering a question that needs to be answered, but rather developing hypotheses that will spawn a lot of activity in the future." When Charles started out, he oriented himself toward the nitty-gritty, which in his observation is typical for young scientists in his field because working on detailed issues is easier. Now, by contrast, he considers himself a good integrator who likes to construct the big picture. This is precisely the aspect of science he likes best. He also enjoys the hands-on experience of doing experiments. He sometimes wishes he could spend more time in the laboratory, "rather than deal with all the administrative kinds of things."

Charles is aware of his prominent position within the scientific hierarchy. "I have a significant amount of prestige and power in my field; I'm recognized as a leader." He agrees in principle with the current system of deciding about the funding of research. In his opinion, this system strikes a fair balance between being elitist (giving resources to laboratories and individuals with established scientific track records) and democratic (providing opportunities to researchers who have not yet proved themselves).

In terms of time, his work takes clear precedence over his private life, "but when conflict arises, my private life is invariably the winner." Currently, he does not feel a tension between the various roles in his life. His marriage to an artist helped him to become more balanced and sociable.

> There's a lot of science that one can do alone, and so if you are an unpleasant person, that doesn't mean you can't do science. If you get angry, get angry at yourself. People will stay away from you, but you can still do science. That doesn't work in a relationship. So as I learned how to deal with some of those personal things in my marriage, that translated over into how things worked in the lab, and that's changed quite a lot. Most of the people around here would be really surprised to know what an angry young man I used to be. I expect that my growth as an individual would have been less if I had not had the benefit of interactions with a woman who is wanting to develop herself.

Charles considers himself more politically aware than average. He was heavily involved in a failed presidential campaign some time ago, but since then his activism has "dropped back pretty much." He characterizes his political views as liberal. He also identifies with his religious heritage. He thinks that this heritage has had an impact on his professional life because it "has always put a premium on academics as something that was to be valued."

His idea of the good life is to have "relationships that are fulfilling, working in something that you enjoy doing, making enough money at it to not have to worry about where the basic necessities are going to come from." He is satisfied with his own life.

Key points:
- Has unintentionally followed a straight career path
- Became sophisticated in the politics of science
- Experienced "de-nerdification"

Although other scientists, particularly women, have a strong internal predisposition to be scientists but follow circuitous career paths, Charles does not necessarily present himself as a "natural" scientist even though his career path was extremely linear. He even regrets that his path was so straightforward and wishes that he had taken some time off between stages of his education to reflect on his future. His linear career path is somewhat paralleled by his proclivity toward linear thinking, although here, too, Charles has increasingly taken a more reflective, "global" position. The internal force countering all this linearity has been his restlessness. He still thinks of abandoning science because he lacks patience, likes new challenges, and gets bored easily.

Charles describes a profound transformation in his life that could be termed "de-nerdification." From childhood on, he was shy and felt uneasy in interactions with other people. Unhappy about his lack of social relationships, he fled from his ordinary loneliness into the dignified loneliness of the laboratory. He became an angry and short-tempered science hermit who barricaded himself in the lab. His graduate advisor, who was similarly unsocial, served as a role model and legitimated this life-style. Charles credits his marriage to an artist with making him more sociable and mellow. He now increasingly enjoys teaching and has made the training of his students and postdoctoral fellows a priority.

David

David is an assistant professor at a prestigious university. In his midthirties, he has recently married and has no children.

David had a childhood interest in topics of the scientific discipline in which he now works, although he had no particular desire to be a scientist or researcher. In his late teens, he taught science as a counselor in summer camps.

David hardly mentions his years at a lesser-known college. Although he majored in his science, college "didn't really prepare me in the least to do research science. Even my science courses were not oriented towards research. I think as an undergraduate, I really only had to write one research paper, in my very last course as a senior. That's just appalling, when I look back on that. Most of it was pure memorization. There was little conceptual development, especially in terms of getting across the really interesting part of research, the looking and finding, the testing of ideas. That part was totally lost." After obtaining a bachelor's degree, David resumed his counselor-type science teaching for some time before he decided to enter graduate school. "I think it was the decision to go back and try and learn more about what I was teaching, for a master's degree, that got me sidetracked and interested more in the science part and the research part. For me it was very valuable to have taken time off between a bachelor's degree and a master's degree, and later I took time off between master's and Ph.D." During his master's studies, interactions with fellow students and faculty increased his interest in science; but at the end of the program "I still wasn't sure what I really wanted to do, and I was applying for positions and looking for either work in education, not at the college level, or a research position." Part of the reason for not staying in graduate school to obtain a doctorate was the terrible employment situation for Ph.D.'s in his field at that time.

For two years, David worked in research positions. He did not like the first one, which "taught me what I didn't like about research," but enjoyed his second job, when he worked for a very good researcher. The interesting work that he was doing greatly influenced his decision to go back to graduate school for a Ph.D., "regardless of the job consequences. Meaning that I decided to do it because I wanted to get the Ph.D., to do the learning part. I knew that the future job market was so bad that I couldn't be assured of anything."

In hindsight, David believes that the years spent not working on his degree were not lost time. "Those in-between years were extremely valuable in shaping events that happened for me, I guess. Connections I made when I wasn't in school helped tremendously in getting research money and so forth to make it through the Ph.D." He did not receive much help from his doctoral advisor, a woman who did not have "a large outreach with other people. She was not a person that helped place her students in jobs. There is definitely an old-boy network, and I've found that to be somewhat of an obstacle, because I didn't have particularly an entrance into that network." Moreover, his advisor was "more involved in being a single parent and doing other things in her life."

Even during David's doctoral training, "it was very, very hard to commit myself to go down that path" toward a research science career. But his research went well. "I was able to work on something kind of unique, and that got people's interest." His successful research also led to the award of a postdoctoral fellowship that "was pretty critical in a lot of ways for me." The fellowship gave him time to publish his doctoral work. It provided "that lag time that was so important for those credentials to be accepted. When I was applying before I had finished my Ph.D., the year I finished and the following year, I got very few nibbles, and yet when I was applying a couple years later—it wasn't that much that was different about me except that my dissertation work was now published—people were interested enough to hire me." David also considers the post-doctoral fellowship a time of intellectual growth because he worked with colleagues who did good and interesting science. In addition, he made a number of useful connections with other people through his postdoctoral collaborators.

After his fellowship, David obtained an assistant professorship at prestigious X University, where he had worked for about two years at the time of the interview. He knows that it is highly unlikely that he will receive tenure in his department. The transition from postdoctoral fellow to faculty has been quite a change for him, not all of it positive. As a postdoctoral fellow, "I had few restrictions; I had few responsibilities other than just doing my own research. The difference between that and now, where I am constantly bombarded and interacting with students or committee assignments or things like that, is something I think about now and again." He also realizes how his "connection with a first-class university makes a distinction in how people are willing to view [him]."

Both of David's parents are college-educated, and they were generally supportive of his plan to go to graduate school. But "by the time I was three quarters through my Ph.D., they were wondering if I was ever going to stop studying this [research problem] and do something else with my life, like get a real job and settle down. They had certainly a lot of concerns about the circuitous kind of path and the different sort of interim positions I had had before I wound up settling down."

David describes his success as a combination of good luck, hard work, and perseverance as well as taking risks that paid off. In a sequence of lucky coincidences, he was able to secure several research grants—they "just sort of snowballed, one thing on top of the other." He thinks he "just happened to sometimes be at the right place at the right time." For instance, when he applied for a research job after his master's degree, "I also decided to knock on a few doors" at other institutions in the area, which eventually led to the grant that funded his doctoral research.

But taking advantage of such lucky turns of events also required "a lot of hard work along the way, mainly in the way of perseverance. . . . I had the attitude that I was going to just keep trying, and that helped me. When I failed I would try again. The first paper I submitted for publication got rejected; it wasn't very good. But I tried again; I rewrote it and reworked it and so forth" until it was accepted. It was clear to David that he had to focus on the "publication process, because that seems to be where so much of the emphasis is put. . . . My perseverance to follow through with these things until they were finally published has made a big difference. A lot of my colleagues or friends don't always do that, and whether we like it or not, unfortunately that's how we're being viewed, by this publication yardstick." David sees the source of his resilience in the work ethic that his parents instilled in him.

His "willingness in several instances to take a risk paid back in big ways." For example, he used all his dissertation funds for thorough data collection, which left him with no money for the writing-up phase. Fortunately, he then gained another fellowship that allowed him to complete his dissertation.

His greatest career obstacles are the general lack of jobs and funding. A particularly difficult period occurred after his Ph.D., when he had no appointment for a year. As another obstacle, he mentions a certain narrow-mindedness in academe that shuns interdisciplinary and applied efforts that are more to his liking. He considers his Ph.D. advisor a career liability "because she just wasn't connected into the scientific community." He also had to endure a period of bad luck when his research project would not progress. David notes that "one of the things that has been different about my career than the careers of my other colleagues is that pretty much most of the research I did was work that I set up. A lot of times, master's or Ph.D. students are plugged into research problems by a major advisor. And my work wasn't that way at all." Thus, unlike most of his fellow students, David could not benefit from the background work that others had already done.

As internal obstacles, he mentions deficiencies in language and social skills that go back to his childhood. He describes himself as "an awkward, gawky teenager in junior high school. My verbal skills weren't as strong as they could have been." He also had difficulty in behaving strategically toward people in positions of influence. "I wasn't particularly very good at massaging people's egos." His interests outside science used to distract him from his research. "My broader interests were at times very much an internal obstacle towards moving ahead in this scientific endeavor. I was spending time doing things like volunteer work within a community, instead of devoting all of my energies to the science part. Those things sometimes were viewed negatively by my professors. And eventually, you sort of clip down those parts of your life. They get hedged away and turned off as you go through this process."

During his education, David often felt that he did not belong in his chosen field and doubted his intellectual abilities. Now, however, he has overcome this insecurity and feels self-confident. He thinks that the social system of science is set up to crush the beginning scientist's self-confidence, almost as a rite of passage. "They make you lose your self-confidence. It just seems like it's part of the process."

David started with "relatively modest" career aspirations. "I liked teaching and so I had thought that I would want to do some teaching. I also liked research, and I looked at the Ph.D. as a Red Cross certification as a [scientist]. This meant that I had done my basic swimming instruction and I could now teach someone else to do that." In the course of his career, he revised his ambitions upward and now rates himself as more ambitious than his average male or female colleagues. He is satisfied with his career so far and feels he has surpassed his original aspirations. In the past there have been times when he contemplated abandoning science, but now he is settling into being a scientist. Still, he does not consider himself a naturally gifted scientist. "The science part didn't seem like it came as natural to me as it seemed to come to other people. I had to work harder on those kinds of scientific skills."

In his scientific work, David does "very little theory development. I've been mostly involved in testing basic theory, and then oftentimes applying that to [more concrete] problems." He thinks his work falls somewhere between basic research and applied research, although applied work used to carry less prestige in the academic community. He mentions several main characteristics of good science. First, it is "a rather creative sort of infusion across different disciplines or across traditionally different ideas, perhaps, to assist in development of theory." Second, it is rigorous theory testing. And then the "icing on the cake is if you can apply it to something that someone outside of the university is interested in." Compared with the overall standard in his field, David considers himself somewhat more theory-oriented and interdisciplinary. He chooses problems "that have had some kind of unusual twist to them," that are important to theory and have some practical applicability.

David believes he might have more power in the social system of science than his average cohorts because he is located at a very prestigious university. But he considers this difference in power to be small.

He thinks that women face unique obstacles during their education, but if they successfully complete it, they receive some advantages in the hiring process. "Right now, it's favorable to be a woman in my field. Women are to some degree sought after because of the imbalance of sex ratios in the departments. For instance, the job I have now was first offered to a woman who turned it down, and many of the recent positions that we've offered here have been offered first to women."

The women's movement has had a profound impact on David. "It's influenced me in terms of my own personal philosophies. I became aware, and I think it's been a positive influence. I've been personally involved with women who were very involved in the women's movement, and I also look at it as being something that will be good professionally as well."

In David's opinion, gender plays a lesser role in the ways men and women in his field do science and a greater role in the social hierarchy of science: some men may "feel that they can dominate" the women. In general, he sees no difference in his interactions with male and female colleagues, but "there have been times that there was underlying sexuality that either caused difficulties or made it easier for things to happen professionally." David thinks that the fact that his doctoral advisor was a woman did not affect their interactions, but it did negatively affect his career development. As already mentioned, his advisor had the difficulties, somewhat typical for women in science, of being relatively isolated in the collegial network and heavily involved in child rearing.

David says he is especially aware and engaged politically, much more so than his average colleague. He used to work actively to remedy social problems, but this involvement gave way to the demands of his work. He considers himself a liberal and a humanist. He identifies strongly with his ethnic heritage, but this identification does not influence his professional life.

Science has clear priority over his private life. He notes that his discipline requires a higher degree of dedication to, and identification with, science than other disciplines do, depending on the particulars of the scientific methods in those disciplines. He feels tension between the various roles in his life and wishes it were more balanced. "At the early stage of academia, you're not rewarded for balancing particularly; you're really rewarded for being maniacal about doing science."

David married only recently. Earlier, he had consciously refrained from marriage to maintain his independence and freedom as he furthered his science career. He was extremely flexible geographically "in order to take best advantage of what was there for my career. . . . Not having great debts or sort of family commitments made those things more feasible for me than for some of my other colleagues. So I wound up delaying those kinds of things in my life, which other people aren't always willing to do." David especially observed a severe strain on scientists' marriages in graduate school. "For both men and women, graduate school is extremely difficult on personal relationships. Many of my friends who were married through that time have gotten divorced. I don't know if it's particularly more accentuated in sciences than it is in other fields, but it seems like it's just a very trying period for relationships for both men and women."

His idea of the good life comprises the freedom to work on the scientific projects in which he is interested, a life in a naturally beautiful and culturally developed environment with people he loves, and the conviction that he is "contributing in some way to society." David is "relatively satisfied" with his own life. "If there's a place that needs work, it's the balancing part between the science and the private life. I would like to be able to have more time to do the things that I used to do ten years ago, before being involved in the fast track, and all this stuff."

Key points:
- Understood the importance of networking and publishing
- Took large risks that paid off
- Succeeded despite difficult job market
- Put family life on hold while establishing career

David has always had a diffuse interest in the topics of his science, but his path into research science was circuitous and obstacle-ridden. He committed himself only very late to a career in research science; and among the successful male scientists we have described, David had to struggle the most, owing mainly to a bad job market in his discipline. Although he believes he is not a naturally gifted scientist, David advanced in his career through hard work and perseverance, risk taking that paid off, and several lucky breaks. A crucial career advantage was that he clearly understood the importance of putting out publications and making networking contacts with people in his field.

Another contributing factor to his success against all odds was his choice to delay marriage and parenthood. He was very flexible geographically and pursued all opportunities for career advancement regardless of where they were located. Now, after obtaining relatively stable employment, he is married.

A crucial question is whether a woman could have sequenced career and private issues in a similar fashion. David's "one-after-the-other" solution may not resolve a woman's "either-or" dilemma. It was relatively unproblematic for David to postpone marriage, and possibly parenthood, until after he was established professionally. Women, however, cannot delay child bearing indefinitely. Thus, the potential costs of the postponement strategy are higher for women; and at some point they may feel forced to focus their energies on family matters while their career is put on hold. Especially if there is a high risk that the career might fail any-way, women may be less willing to jeopardize their private plans in the hope of achieving professional success.

Erik

Erik is a successful scientist in his mid-forties who works at a presti-gious university. He is married for the second time and has two children.

Erik comes from a farming family. After graduating from high school at the age of fifteen, his father received a full fellowship to attend a uni-versity. "He was the oldest of three sons, it was the height of the Depres-sion, and his parents refused to allow him to leave the farm. That was the end of his education. And he was basically trapped in that situation the rest of his life and was quite unhappy about it." Erik's father, always bit-ter about this denial of opportunity, was determined that his children, Erik and an older sister, would receive the benefit of a university educa-tion. "And I honestly don't ever remember thinking that I would not go to college. It was just assumed that would happen. . . . My folks would have killed me if I hadn't."

Erik's early career plans mimicked those of his sister, who first in-tended to go into medicine and then into law. For college, Erik applied to the Air Force Academy because he had "always wanted to fly." When this plan fell through, he attended X University, where he had already taken part in a summer program in science.

At the university he "went through a variety of [crucial] switches and other things," including a change in majors. Erik received a positive im-age of an academic's life-style through a professor who taught in the sum-mer program. Not only was this professor an exciting teacher, but he also belonged to Erik's church group and shared an interest in jazz. "So it made me see a more human side of the academician, aside from the professor standing there."

Erik's first research experience was working for two years in a re-search program as an NSF undergraduate research trainee. But he be-came interested in a research area that the professor he worked for detested. When the professor found out that Erik had applied to a gradu-ate program in this area, he canceled Erik's undergraduate fellowship. Fortunately, Erik was then hired as a research assistant by a newly ar-rived professor. He liked the work so much that he decided to stay at X University for graduate school and to work with this professor as his ad-visor. A graduate fellowship secured financial support. His advisor pro-vided training "not just in dissertation topics, but we were well schooled in the politics of science and got a full critique of every faculty meeting afterwards. I learned an awful lot about the politics of science as well as other aspects of an academic career. And we have collaborated ever since. So he probably was the person most responsible for where I am today." Erik considers him "probably my best friend as well as the most academically important person to me. I've talked about probably everything in my life with him."

Erik finished his graduate studies more quickly than planned and went abroad for a postdoctoral fellowship to avoid being drafted for the Vietnam War. After returning from the fellowship, he joined the faculty of prestigious Y University, where he moved through the academic ranks and still works there today.

Throughout his career, Erik was rather insecure, always afraid of stumbling at the next hurdle. "You're always looking ahead one step. I can remember being a graduate student, thinking that it was impossible that I could ever pass my orals. And then when I passed my orals, how could I ever write a hundred-and-fifty-page thesis? I had never written anything more than three pages. And then when I got to that step, how could I get a job? And once I got the job, how could I ever make tenure? And so I've always set sights relatively low." Even now, he considers himself not particularly self-confident.

> I've always in one sense been confident that intellectually I could do what I needed to do. But I was never particularly driven to excel. For a long time, and this goes all the way back to grade school, I always could just get by by not doing very much. I was very proud of the fact that I never studied in high school. I never took a book home, because I could always sort of get by. One, I don't think I ever knew what I really could do, and secondly, I guess I never really developed a lot of the drive that I needed to find out what I was capable of. There was always this nagging feeling that I haven't really quite made the most of my potential. And I have lowered self-esteem.

Erik does not want "to be a dean or vice-president or anything like that. I'm perfectly happy here." His professional ambitions are waning. "I think I'm starting to see some other qualities of life that I hadn't seen before and I'm more content. That's a natural process of getting older." Although Erik mostly fulfilled his original aspirations, he is not totally satisfied with his scientific career because he has not built "a sound financial basis for my science. I'm still having to scrounge too much for money [for my research program]." In the future, he would like "to play more of a role in the development of [his] profession" in terms of policy-making. He contemplated abandoning science maybe "once or twice, but I always felt I was totally unqualified to do anything else." Erik thinks that he has made the most of his advantages and opportunities, except for his postdoctoral fellowship. "That was a real opportunity to work with the very best people in the world in my field, and because of various personal crises, I spent much too much time worrying about personal matters."

As a particular career advantage, Erik names his series of fellowships in high school, college, graduate school, and the postdoctoral phase. "Every one of them was a key stepping stone. Without any one of those four, I don't think my career would have tracked the way it did." Erik also recalls several serendipitous opportunities that enhanced his career. In his opinion, luck played a substantial part in his career success. "I think the way people really succeed is being able to recognize when a good thing has happened and take advantage of it."

Among his advantageous personal traits, Erik mentions high intelligence and his upbringing in a family who taught him strong moral values, expected a great deal from him, and offered support. He also alludes to his even temper, which helps him avoid making many enemies. Although he does not consider himself a particularly social person, he has the required degree of political savvy. "I was well enough educated in the politics of academia that I came into a profession and was able to play the game to get through the tenure process, even if my science and teaching wasn't maybe as strong as it should have been. I think if I had been totally naive, I might have had a lot more trouble. In a place like [Y University] you certainly don't have individuals holding your hand. I've seen a lot of people who didn't make tenure because they didn't know how to play the game." Erik also thinks he is fairly resilient, "probably because I've never been totally knocked down."

Erik considers the draft for the Vietnam War a career obstacle. "That was a minor obstacle in retrospect, but at the time it was the most important thing in the world." He also experienced a difficult period in his mid- to late twenties, especially his postdoctoral years, which he describes as "a mess, personally. It was a pretty lonely period." He further notes the low salaries at Y University before the late seventies—another career obstacle.

At Y University, Erik's career path was generally smooth, with the major exception of a reorientation in terms of research fields. In his early years there, he found that he was stretching his capacities too thin by working in two distinct research fields. "My former mentor and I had lunch and said, look, both of us are trying to do the same thing, and we can't do it. So he took [one field] and I took [the other] and diverged at that point."

As an internal obstacle, Erik mentions that he is "basically a fairly lazy person. I can easily procrastinate and not do something that I should do. And usually things have to build up to the point where I get very nervous and uptight about not having done what I should have done, before I can push myself into doing it." He does not consider himself hardworking. "I enjoy just not worrying about anything. So I can lose myself in a book or a movie or the most ridiculous, inane television program on the air. I have the capacity just to sort of become a vegetable." On the other hand, he possesses a manic energy that enables him to "work twenty hours a day and refuse to take five minutes off." In that respect, he resembles his father, who "worked incredibly hard throughout his life."

Erik feels he faced smaller obstacles than his average male colleague. The half-dozen women he knows from graduate school all had very successful careers, in part because they came onto the job market when there was a demand for women scientists.

Erik believes he was strongly influenced by the women's movement. "Certainly the women's movement has made me more sensitive to my own cultural biases and I'm trying in some cases rethink them, in other cases at least keep my mouth shut when it [isn't] appropriate. It has certainly caused me to reevaluate what should be done in terms of providing more opportunity to women. I have a lot of trouble with affirmative action and the concept of affirmative action. In some definitions of it, I certainly subscribe to it, and in other ways I don't at all." In his favorite type of affirmative action, the scope of the search for an academic position is wider for women than for men applicants. For instance, men candidates should be considered only if their profile of prior research experience matches the position precisely, whereas women candidates should also be considered if they come from related subspecialties.

In Erik's opinion, women in science face the problem that too many demands are placed on them and they try to fulfill them all. "Every two or three years, I sit on a tenure decision case [of a woman], and the problem can very frequently be traced in part back to the fact that she tried to spread herself too thin. She thought she was expected to do too many things, and there were things she really wanted to do too. And she tried to speak to every third grade who called up and accept every undergraduate who wanted to work in the lab."

In a university setting, Erik sees no difference in the way he interacts with women and men. In the field, his behavior has depended on the personalities of the women scientists. While some women completely ignore the gender difference, he understands that others need some degree of privacy and consideration. He also reports that on a few occasions "interactions with women have become more personal than professional and then became uncomfortable, at which point I had to extract myself. But they were rather few and rather predictable and not really much of a problem."

Erik believes that, to some extent, genetic differences underlie the gender disparities in the selection of subspecialties and mathematic ability, but he thinks that cultural factors play a larger role. He notes that any allusion to genetic differences is a sensitive issue and particularly unpopular for a man to make. In terms of scientific approach and professional conduct, he sees no gender differences.

Erik's working style is "sporadic: fits and bursts. . . . The thought of an eight-to-five job always has terrified me." For him the hallmark of really good science is "integrity. There has to be absolute confidence that the work is as reported. Everything from initial hypothesis formulations to the actual methodologies that are carried out to the analysis and the writing up—the work has to be done and be presented in such a way and by such a person that everyone who contacts it believes that it was good science. That doesn't mean they have to believe it; they have to believe that it was good science." Top-quality science also "integrates a result into a larger body of evidence and knowledge. I think the really important science [breakthroughs] are those cases where somebody has either synthesized information—provided a key piece of information which allows us to make connections—or looked at things in a whole new way. And not everybody can do that." Erik considers his quality standards pretty much average in the field. He does not believe it is necessary to identify with one's profession to do good scientific work. "I don't think you have to be wedded to it a hundred percent of the time." What he likes most about science is the hands-on fieldwork and the presentation of the work in talks. He does not like writing up the research results, although he has published a fair amount of work.

Erik does not think he has a great deal of power, although he has served on some influential committees within his department and also in research-funding organizations. "People are aware of that, and they're very nice to you until you get off the committee."

His science career "and the rest of [his] life have been pretty constantly intertwined." He feels role conflict between professional and private demands. His marriage and his two children have reduced the time he can spend on research. The couple has faced severely limited job opportunities because they must look for two positions in the same field and location. The career of Erik's wife, who is junior in rank, would have greatly profited from a geographical move; but Erik could not move. Nevertheless, he considers marriages between scientists in the same field a frequent and natural event. "It's the nature of people to meet and fall in love and marry people that are like them. And I have never had a laboratory where not at least one of my graduate students was married or getting married or heavily involved with another person in the same field. It's just a fact of life."

Erik's idea of the good life includes the ability to explore ideas and the absence of a "routine work environment." Good health and having a family are also important to him. He is fairly satisfied with his life.

Key points:
- Succeeded despite having little drive
- Focused on limited research area
- Was aided by mentor's lessons in politics of science

Erik's early career path was to an unusually high degree determined by external influences: his father's frustrated ambitions for a university education and his older sister's career goals. The absence of a strong drive and inner direction, in combination with his somewhat erratic work habits, might have been the mark of an underachiever who could not fulfill his great scientific potential. But through serendipitous turns of events, Erik achieved a highly successful career in academic science.

His career also illustrates the benefits of having a good mentor who trains the aspiring scientist not only in research but also in the politics of science. His long-standing association with this mentor, which started in Erik's undergraduate years, goes beyond the professional sphere; it has developed into a close personal friendship.

Erik's wife, a scientist in the same field but with junior rank, experienced some career problems caused by limited geographic mobility, a situation typical of dual-career couples in science.

The people we have met in this chapter achieved great career success in academic science, but their paths to success differed. Some had charmed careers with few difficulties; others went through periods of adversity and hardship. Some were determined from early on to become leaders in science, while others ended up in this position more accidentally. In chapters 4 and 5, we will interpret the experiences of our profiled former fellows in light of the findings from our larger samples.

CHAPTER 3
▼ ▼ ▼

Taking a Different Road

Not everyone among the former postdoctoral fellows still works in research science; a small proportion of the interviewees (11.5 percent) left the field at some point after the fellowship. In some respects these people form a more diverse group than the successful academic scientists because they have abandoned research science for a variety of reasons and now work in different areas. The experiences of the men and women in this chapter offer valuable lessons about the obstacles, difficulties, and dissatisfactions that you might encounter as a researcher.

We emphasize again that leaving research science does not automatically mean career failure. Some of the former fellows have had very successful careers outside of research science. Moreover, society benefits from well-trained scientists who choose to work at the border between science and other areas.

FIVE WOMEN

Florence

Florence is a high-level academic administrator. Close to fifty years old, she has never been married.

Florence comes from an academic family. Her father was a science professor, and her mother was college educated. Her parents were "enormously supportive and helpful" throughout her career. "I grew up with this feeling that, of course, you would go into some kind of profession. I do not remember ever feeling particularly pushed." Florence was a good student without having to work very hard. She did fairly well in her high school science classes, but science "was not the great love of my life." The students at her high school were a "pretty select group. We all assumed, or most of us assumed, we were going to college, going to get advanced degrees or something like that. It was okay for girls to do well.

It is as if I was living in a very comfortable world. We were all going along doing about the same kind of thing, and you could take part in plays, in musical stuff, and wherever your interests led you. It was a very supportive environment." Her career plan during high school was to become a physician.

Although Florence had a good relationship with her parents, she "did not want to follow in their footsteps" when it was time to decide which college to attend. "I swore that I was not going to be involved in any place that my parents had ever been. I was not going to major in anything that either of my parents had anything to do with." In spite of these intentions, Florence did end up at prestigious X University, her parents' alma mater. It soon became obvious to her that she did not want to go into medicine, but she had no other clear plan. She pursued an interest in a modern language until she discovered that she had no particular talent for languages. This led her to a language-related field and an association with an impressive advisor. Still, "at that point, I was not particularly going into science, and it was not clear where I was going." Finally, somewhat accidentally, she got interested in the very science in which her father worked. She mentions one female teacher in this field who was particularly inspiring. Florence majored in this science and graduated at the age of twenty.

Although she took the Law School Admission Test (LSAT) in addition to the Graduate Record Examination (GRE), she decided to attend graduate school in science. Following her father's recommendation, Florence chose a small, personable, good-quality graduate school at Y University. There she held a teaching assistantship and was, for part of the time, supported by an NSF fellowship. Working with her advisor was "a wonderful experience," but the advisor did not publish much or train his students to write articles. When he received a fellowship from another university, he left Florence and another graduate student behind during their last year in graduate school. The school provided all kinds of support, but Florence suspects a continuing relationship with her advisor might have been preferable.

After graduating, she went abroad for a postdoctoral fellowship. Her research there was hampered by mishaps beyond anybody's control, but "I [also] made a couple of foolish mistakes in research that came out of my ignorance and my not having the guts to ask [the advisor] what he meant." She was somewhat lost and in want of direction, which she did not receive. "I could have done a lot more preparation and got more out of [the postdoctoral fellowship]. I did not bring as much to it as I should have, but I would have been better off in a less laissez-faire environment. In terms of my own life, I do not think [the fellowship] was wasted, but it was wasted in terms of research training." During her postdoctoral fellowship Florence started a job search, which was aided by a professor at Y University. While still abroad as a fellow, she was offered, and accepted, a position as an assistant professor at Z University.

Research was not emphasized at Z University, and Florence did not find a group of research-minded colleagues. Although she did some research of her own, "it is an uphill battle to do research by [oneself], particularly if it is scientific research that requires some skill, some assistance, some equipment. A mixture of my not having somebody to prod me there and not having developed as good work habits as I probably should have made it much easier for me to go towards other interests."

Florence was urged by senior faculty members to run for a faculty government post. "I got into faculty government that way, which really is what led me into administration. I did not plan to go into administration, but again, I was apparently relatively good at it and articulate and I survived." She went on to hold several, increasingly senior, positions in academic administration. When she entered administration, she carried a reduced teaching load, but she completely abandoned research.

Florence does not like administrative paper shuffling and the sometimes rude and cruel interpersonal style in her present job. "I can play the politics; I just do not particularly like it." But on the positive side, "I like being able to have an effect on things. I like knowing what is going on. I think that is probably what kept me in faculty government for a few years." Moreover, her administrative position allows her to draw on her special talents for understanding and empathizing with other people. "I care about other people a lot; I care about how they feel. I seem to be able to pick up other people's meanings and needs and where they are coming from. I am good at handling people in a group or individually. . . . From my high school days, my father told me that I could always see both sides of the question. Maybe that is part of my not having a single-mindedness that might have done me better if I had gone on in research. But I have always been able to see both sides of the questions from, like, three sides. I articulate them for other people. They are useful skills in a people-oriented administrative job."

When she started out in her career, she wanted to become a professor in her science. Beyond that, she had "[no]" explicit aspirations for the future, except that life had to be valuable, and useful, and interesting. . . . I have never been able to understand people who say, well, I am going to do two years here and three years there, and this is where I want to be in ten years. I understand maybe that is necessary, but I have never been able to do it." Currently, she rates herself as about average in terms of ambition.

Luck played some part in her career, mainly in helping her gain her first faculty position through personal connections. Her graduate advisor had taught a course at Z University. "So we knew them; they knew him; he recommended me. People also knew my father and so I got it: the classic old-boys' network." As further advantages, Florence mentions the fellowships and grants she received at various phases of her education. She also has a couple of close friends who have been very supportive.

Florence considers herself bright and quick in understanding research findings, but she thinks she lacks a firm formal training in mathematics and other disciplines. In hindsight, she regrets that her intelligence and ease of comprehension prevented her from forming solid work habits in her youth. In high school, "I could get by relatively easily; I did not have to study enormously. I could pass stuff with an *A*." She now characterizes herself as moderately hardworking and energetic. "I am not a workaholic. I can work very hard when it is necessary and when something has to be done, and I do not like doing things poorly."

Florence does not think she made the most of her advantages and opportunities. "I think I should have been able to, in some cases, be better organized and take more initiative. I recognize a timidity that I ought to be perceptive enough to overcome. But it is easier now that I am fifty than it was when I was twenty-five. But basically I think at times I have been a coward." Thus, she locates her major career obstacles within herself. She thinks her personality has sometimes prevented her from dealing with problems in an effective way. For instance, she should "have been able to have the self-possession and the initiative to have got more out of that final year of graduate study and that postdoctoral year." She also regrets the lack of mentorship during that period. "I do not think I was mentored in the way that, in retrospect, probably would have been helpful."

Professionally, Florence feels self-confident, but on a purely social level she does not. "I am still basically a somewhat timid coward at times." She regards herself as shy but not self-centered because she is able to see other people's perspectives. She has little trouble meeting people socially, but "I am not terribly good at the large social chitchat activity."

She is able to cope with the demands of her current position, although the interpersonal dynamics are sometimes unpleasant. "If resilient means being able to take it, cope, and come back again, I am resilient." Florence is also good at solving problems. "I am usually the one who can think of the way out of a predicament, if people are caught in a predicament, whether it is a matter of how you get from here to there when a rental car is not available or something far more theoretical."

She still identifies herself as a scientist and has plans to return to teaching, but "I think, realistically, I would probably not do any research." When it became clear that she would not be a research scientist, she experienced some feelings of guilt. "It is mostly the awareness that I have not used what I was trained to do as well as I should have that led to a feeling of guilt." Florence is not satisfied with the course of her career. "I wish something, either myself or something external, had caught me at a much earlier stage and turned me into a somewhat more thorough, disciplined person so that I had continued on with research. Because if I had continued on with research, I would frankly have more degrees of freedom now in what I wanted to do, even if I wanted to continue in administration."

Florence notices gender differences between scientists. She thinks that women scientists tend to be less single-minded in the pursuit of their research and more socially responsible and reasonable. But she also notes plenty of overlap in female and male distributions of these characteristics. Moreover, an assertive woman is likely to be seen as "bitchy," whereas a man with the same degree of assertiveness does not elicit such a negative reaction. In her opinion, older women were socialized to have other interests besides science and not to identify solely with their scientific profession.

In respect to her interactions with female and male scientists, Florence says that she works as effectively with men as with women; but she has never mentored any men in the way she has mentored some younger female scientists. She has more female than male personal friends among her colleagues.

Although a female professor in college warned her that "it is very difficult to go on in [this science] because you will find a lot of prejudice against women, I do not really think I have experienced anything like serious sex discrimination. I have certainly seen and been in a general sense subject to sort of macho sexism, but not in the way that has had any significant effect on my career, partly because I could always talk back smarter than they did."

Although Florence is not active in the women's movement, she is sympathetic to its goals. She rejects the claim that women scientists face no special difficulties. "It is clear to me there are difficulties, and there are certainly prejudiced men. However, I find it is easier, and I think one is more effective, if one finds a nice, joking way of conveying that rather than being hostile." This low-key approach also corresponds with her self-described personality. "I was never a terribly assertive sort of person, always very socially aware of how other people reacted to me and things like that, so I am certainly not suggesting that I was anybody's role model for going out and making great waves in a place where women were not appreciated."

According to Florence, really good science consists of "a sophisticated experimental design to address a well-articulated problem that is, in fact, a genuine problem." By contrast, poor science is sloppy work that neglects to control or eliminate very obvious alternative explanations. Designing an experiment is the part of science that Florence likes the most. She hates writing up her research, and that "has usually been a stumbling block." She does not think she has been able to do top-quality work and rates her ability as a researcher as about average.

Florence says, "I always expected to get married and have children and work in a profession on the side; I did not see myself as a single career woman. Never happened. But in some ways, I still like things like gardening and cooking and stuff like that. And it is very clear, as my other single friends and I agree, everybody needs a spouse, a wife, somebody to do some things for them, if only to take the cat to the vet. But I mean there are some things in which I am [a] very traditional female. . . . There were times I saw myself going on as a single career woman and not wishing to do that. There were times when I was in a sense more successful administratively or getting elected to things than I really wanted to be. But there was not, at any one of those times, any reasonable alternative." Thus, remaining single did not result from a conscious decision to put her career first; it was due to not meeting the right man. "Had I been married, had I had children, I do not know what I would have done. I am not at all sure that I would have continued. It is not that I had ambitions to end up in this particular direction."

Politically, Florence considers herself aware and engaged and holds moderately left-wing views. She also identifies with her religious background and belongs to a church-related group that works to alleviate the plight of the homeless.

Her idea of the good life includes "living with people you like as well as respect and doing something to contribute to the world." Another aspect is "being able to live a comfortable-enough life which means enough money and time that you can enjoy the world, flowers, vegetables, animals." She says she is moderately satisfied with her own life. For the future, she entertains the plan of buying a farm because she loves growing things.

Key points:
- Lacked mentorship and guidance
- Began academic career in department with no research support
- Was promoted into academic administration

Florence's family background seemed to foretell a scientific career for her. Indeed, at one point she even tried to distance herself from her parents by selecting a different college and concentration; but in the end she closely followed in her father's footsteps. Nevertheless, she had neither strong ambitions nor any substantial long-term plans for her career—she merely went along with the flow of events. Like Deborah, Florence has reflected intensely about her internal personality flaws. She thinks that she lacked work discipline and was too timid, especially in the early stages of her career.

Florence's career testifies to more resilience and strength than her self-characterization as a "timid coward" suggests. She appears to be more critical of herself than an outside observer might be. After all, she has become a resourceful, high-level academic administrator who, although she does not enjoy the competitive atmosphere of her workplace, can certainly hold her own in confrontations.

The most likely cause for Florence's departure from research science is that she took a position in a department that was not research-oriented—probably because earlier factors prevented her from compiling a track record strong enough to make her a plausible recruit for a prestigious, research-oriented department. She appears to have been held back by a lack of mentorship at the graduate school and postdoctoral levels and have struggled with unforeseeable problems during her postdoctoral research. At a critical period in her career, Florence needed strong guidance because she was not independent, self-motivated, and outgoing enough to carry out a research program alone. With the right direction and guidance, she could have become a successful research scientist because she appears to possess the necessary talent.

Florence's career in academic administration is, by most standards, a success rather than a failure. Moreover, from a societal point of view, women should hold positions that influence science policy as her position does. But she personally regrets leaving research science. Although Florence wanted a family, she never married. Thus, she ended up as a career woman—almost, she says, "by default."

Like Erik, Florence had the talent for science but lacked the drive. Both were potential underachievers, but Erik became a successful scientist while Florence left research science. The crucial difference? At the end of his college education, Erik met a mentor who became an important influence on his later career; but no one gave Florence guidance when she needed it. As a result, Erik secured a job at a premier research university while Florence joined the faculty at a less prestigious university.

Gail

Gail works as a science consultant for the government. She is in her mid-thirties and married but has no children.

Gail developed a particular interest in science in high school. "In grade school, there wasn't much emphasis on science at all, and I never thought about it. But when I went to high school, I had a really excellent [science] teacher, a woman. I went to a girls' school, and I think that made a difference, too. [Science] was fun, and, all of a sudden, here was something that just made sense. I still wasn't planning to become a scientist at that point, but at least I got into it and I played with it a lot, and I liked it."

When Gail started college, she did not intend to major in a science.

> I spent a year doing other things, and I found that I really missed taking science courses, and I missed playing around in the lab, so I started taking [one science], and at the end of my sophomore year I decided to major in [a second science]. But there was no particular person or event that really triggered that. Part of it was just dissatisfaction with the other courses I was taking, and courses in the social sciences in particular would just not be as exciting. I liked the idea of studying something that wasn't about human activities, but something that was about the world at large. I also liked the fact that [science] was supposed to be something that girls weren't good at. I know a lot of women are turned off by that, but there were a number of us who really were turned on by that and felt challenged by that.

After college, Gail worked for two years as a laboratory technician because she did not have a clear idea of what she wanted to do next. The laboratory proved to be an inspiring environment. "The person I worked for was somebody I had a lot of respect for—it's hard to call him a mentor because in a lot of ways he really wasn't—but he was somebody who was very thoughtful and very rigorous in his thinking, and somebody I wanted to be like. Working with the postdocs in the lab gave me the same kind of feeling. I liked the way they thought about things and their approach to things, and I wanted to be like them."

This experience prompted Gail to go to graduate school—which turned out to be a very trying, frustrating time. The laboratory she joined was in turmoil. A graduate student who had recently earned a reputation as a young superstar had just left, and the people in the laboratory were discovering that the main findings of his "groundbreaking work" were irreproducible. Thus, laboratory members spent a great deal of time disproving much of their earlier work. "People were stuck in this ugly and depressing and frustrating situation for a period of years, and there was a lot of general, free-floating anger and frustration. The situation was made worse by a lot of ancillary factors—various personalities that were involved, even the floor that we were located on. Our lab shared a floor with two other labs that were basically world-famous and full of extremely hyper and competitive people, and so we shared a lot of facilities and space with basically crazy people." Despite the unfavorable conditions, Gail managed to write a thesis and graduate. Yet she started to question her commitment to research science. "I suspected that one of the reasons why I was unhappy was because I really didn't like doing bench science, but I was so miserable for so many other completely legitimate reasons that it was really hard to figure out what was going on. I decided I was much too depressed and unhappy to make any kind of important decision about my life."

To give research science another try, Gail took a postdoctoral fellowship in a slightly different setting and research area. The fellowship was a much more rewarding experience than graduate school. The head of the laboratory was a woman who ran it in a more formal and open fashion than her graduate school laboratory had been run. There, the "old boys" had made the decisions in a totally informal way, thereby excluding Gail from participating. In the postdoctoral laboratory, however, "decisions would tend to be made at group meetings, instead of informally at the bar with whoever was there. [The director] would go out of her way to make sure that everybody had a voice, that everybody knew what was going on. If there was information that everybody needed to know, it would get posted or it would be sent around the room with a routing slip. She didn't rely on informal ways of transferring information. And it was just little things like that that made such a difference."

Gail's postdoctoral project was interesting, and she completed it successfully; but "as much as I liked thinking about science and talking about science, I really didn't like doing science—I really didn't want to be a research scientist. And at that point, I felt like I could make a choice to be something else. It was more a free choice. I wasn't running away from something, and so at that point I decided to move more toward policy. It has been the best decision of my whole life. I love what I'm doing now, and I'm having so much fun." Gail became a consultant for the federal government and has worked in the policy area ever since. Although she has left research science, she still uses her scientific training in her present job. She wants to keep open the option of returning to academia at some point in the future—most likely, however, to a school of public policy rather than her science discipline.

Gail's original career aspirations focused on academia. "When I was working as a technician, I really saw myself very much like the person I worked for. I never had fantasies of Nobel Prizes, but I could see myself being a professor, running a small lab, doing interesting and respected solid work." Her actual career diverged from these original aspirations, but she is satisfied with its course and her achievements. She considers herself less ambitious than her average male colleague and equally as ambitious as her average female colleague.

To a family who was "totally blue-collar," Gail's science aspirations seemed somewhat strange. "My family has never been able to figure me out. But my family has a real live-and-let-live attitude, so when I zoom off and do something, they just shrug, like, 'well, there she goes again.' [Science] was just another one of those wacky things I was going off to do. It's not as if they weren't supportive, but it's not something they would know how to be supportive about. My parents always gave me the impression they were proud of me, but there wasn't much beyond that." Sources of support included her friends, many of whom had similar interests, and her brother. Yet the most important help in times of difficulty has come from her husband, whom she met in graduate school. They worked in the same department but in different laboratories.

Gail's postdoctoral fellowship was a crucial career advantage. "When you come to a lab with your own money you're definitely treated differently. Fewer demands are made on you, and you have a lot more freedom, so that was very nice." She thinks that luck is always involved in doing research. Sometimes experiments work as hoped; sometimes they do not. Although she considers herself lucky in her postdoctoral research, her graduate school experience contained "an element of bad luck."

In Gail's opinion, she has encountered greater difficulties than the average male scientist in her field. "It's obvious men are taken more seriously; men do have it better, I don't care what people say. It's not as bad as it used to be, but it's still true." In hindsight, she feels she should have been more assertive during her graduate training. "There were points during that period where I could have taken the initiative more, where I was being pushed by certain postdocs into projects that were less desirable. I should have fought back. But I also felt very dependent on these postdocs to teach me things."

Moreover, she says she did not have the "entrepreneurial spunk" she considers necessary for scientific success.

> Being a successful scientist really means getting the grants, making yourself visible in the scientific community. You can't just be a quiet little scientist holed up in a small lab. P.R. is important. When I was in graduate school, some of the people down the hall from us had some little slogan about "who needs data when you've got style?" And it was very much the atmosphere—being able to talk a good game is always more important than anything else. Certainly when you watch tenure decisions at major universities, it becomes very clear that what matters in getting tenure is one's market value more than anything else, and that's really a function of going out and speaking at meetings, and developing some sort of presence in the scientific community. And that's something that I find totally weird and can't do.

As a further career obstacle, Gail mentions that she lacks the enormous amount of optimism that she regards as a prerequisite for a successful science career. "I don't have a high enough tolerance for frustration that you need to be a scientist. Most of the people I know who are really successful scientists are incredibly optimistic people. No matter how bad things get, they know the answer is right around the corner."

In her view, she has always been resilient, hardworking, and energetic. But her self-confidence was fragile during her somewhat traumatic graduate school experience. Now, however, she feels self-confident. "Having a little success makes a big, big difference. My postdoc position did an awful lot to restore my own faith in my abilities. And being here [with the government], I feel like I've really found my niche. I love what I'm doing here and I'm good at it."

As to gender differences in doing science, Gail notices differences in professional conduct. "The men were much more likely to fight over who got credit for what. They have a harder time pitching in to do the kind of shitwork that everybody has to do in order for it to get done. You always hear that women have never played team sports and have a hard time working cooperatively, but that's not what I saw." Gail "found it easier to collaborate with women, and easier to share space with women because they were never as demanding as men and didn't expect so much from me."

Gail thinks she was subject to subtle forms of discrimination. In graduate school, the male postdoctoral fellows treated her and other female graduate students in a very condescending way, which she partly attributes to gender. There was also an informal old-boys' network that excluded women. "The lab had a lot of male-female problems. The head of the lab was your basic absentee landlord. Most of the postdocs were male, and there was a lot of going out to the bar to watch football together and that kind of thing that I really felt excluded from."

She also felt alienated from her male co-workers because of their different culture, preferences, and tastes. "There were lots of times when I felt they had all these things in common that I didn't share: their love for science fiction and 'Star Trek,' for example. And other people seemed to also have a greater interest in science at a level of detail that bored me stiff. I could just see that I didn't always have the same interests that other people had. And that's when I felt like I don't belong here." There were also entirely different ideas of fun. "I remember they used to do this old stupid frat-boy stuff, and I didn't feel like I was a part of this at all."

Good scientific work is characterized, according to Gail, by simultaneous attention to the big picture and minute details. "Really good scientific work requires that you think on two levels at once, which very few people can do. You have to be able to see the global picture—what are the important questions in the field now. And then on another level is this very fine and minute thinking of choosing a model system and experiments in which you can address very specific questions and gather data on a very precise and minute level, but which have relevance to this bigger picture." Furthermore, top science "involves addressing new questions, or really breaking new ground. And that requires not only a lot of intelligence but a great deal of courage and self-confidence. The best people have not only smarts, they're brave enough to take those risks." In contrast to high-quality science, "the worst science is stuff that's just really sloppy—where people make claims for things that they haven't really demonstrated in their work, that the data doesn't show. Next to worst stuff is [work that is] just irrelevant. I mean, you did it well, but so what? Who cares?"

In her own scientific work, Gail tended to avoid high-risk problems. "Since I really hated dealing with frustration, I wasn't the sort of person who would go out and develop new techniques. I wasn't one of these people who took the hugest risks. Mostly I liked to look for things that had a little bit of a twist to them. I liked problems that I could solve with a little bit of creative thinking rather than by brute force."

Gail thinks she was not able to do top work in science and rates her ability as a scientist as average. In her view, the quantity of publications is an important but generally overrated aspect of being a good scientist. Her own publication output was "definitely unspectacular."

She liked two aspects of science best. "I liked planning the experiments, and I liked it when you had some new data and you could sit at your desk and think about it and figure out what it meant, especially if you got something you hadn't expected. It was the part in between that was the problem." The basic attraction that science has held for Gail since her high school days is its practical usefulness in "explaining the things that you see every day. . . . It's just a style of thinking that I really enjoy— and a way of thinking about the things around, rather than thinking about some exotic, wacko, outer-space thing."

Gail is married to a scientist in the same discipline; they have no children. He works as a professor in a different city, which is a few car-hours away. The couple has two apartments, one in each city, and lead a commuter marriage. Gail's career has "always been more important than my private life." She does not feel any tension between the various roles in her life "because my private life is very quiet, and I don't have a lot of demands there." Career considerations have played a role in the decision not to have any children yet. "I've always felt that I wanted my career to be at least somewhat settled and moving in some stable direction before having children, and it's taken me a long time to get to this point where there is some stability. Of course, now that we have this wacky commuting thing, these are not the ideal circumstances in which to have children either, so this is all still up in the air."

She sees a general incompatibility between the structure of science careers and the life cycle of women. "The years in which you have to work the hardest and be the most dedicated are child-bearing years. And for men to have to commit so much of their twenties and thirties to working like maniacs is doable, but for a lot of women it's not. When women stop and have children and then try to go back, they have a much harder time. I remember once one of my friends had a long heart-to-heart talk with the chairman of my department when I was in graduate school. He was a very successful scientist in his fifties, a member of the National Academy, very liberated and correctly thinking and all that stuff, but I remember him telling her that at the better schools there was an age cutoff for assistant professors, and you would not be considered for one of those positions if you were much older than thirty-four, thirty-five."

Gail considers herself especially politically aware and engaged, much more so than most scientists. She characterizes her views as "middle-of-the-road Democrat." The women's movement had a great impact on her life by showing her that she had other options than becoming a housewife. Ethical principles rooted in her religious background influence her professional life in science policy.

"I think the ideal life is one where you use the gifts you have as best you can," whereas "spending your life using the talents you have for ends that don't really accomplish anything or won't ever benefit people in the long run" would amount to a bad life. She is very satisfied with her life in general.

Key points:
- Left research science at her own volition
- Attracted to practical aspects of science
- Was alienated from science culture
- Has a commuter marriage

A key issue for Gail was when to leave research science. She did not want to quit under the cloud of an unfortunate graduate school experience, which for her would have implied incompetence or failure. A successful postdoctoral fellowship enabled her to review her preferences freely and leave research science on her own terms, without any hint of inadequacy.

Gail prefers the down-to-earth aspects of science. She enjoys the scientific way of thinking as a means of explaining the environment around her and has less interest in the more esoteric and speculative facets of science. She also does not like doing the actual experiments. Given her attraction to the practical aspects of science and her lack of enthusiasm for the actual scientific work, her switch from research science to the policy area looks like a logical choice. She has since been a successful professional at the intersection of science and politics, a place where it is crucial to have competent scientists—including, of course, women scientists—in policy positions.

Although Gail does not recall any blatant discrimination in science, she thinks she was subtly excluded from the male old-boys' network. Moreover, she felt somewhat culturally alienated from her group of mostly male co-workers because she did not share many of their attitudes and tastes. Her preference for formal decision making in her female-run postdoctoral laboratory, rather than the entirely informal ways among the "old boys" in her graduate laboratory, may have a more general implication. The coziness of informality grows in the substratum of an implicitly shared culture. That is, certain sets of background assumptions do not have to be explicitly evoked; they are known as a matter of course. Outsiders (women and probably also minorities) may not share all the elements of this culture. Thus, a more formal and explicit way of running things may better safeguard their equal participation because it counteracts the hidden handicap of not knowing all the background assumptions of the dominant culture.

Gail and her husband have experienced the two-body problem of the two-career couple. Currently, they lead a commuter marriage and, partly because of this, have delayed starting a family. This delay cannot be indefinite, however, and at some point a decision will have to be made about whether to have children or not. If the couple decide to start a family, this may entail difficult adjustments in living and working arrangements.

Holly

Holly works for a major company doing technical work. She is in her mid-fifties, married for the second time, and has two children from her first marriage.

Holly grew up as one of eight children in a foreign country. Her father, a judge, was a major influence on her career; he valued learning and wanted his daughters to get a good education, which "was not at all common in [that country] for a woman in those days." Holly entered college but had to leave after her father died. When the family could no longer afford a college education for all the children, only the boys' education was supported. "Somehow money was found for my brothers, which I didn't even resent at the time. That's the way it was in those days."

Subsequently, Holly immigrated to the United States and became a housewife and mother. During her early thirties, she decided to go back to school. The initial impetus was studying American history for her citizenship examination. "It was much more fun than staying home and being a housewife, so I started going to school a bit more frequently." In this way, she finally completed her bachelor's degree at X University, although at that time she had no particular career goals. Several professors were "very encouraging and would suggest that I should go on [to graduate school]." Although her husband strongly opposed this idea, Holly pursued it; and in the process their marriage broke up. Thus, going to graduate school "did mean leaving my husband and my family. That was grim. For several years, I didn't have any money, and I was living in a slum. It was pretty rough. But I enjoyed the university. It was fine, and I got a whole lot of support." In her social life, however, she felt somewhat isolated. "I always felt a bit out of it, because I was older than most of the other students. . . . As far as faculty was concerned, they were my age, but I was a student, so it was quiet per se."

Around the time when Holly received her doctorate, her ex-husband remarried, and Holly took their two children to live with her. Holly's job search for a faculty position was unsuccessful, because the academic job market was bleak at that time. Consequently, she took a postdoctoral fellowship. After the fellowship, she obtained an assistant professorship at Z University and greatly enjoyed working there. Then she married a professor who worked at X University, her undergraduate school, which was very far from Z University. Her second husband, a tenured full professor, "couldn't get a job at [Z University], so it seemed it would be easier for me to find something over here rather than for him to find something over there. So I moved back."

She took some courses in another science and after a while found a job in industry with a major company. There she does mainly applied and technical work that is somewhat related to science, but she no longer considers herself an active scientist.

The women's movement has changed Holly's life. "Hearing about the women's movement and the realization that there were other possible careers beside mommy was very liberating." She recounts the occasion when she realized that a wider range of choices was available to her.

Years and years and years ago, when my children were very, very small, maybe in the late 1960s, I read in *Time* magazine about some woman who was at that time in her late thirties or her early forties. She had a seventeen-year-old child, and she was going back to some university that she had attended in her youth to get her master's degree in [a science]. I remember being astonished: could you imagine somebody age forty or thirty-eight, whatever, going back to school? And that's the first time it occurred to me that such a thing was possible. I thought the only people who could go to universities were people age seventeen-and-a-half. And that really opened the door for me.

When Holly started out in graduate school, she did not have a concrete career plan. "I was really more interested in learning about [a science] than I was in thinking of a particular career. I mostly went to school because I liked going to school. It wasn't to achieve something as far as reaching some particular professional goal. I assumed I would end up in an academic environment, probably. My models were academics, and I enjoy being around universities." Her intention of going to graduate school met with rejection all around. "My mother thought I was crazy. My brothers and sisters were amused at this middle-aged person's doing all this stuff. My husband was hostile. My children were suffering. The other housewives that I knew where I lived were very disapproving. So I was really pretty much on my own." Only some professors at X University were supportive. "They were about the only people who were working for you. Nobody else in my life was."

A crucial career setback was not finding an academic job after leaving her position at Z University. She needed a job and had to accept one at a major company, "but that wasn't what I had wanted to do, and that was very disappointing at the time." In the company she has seen "a fair amount of sexism, which I find frustrating. Sometimes, your opinion is discarded and people won't even listen to what you are saying because you are a woman. They assume women don't know anything." But Holly thinks that these incidents of sexism have not hurt her career. "I don't feel I was discriminated against. . . . They just kept promoting me, since I have gone there, and so things have gone well in that regard." But a recent disagreement with company policy has blocked her chances of further promotion, and she is thinking about leaving.

Financial support was a problem not only during graduate school but also when she was an assistant professor. "I was making an assistant professor salary, something like $18,000 a year, and I had two teenage children. They ate all the time. Money was very tight come the end of the month, and that was very hard. Assistant professor salaries are not geared to raising children."

Holly does not think she should have handled the obstacles she encountered differently. At her present position, she had a particularly supportive manager who helped her in difficult periods. She acknowledges the role of luck in her career. "I think luck always plays a role. [You] have to be in the right place at the right time." She also experienced instances of bad luck. She recounts how a program in which she worked was suddenly cut because the government canceled the research contract supporting the program.

As internal qualities that have helped her, Holly mentions energy and patience. She also considers herself resilient and hardworking. "I like working. I get a lot of satisfaction out of it. I like that feeling of achievement, of coming up with something." Holly considers herself self-confident and traces this trait to graduate school, where she learned how to handle intellectual challenges to her work. Graduate students had to give frequent presentations in the presence of several faculty members. These professors "would just lay into you, not in any personal way—in fact they were very nice—but they were pretty sharp folk. They were really interested in what you had to say, and they would challenge your conclusions and your interpretations." Thus, she developed a great deal of self-confidence "by the time I had gone through four years of constantly having to stand on your own two feet and speak for yourself."

Holly says she is straightforward in dealing with other people. "I am not political at all. I think people know that. I don't play any games." In her opinion, her "telling it like it is" has its advantages; but she also recognizes that, on occasions, it would be more appropriate to be tactful.

Holly does not think that being female has influenced her way of doing science in any way, nor does she believe that, in general, women and men do science differently. Her day-to-day interactions with male and female colleagues do not differ much, but she has "bent over backward to give [women] a break, to encourage the younger women more than I did the men, which may have been unjust on my part, but somehow I figured that men could take care of themselves."

Holly's working style as a scientist was to be very thorough and do very detailed analyses. But she also "sees a big picture" and does not get lost in details. According to her, really good scientific work has "to stick close to data." It also has to ask an important question and finally must achieve a theoretical synthesis of a variety of other findings to create "a bigger picture." The aspect of science she likes best is doing experiments. She rates her scientific ability as above average.

Holly is "not ambitious for power." All she wants is interesting and satisfying work. Although she did not fulfill her original aspirations of becoming a college professor, she is satisfied with the course and achievements of her career. "I had opportunities to go the management route at [my company] and I have always turned them down. I much prefer to do the technical work than to do managing work. But management is where you make big money. People build up their empires and all of that, and I have no interest in that at all."

Holly's professional life has priority over her private life, although it is sometimes difficult to reconcile these two areas. "If I were on my own, I would work longer, and maybe some weekends and so on. When I do have to work on weekends, I feel guilty about it." Her second husband is "very supportive" when she encounters difficult periods at work.

Holly is politically aware and engaged and holds liberal views. She has worked actively for a presidential candidate and has organized her neighborhood over a local issue. She identifies with her foreign heritage, but that has no impact on her professional life. She follows an ethical code that requires honesty and standing up against injustices.

Holly says that becoming a scientist was "very rewarding. I don't regret it at all. I am satisfied with the way things have gone." The only exception is her feeling that her departure for graduate school was hard on her children. "I regret that my children suffered. That's the only thing that I regret." Holly has now begun teaching one course at X University, and in the future she hopes to teach part time at another university. "I am too old at this point to be able to get a full-time job. Nobody would hire you full time at this stage."

Holly is "pretty satisfied" with her life, and her idea of the good life is close to her own. "I am doing work I like. I am married to somebody I like. I have children I like. We are comfortably off. [We are in] good health. What more can anyone want?"

Key points:
- Began science career at older age
- Enjoyed graduate education but was isolated socially
- Had to confront clashes between career and family life

Holly's career path exemplifies some of the problems experienced by many women who enter or reenter a science career at an older age. Her main problems lay at the intersection of family life and career. Twice, these two areas of her life clashed.

The first time, she decided in favor of her career. The emerging women's movement had opened her eyes to options beyond family life.

The choice to go for a doctorate was probably more difficult for Holly than for most scientists because it involved significant costs: leaving her marriage and her children. She acknowledges that her children suffered because of her departure.

The second time, she decided in favor of family life. If Holly had held on to her faculty position, she would have probably stayed in an academic science career; but her second marriage to a geographically immobile academic led her to quit this position and move to her new husband's place. This move, in effect, terminated her research science career.

Holly's educational experience was very positive and gave her strong self-confidence because she constantly had to overcome intellectual challenges. Socially it was more difficult because she felt isolated from younger fellow students as well as from professors of her own age. This feeling may be common among older students, both women and men. Social support groups, such as clubs for mature students, might easily address this issue.

In her overall evaluation of her career and her life, Holly sounds more positive than she does when talking about the details, such as the negative aspects of individual career decisions and her current job. It may be a general tendency to make a global statement sound more positive if one believes that, in sum, the positive aspects of a situation outweigh the negative ones. Or perhaps Holly needs to assert that her choices were right because she made particularly painful ones.

Irene

Irene works at a university in an administrative position. She is in her late fifties and married, with one child.

Irene grew up in a small rural town where educational aspirations were typically low. After her parents separated when she was six, Irene and her three younger siblings lived with their mother, who had started college but never finished. Although her family "was not the kind of family where for generations back everyone had been going to college, it was clear to me, without its ever having been formulated directly, that I would go to college when I finished high school." In contrast to prevailing attitudes in the town, the family expected educational achievement: "It was assumed that all the children would go to college." They all did, and all earned advanced degrees. Irene's father, who had dropped out of college, later resumed his education, earned a Ph.D., and became a scientist.

In her rural high school, Irene received an abysmal science education.

"The science courses I had in high school were unspeakably bad. There was no equipment. Basically we simply read through a science textbook with the aid of the high school principal who I don't think knew the first thing about either chemistry or physics." Consequently, during high school, Irene "never considered [science] as a possibility" for her future career.

Through some courses at X University Irene finally discovered her interest in science. She especially mentions one female science professor who had the talent to make even "quite deadly material become interesting and engaging." Generally, college was liberating for Irene. X University provided an environment that fostered intellectual excellence. "It was a place where it was assumed that everyone was interested in things of the intellect, broadly defined. And I found it a liberating experience to be somewhere where being thoughtful, being intelligent, wasn't a social drawback in the way that it was in high school. And having friends who were themselves very smart and articulate and interested in things was wonderful." Irene enjoyed the high-quality education at X University and found that she liked a particular science (her father's discipline) so much that she decided to continue studying it in graduate school.

"Graduate school itself was relatively uneventful." Irene spent two years in a master's program at Y University, which she did not finish. In a somewhat accidental way, she transferred to prestigious Z University. The faculty there "were not especially supportive, but that was their mode for anybody. I always thought it was a kind of 'sink or swim' graduate school." She married a graduate student in the same department. When they both graduated, he was recommended by faculty for jobs and received a number of job offers, but she did not receive any. "So I assume from that that nobody recommended me for any. And I also, looking back on it later, assume that that's probably because I was a woman. But at the time, I didn't ask about it, and didn't think a great deal about it."

Irene followed her husband to the place of his postdoctoral fellowship and found a research job relatively close by. After that year, she again followed her husband to another university, but this time she could find no job. The next year, they received and accepted a dual job offer at W University that entailed a full-time faculty appointment for her husband and a part-time appointment as a lecturer for Irene, with the understanding that, when the department expanded, Irene would receive a full-time position and a promotion. She found this arrangement agreeable because she was pregnant, and "working half time was a good solution to combining working and having a baby. I did not find it terribly difficult working a half-time schedule. One nice thing about academia is that you have a lot of control over your own schedule. You can decide when you're going to put your time in, and that means that you can coordinate that with the availability of baby-sitters."

After several years, Irene's position was converted to full time; but she initially did not receive the promised promotion to assistant professor. When asked, the university president said "he had thought that since I was a wife and a mother, I would not want to commit myself to a tenure-track position like assistant professor, but would prefer the flexibility of a lecturer's appointment, which I thought was rather insulting." Only after Irene insisted on becoming an assistant professor did she receive the appointment. She enjoyed teaching and doing research at W University, a great deal of which was done jointly with her husband.

The critical turning point for Irene's career was the denial of tenure. "That was, professionally speaking, a disaster." Irene thinks that she came up for tenure at an inopportune moment, when many universities thought they were overtenured and in need of new blood, thus raising the criteria for awarding tenure. At W University, "which prior to that had essentially almost always given tenure to someone who had stayed around for the full seven years, 90 percent of the people who came up for tenure that year did not get it. I was one of them. I felt then and I still feel that it was an absolutely wrong decision." Irene believes that by terminating her appointment, W University got rid of a good role model for potential women scientists because she "was successfully combining marriage and a baby with a teaching and research career."

The tenure denial effectively finished Irene's science career. "Since that time I have been unable to find an academic or full-time research appointment." At first, she tried hard to find another position and was even willing to consider a geographic move. But after five years, she gave up her fruitless efforts. "I don't think I ever even got an interview, and that's very discouraging. You feel that you're competitive, but you don't get any reinforcement for that belief." For a number of years, she worked as a research associate on her husband's projects. This was "not a wonderful solution. I missed having colleagues, and I felt rather strongly that it was a humiliating position to be in, but it was not bad in the sense that it certainly did give me an opportunity to do research." When research grants dried up, Irene could no longer be her husband's associate. She found a postdoctoral fellowship and several visiting positions, "an appointment as a visiting lecturer or professor here and there, but this never evolved into anything more long term." Eventually, she quit her science career and is now an administrator of a student-related service at W

University. "I regard it as a very low-level job in that this essentially requires administrative skills and a kind of savvy about what goes on in the academic world, but not much more." During the summer, she does some research with her husband without any official position or pay.

Rather than follow a long-term plan for her career, Irene always just took the next step, sometimes in a less-than-decisive fashion. "I always assumed I would go to college. At the end of college, I assumed I would go to graduate school. When I finished graduate school, I sort of assumed that I would get a job, but I didn't do anything to secure a job." She contrasts her lack of clear career aspirations with the explicit plans of cohorts, whom she calls the "potential Nobel Prize winners. They know from the start that they're going to end up with a professorship at Stanford or Harvard, and that they are going to do very important research, and that they're going to be recognized. And usually they're right."

For Irene, research has its intrinsic rewards as a "very intellectually satisfying activity." Receiving acclaim for it is not of primary importance. "It wasn't that I wanted to do research that would be universally recognized as terrific stuff. It was more that there were questions I was interested in answering, and doing research was a way of finding those answers. And as I enjoy the research process per se, I enjoy turning a question into an answerable question, designing the experiment, collecting the data. I enjoy all those aspects of doing research." Irene considers herself less ambitious than her average colleague, male or female.

She believes "luck is the great unacknowledged factor in everybody's career. It's not the only thing, but sure it makes a difference." A fortuitous event was getting the dual job offer at W University. An acquaintance from graduate school had joined the faculty at W University and recommended Irene and her husband when the university quickly needed to fill a vacancy. Irene considers it bad luck that she came up for tenure at a particularly inauspicious time. "If I had come up one or two years earlier, I would have had tenure without any question."

As a personality trait that has been advantageous for her scientific work, Irene mentions "a particular kind of analytic intelligence, a pretty high degree of verbal ability, reasonable quantitative skills, and a [scientific] point of view." She considers herself self-confident. When she was a teenager, "it never occurred to me that I couldn't do anything that I wanted to do. And I suppose that is a constant in the family." Throughout her life, "I think any job I have ever taken on I have been able to do at least as well as the average person and usually better." She also links her self-confidence to being "not as sensitive as many people to social expectations, social influences. Stuff goes over my head or off my back that other people who are more attuned would catch." Thus, she may have ignored signals in her environment that discouraged her from a science career. Irene thinks of herself as reasonably resilient. She works hard when she is involved in a particular project, but "I don't put in the kinds of hours at research that I think most successful researchers do." She thinks her energy level is "a little above average," which she believes is to a large part physiologically and genetically determined.

As a negative quality, Irene mentions that she has been too passive in pursuing job opportunities. Also, "in hindsight I can see that I could have behaved differently after I lost my job here. I think I was so reluctant to give it up that I spent a lot of energy trying to get it back and also feeling very bitter and angry. And those were wasteful emotions; they were nonproductive." She thinks she should have channeled her energy into her research, which would have made her more productive and improved her long-term chances of getting funding for research.

Irene rates her ability as a scientist as better than average and never felt that she did not belong in her chosen field. Consequently, she is not satisfied with her career. She would like to devote more time to research than she currently does. An academic position that combines teaching and research, just like the one she had at W University, is still her ideal. Irene regards her departure from science as a waste of human resources. "In some sense, it's society that gave me my training, allowed me to make my choices, but having invested really quite a lot of money in a graduate education, ended up not being able to use me in what I regard as a sensible way. A lot of training went to waste in the twenty years that I have not been able to find a job doing what I'm trained to do." She sees herself as a victim of the "Kleenex decade" of the seventies, when "institutions hired people for three years and then tossed them out."

Irene has not interacted differently with women and men colleagues. She believes that, on the average, there are no differences in the way they do science except in the area of professional conduct. "I go to conventions and watch male colleagues do what a friend of mine, another woman [scientist], calls displaying themselves. They start talking immediately about their research; they're not particularly interested in what you have to say about your research. It's an occasion to make a professional display of yourself as a competent, hardworking person. I don't do that and I don't think the women [scientists] I know do that either."

Except for the episode with the president of W University and possibly the lack of faculty support in her job search after graduate school,

Irene experienced "very little overt discrimination." She expects few women scientists to be conscious of discrimination against themselves; but in her opinion, substantial gender disparities on the aggregate level clearly indicate the persistence of discrimination. "So the fact that I or other women are not conscious of discrimination seems to me less important than the fact that many other indices indicate that discrimination does occur." She experienced a minor instance of sexism when the head of her department introduced one of her talks by dwelling "more on my physical appearance than my research capabilities. That made me uncomfortable and I think indeed it's a case where professional identity and personal identity were being confused by him."

Irene chose her research area as a graduate student and stuck to it. Her choice of methodology was determined by the particular graduate school and the supervisor with whom she did her research. She does not think good scientific work requires complete identification with one's work; but she recognizes that the more time scientists spend on their research programs, the farther they get. Good science, in her view, addresses an important problem. "You can ask lots of questions, but many of them are trivial, and a lot of people waste a lot of time on trivial questions." Good work is also characterized by a systematic approach, an attempt to disconfirm one's hypotheses, and the effective communication of results. Irene rates her own quantitative output of research as low, "but not so low as to be insignificant." The number of publications, in her mind, is one, but not the only, factor in determining the quality of a scientist. She thinks about power in science in epistemological rather than political terms. Science has "power in the sense of control over natural phenomena, the power that understanding gives us." What Irene likes best about science is "figuring out relationships" in her subject matter. Her moral and ethical standards, which place a "very high value on honesty," also influence her work as a scientist.

Except for regrets over the scarcity of time for the laboratory, Irene feels no tension between her various roles. In her present situation, she does not "have any trouble integrating various aspects. They all seem to me to be harmonious, but I don't have as much time as I would like to devote to research." Being married to a scientist in her own field had positive and negative effects on her career. On the positive side, "my husband and I have been collaborators, and I think we make a good team. And when I haven't had a job, he has enabled me to continue doing research. . . . I think having a supportive husband has been extremely important." On the negative side, there is the problem of finding two positions in the same location. Moreover, her husband is very conservative in terms of publishing research, and she thinks more of their joint research could have been published. But overall, "I would say that the pluses outweigh the minuses by far."

Irene does not think the women's movement influenced her professional life because "I always expected to have a career. I always expected to work. I always expected to be productive." In her personal life, however, the women's movement had a considerable influence. "It's made me rethink the relationship between men and women and aspects of marriage—what is reasonable to expect from marriage, from your marriage partner, and whether that should depend on gender."

According to Irene's view of the good life, "it is important to be productive in the sense of providing material goods or services that benefit other people." Other aspects of the good life are good companionship and at least a minimum of physical comfort. Finally, "one needs aesthetic pleasures, needs a little beauty one way or another." Although Irene feels that some aspects of her life could be better, she is fairly satisfied.

Key points:
- Took junior position in same department as husband
- Ignored strategic career planning
- Was denied tenure

Irene was forced out of research science against her will. She likes nothing more than being a professor, but she was denied tenure and has not been able to find a permanent position in academia ever since. In this case, the career paths of husband and wife started at the same point and later diverged radically. They met each other in graduate school and received their doctoral degrees in the same field at the same time. Then the husband got higher-quality positions while Irene had lesser positions or none at all. When her husband became a full-time assistant professor, Irene became a part-time lecturer. Her insistence led to a full-time, tenure-track position; but the denial of tenure precipitated a long process of marginalization that progressed through research associateships, fellowships, and visiting appointments and finally forced her out of science.

The major cause for the tenure denial appears to be bad timing. Another reason might have been that a tenure denial vindicated those who felt that Irene should not be on the tenure track in the first place. Moreover, the fact that most of her research was in collaboration with her husband, who was senior to her in the academic hierarchy, may have created the impression that she was only her husband's assistant, not a productive research scientist in her own right. Finally, Irene is an example of the "pure" scientist who is almost exclusively interested in the intellectual challenges and pleasures of science. She does not care much for recognition or work hard for career advancement. This disregard for strategic career planning might have hurt her career in general and her chances in the tenure decision in particular.

Remarkably, Irene's high degree of self-confidence was not undermined by her failed science career. By contrast, some of the highly successful scientists, both men and women, were much less self-confident and had a weaker sense of belonging in science than Irene did.

Jane

Jane is working toward a teaching certificate and plans to teach science in elementary school. She is about forty years old and married, with two children of her own and two other children living in the family.

Jane's parents were both college-educated professionals, but she hardly mentions them as an influence on her career path into science except to say that growing up in an "incredibly disruptive" family may have made her more resilient. Her formative influence came from outside the family, from "a wonderful [science] teacher in high school who had had a career as a research scientist before she was a high school teacher. She did special projects after school with a few students, and encouraged us to do science-fair projects. She really guided us toward self-defined and -initiated projects and helped us a lot in honing them down." This teacher also encouraged Jane to apply for a very competitive science program for high school students at a major university, but Jane did not get accepted.

She went to college at renowned X University, where she "just flew through science courses and did really well with minimal effort." Soon, however, academic pursuits were eclipsed by political activism. When a wave of "extreme student turbulence" swept X University, Jane participated in the student protest and dropped out of school. About a year and a half later, she decided to resume her college education. Because her parents insisted on keeping her at close range, she joined nearby Y University and majored in a science that she found enjoyable and easy. "I didn't have really good ideas of what you did with it, or what goals you would have after that, but I knew I could get a degree in [this science] without a lot of fuss and bother."

Jane enjoyed her studies at Y University but notes "an absence of advice and mentors." Her advisor was a woman in her mid-fifties, a "very capable and well-known scientist" but not a role model. "The more you got to know her, the more you realized she'd given up all personal life to be a scientist. She had a very lonely and isolated life." Jane applied to graduate school in her science because it seemed to be "the logical next step" given the ease with which she had mastered college-level science. At that point, her advisor "asked me to swear to her that I would never try to have a family at the same time, because it was impossible to juggle the two if I really wanted to be in science." When this happened, "some little warning flag went up, but I kept going."

"Without really knowing what I wanted to do," Jane entered graduate school at W University and chose her subspecialty because "it would give me a practical skill and application that would be useful to the world, and would give me something different to do than just being in an academic setting." In graduate school, she at first "fumbled around for a while without any sort of mentor, just not having a lot of respect for my professors." Finally, however, she connected with an excellent mentor, "a very wonderful man, and probably the best scientist I ever worked with—very supportive. I think I was the first female he'd ever had as a Ph.D. candidate." Although Jane enjoyed working with this mentor, she realized that he treated her differently from her male cohorts. "What I started to notice was that although I had his support, he wasn't tapping into his network for me the way he did for his male grad students. There didn't seem to be, in his mind, the push to have my career be a success. Or he was uncomfortable with a female. I don't know what it was. But there was less introducing me at meetings."

After her doctorate, Jane went on to a postdoctoral fellowship at prestigious Z University, where she disliked the extremely competitive "dog-eat-dog" atmosphere. People had to "hang on to their own little pieces of research, because somebody else might steal them, literally." She also felt too tightly integrated into larger research projects over which she had no control. "I don't think I'm a person that functions very well in lab settings where there are lots of people doing little pieces of a problem. I like to have a sense that I have my own area, and I also think my talents are more for observation and my own deductions than for being a cog in a whole string of reasoning of somebody else's."

At the end of the fellowship, when it became time to apply for assistant professorships, Jane was so disillusioned that she seriously questioned whether she should embark on an academic career. She still loved doing research, but the required "level of commitment and sacrifice of the personal life just didn't seem worth it. I began to feel this emptiness, that I was giving up all the other aspects of life to be around these people I really didn't care for. Really the question was 'Do I love research so much that I can put up with all this other garbage?'" Jane "kept coming in second" on several applications for assistant professorships; and "when the chance for a married life and a more normal kind of existence came along, it just didn't seem like a choice at all." She got married and became a part-time research scientist in a federal research laboratory. Although she loved her research, the work conditions were miserable. She earned very little money, could only come home during the weekends because of a long commute, had no health benefits, and worked on month-to-month contracts. Moreover, on the publications of her own research results she was listed as second author.

After a few years at the laboratory, Jane received word that the grant that supported her work had not been renewed. On the same day she found out that she was pregnant with her first child. At this point, she effectively left science. She would have continued research if she had obtained a part-time research position at her place of residence, but she did not find one.

When Jane started out in science, her somewhat fuzzy career aspirations centered on teaching and doing research in academia, "and not more ambitious than that. I didn't think that I was going to aim for a Nobel Prize or anything." In general, she considers herself much less ambitious than her average male or female colleague.

As a career advantage, Jane notes that it was always very easy for her to obtain scholarships and fellowships, "I think mostly because they were based on grades, and I'm a natural student." She feels privileged to have received all those scholarships and fellowships during the course of her education. Moreover, she "thinks scientifically, much more than many women I know." A further career advantage was that during most of her twenties, Jane was "fairly satisfied with a solitary life." Only when she approached the age of thirty did her priorities begin to shift toward her social life.

Jane does not believe luck, good or bad, played a significant part in her career. She thinks that, compared with women scientists of her age, she met with about average obstacles. But she recounts several instances of gender-related discrimination and mistreatment during her career as a scientist that ranged from outright job denial to subtle social exclusion. For example, in one case her job application was rejected in favor of a clearly less qualified man. When she asked about the reason, she found that the people who had made the decision had taken it upon themselves to protect her marriage. "They said that they thought I had just recently moved to [this city], and it would be too disruptive for my husband to move for a job that they would offer me. So they didn't want to put me in that position of making that decision. They knew that my husband had a good, special job here, and they thought that my marriage should be supported as well."

Jane also notes that "certain things were clearly closed to me. There were little social hours and stuff that involved male camaraderie, that I really didn't feel like busting in on. But I knew that those were the places where hiring decisions got worked on, and I think there's an enormous ignorance, still, on the part of male scientists about the experience of female ones. And that really is detrimental. . . . You have to be prepared to be totally your own advocate, and in a different way than the males are, because they're taking care of each other. You have to be prepared to just forget about the image of the bitchy female, and go ahead and get what you need."

Moreover, her Ph.D. oral examination was an uncomfortable situation. She was before "a panel of eight men, all over forty-five, who interrogated me for two hours, and there wasn't a woman among them. And I guess I was forced to realize that this was the society I was joining. There were some questions that were pretty off-the-wall, and there was this underlying kind of discomfort: 'What am I getting myself into?'" She recognizes that the examiners meant well toward her, but she perceived an awkward, paternalistic quality in their interactions.

In Jane's opinion, these instances of gender discrimination negatively affected her morale more than her career. "It's hard to keep up your own steam when you have three or four of those experiences, which I certainly did." At the same time, she did not have a clear concept of what happened during those experiences. "I don't think I could have described well enough what I was experiencing when it was happening to get help with it."

She credits the women's movement with clearly articulating, or naming, experiences of discrimination that previously were not acknowledged as such. According to her, the movement enabled women to understand the way in which they were treated, to realize that it was wrong, and to resist it. "Even in the early seventies, most people in academia did not put a name on [the mistreatment of women]. And the experiences were taken for granted. Right now, at [W University] campus, issues of sexual harassment are finally being prosecuted. And female grad students are putting names on it, are just saying what they experienced, what we all experienced. But we had no framework to come forward with it; we just joked about it. . . . Now, I wouldn't tolerate certain treatments that I did receive. In my present state of mind, things that I just swept under the rug would be intolerable. . . . I just couldn't see beyond the limits of what was around me, which women didn't challenge. And there were no women in any positions of power."

Jane's strong work ethic stems partly from parental models, partly from enjoying the work, and partly from feeling a sense of responsibility toward a greater community. She considers herself assertive, more so than most other women she knew in graduate school. In contrast with her female cohorts, she had no trouble changing advisors if she felt they were not good. Still, she thinks she should have been more self-confident and assertive at certain points during her past career. "Now I think that I should have replied in very direct and coherent ways when somebody said, 'Well, we didn't interview you because we wanted to protect your marriage.' I should have come back and said, 'Well, please don't do that to anybody else. I'm sorry.' That was a big mistake in my case. There was a clear point when I should have replied, when I didn't."

As regards her working style as a scientist, Jane liked "to sense that I had my own area, that I wasn't just a cog. And so I tended to generate my own area. I think I probably could be much more cooperative now. But I had that sense that things would be taken away from me." Among the characteristics of really good scientific work, she mentions originality, "a new synthesis of stuff that was already there," thoroughness, and simplicity. The hallmark of bad science is, first of all, dishonesty. Jane thinks that her own standards for scientific quality were more demanding than the overall standards in her field and does not believe that scientists have to identify completely with their profession to produce good work. She rates her ability as a scientist as probably above average.

Jane never doubted that she belonged in her chosen field. "I enjoyed the work. I enjoyed what I was studying." She was attracted to her particular field because the results could have some beneficial practical applications and because it advanced knowledge. "I'd know something that nobody had ever known before." Doing the actual research was the aspect of science that she liked best; she enjoyed "the quiet, meditative hours in the lab." Jane thinks that being female influenced the way she did science, especially in terms of scientific procedure. In what she considers a typically female approach to research, she "loves looking at things closely" and makes close observation rather than "picking up the threads of somebody else's reasoning" the starting point of her research.

Jane feels that the current social organization of science, with its intense competitiveness and separation from a "sense of a greater good" in terms of service and responsibility to society, is inherently "seedy and brings out a lot of bad human behavior. There's enormous damage done, not just to the individuals in the lab, but to their families, and to the people they're supposed to be teaching. . . . If it were a different kind of society, I'd probably be making some kind of contribution with my training that would be far less based on competition, but more on the skills that I have. I'd be working at something that could be done in six- or eight-hour days that would use my skills and my training."

Although Jane does not think she made the most of her advantages and opportunities, she is generally satisfied with her career. She is currently preparing herself for reentering the labor market by working toward a teaching certificate for elementary school. She plans to teach science in public schools.

Before Jane was thirty, her career had clear priority over her private life, but then the priority reversed. Getting married and having two children were important elements in that shift. Her family obligations also limited the geographical options for her science career. "Because I married somebody who was older and settled, I really was not in a position to be applying all over the country." Jane believes that the conflict between family life and career that she has experienced is shared by many women. "I don't think you can minimize that struggle between career and family for young women. You get to that point, and you look for role models of where it's been done successfully, and they are just so darn few. Instead of role models, what you see are negative examples."

Being actively involved in her community, Jane has put in "many hours of work in the public." She is a counselor for an inner-city school and sits on a school advisory council. In addition, she is engaged in various national and international political causes. In her political views, she leans toward the Democrats but does not completely identify with this party. Her major political creed is to further the "representation of the small people in general." Her personal philosophy is humanism combined with a belief in the importance of spirituality. This philosophy made "instances of dishonesty or theft or abuse of power really distressing to me," especially because she had originally assumed that "scientists would probably live by a higher code than the rest of humanity."

Jane's idea of the good life comprises "having the opportunities to have a family and participate in it fully and offer something to the community" as well as having "time and encouragement for learning new things." A bad life would be "isolated and highly structured, with little time for spontaneous interactions, and few meaningful interactions with other people." Jane is very satisfied with her life.

Key points:
- Had feelings of alienation from culture of science
- Chose to focus on family matters following career setbacks
- Retains a strong idealism

Jane embarked on her science education without long-term plans and clear career goals. Rather, she always took "the logical next step." Her science career was driven by her obvious talent for science and proceeded without much effort. Before she entered graduate school, her female undergraduate advisor asked her to swear not to aspire to both a family life and a science career because they were mutually exclusive. This oath turned out to be a sadly true predictor of Jane's later life because the combination of family and science career proved unattainable.

Her decision to quit science resulted from a complex pattern of push and pull factors rather than from a single cause. Dissatisfaction with the social system and culture of science undermined her allegiance to a science career and heightened her sense of the sacrifice that this career path would entail. After several applications for tenure-track positions failed, her resolve to pursue an academic career was further weakened. At that point came a concrete offer of marriage, which Jane accepted. Consequently, she contented herself with a marginal science position. The exit from this last foothold in the science system was analogous to her abandonment of a professorial career. A combination of a career-internal problem—in this case, the nonrenewal of a research grant—and a positive development in the family sphere—in this case, her first pregnancy—made Jane abandon science and become a homemaker.

Her criticism of the social system of science focuses on its high competitiveness; its extreme division of labor, which prevents the autonomy of the individual researcher; and its requirement of single-minded devotion. While these complaints appear to be common among both female and male scientists who left the field, Jane adds the element of disappointed idealism. She has a strong ethical objection to the current science system on the grounds that it has severed itself from societal responsibilities. She also mentions instances of gender discrimination.

Under different circumstances, Jane feels she could have made a useful contribution with her science training. Nevertheless, her level of satisfaction with her career and life is generally high. Partly, this may reflect her low ambitions; partly, it may result from the fact that when her science career floundered, other aspects of her life flourished. In contrast with numerous members of her generation, who traded idealism for career success, Jane abandoned her science career but retained the high level of social concern and activism of her student days.

FIVE MEN

Fred

Fred works for the federal government. He is in his early forties and married, with two children.

Fred's career path into science was "fairly straightforward." His father was an academic scientist, and Fred "was raised in a community where science was emphasized. That has probably been a major factor. The environment was perhaps more science-oriented and technologically oriented than most." Better at science than other things, "I always more or less figured that I would end up in some sort of technical or scientific discipline." His early education was uneventful. In high school he received mediocre grades because "I had an aversion to doing homework, which teachers didn't agree with. So I usually would get an *A* on the exams, and an *F* on the homework, and [finally] would get somewhere in between."

In college at well-known X University, Fred did progressively worse in the science in which he initially intended to major. He finally switched his major to another science field. When he started as an undergraduate, he did not intend to go any further than the bachelor's degree. His reason for immediately entering graduate school, also at X University, was connected with the political situation at the time. "If I didn't stay in school I would have gone to Vietnam." During the first year of his graduate studies, he became ineligible for the draft. Nevertheless, he completed the whole year and received a master's degree. "And then [I] decided to go get more serious about this whole thing, get a Ph.D." He entered graduate school at Y University, which had a good program in his discipline. Fred's research was in a "rather esoteric field." His financial needs forced him to work as a teaching assistant for a long time, which he would rather not have done.

After receiving his doctorate, Fred took a postdoctoral fellowship at Z University to collaborate with a researcher in his specific field of interest. Then he joined a federal research agency. After Fred worked there for several years, his position was terminated because of government budget cuts. "By this time, I had a house here and a wife who was working in a reasonable job, and so I stayed in this area because that's where the family was, and tried to find a job." He was unemployed for over a year. At that time, there was a big rush to develop a particular subfield in his discipline; and Fred, who was not trained in this subfield, found "there wasn't much of a market for me scientifically." He finally joined a company for a year and a half, doing work unrelated to his science, until he heard through a friend about a job opportunity as a grants administrator in a federal organization. He has worked in this position for over five years. Fred likes his work. "It's a lot easier to be on the giving end than on the receiving end of grants."

He does not feel he made the most of his advantages and opportunities. "I think I could have done better research, more focused research. I tended to drift around from too many topics, and stayed too long doing particular things. I worked on some too long and some too short." He was attracted to his research problems by their extreme difficulty. "I liked that challenge. Twenty years later the problems that I was working on still haven't been solved, so I guess I wasn't the only one who failed." Fred came to realize that his research "had not been of the highest quality, and that was disappointing to me." He rates his ability as a scientist as "average at best. . . . And I think that's one reason I'm fairly comfortable in the job I have. Many of my colleagues who do the same kind of thing are longing to get back to the laboratory. In my particular case, I think I do better at this end of it than I did at that. . . . I wouldn't give myself money."

Fred considers getting his present job a big lucky break because it fits his training and experience well. A personal advantage he mentions is that he has "a large ego, which I think is pretty much a requirement for a scientist. And it doesn't hurt for a bureaucrat either. You don't make many friends and you make a lot of enemies. I reject about 95 percent of the grants that come to me, and [people] aren't very happy about that. There are people who can't sleep at night doing [grant administration work]. I sleep." Fred does not mind making decisions about accepting or rejecting grant proposals. He thinks he has "a fair amount" of personal power in his position.

In Fred's opinion, he has met with about average difficulties compared with his male cohorts and maybe slightly fewer difficulties than his female cohorts. He does not think he should have handled the obstacles he encountered differently. He notes that his major career obstacle was the loss of his job. In his opinion, the leading cause for his unemployment was bad timing: he came onto the job market when there were not many opportunities. Currently, "I would be far more employable than I was ten years ago." He still has the vague idea of going back to academic science as an administrator and then doing some research on the side. Another difficulty was working with a highly "excitable" female supervisor during his time as a scientist. "It was like living with a time bomb that went off frequently."

As an internal obstacle, Fred mentions that he is "somewhat undisciplined. If I had stayed in research science I wouldn't be known for a very consistent scientific product. I think there would be some [research] that would be better than average and a lot that would be worse than average—very uneven."

He rates himself as less ambitious than the average colleague. Although he did not fulfill his original scientific aspirations, he appears relatively satisfied with his career path. His present position "wasn't exactly what I started out to be, but I don't mind being here." He does not have much ambition to rise in the bureaucracy. "I guess I could move up one position, but that would be all that I'd want to, because I'm less interested in power and I think I can do a good job at where I am. Maybe it's an antithesis of the Peter Principle."

Fred thinks of himself as self-confident because of an inherently large ego. He also thinks he is relatively resilient. "I haven't hit anything that stopped me particularly yet." He does not consider himself "all that socially inclined, and I imagine that was a deficit, but I don't know how severe it was."

As regards differences between the average female and male scientist, Fred believes many older female scientists try to be "more masculine than their male counterparts" in terms of personality traits but thinks this difference has changed for younger cohorts. He notes that the rise of the feminist movement positively affected the career of his wife, a scientist in his own field.

High-quality science, in his view, is "a major advancement in the particular discipline and gives you entirely different insights into a specific problem or phenomenon." Poor science, by contrast, is characterized by "a lack of fundamentals, the very basics of scientific discipline and thought. A hypothesis must be testable. There are certain very basic things that you're taught in sixth or eighth grade about what science is, and you'd be surprised at how many people forget that. I would say 40 percent of the proposals I see forget that." In his opinion, total identification with science is not required in order to do good scientific work. As a scientist,

Fred most enjoyed the hands-on experience of doing experiments. His working style was "quick and dirty."

Fred married a woman scientist with whom he worked when he was a student at X University. He considers being married to another scientist in his field positive because "another scientist will have a better understanding of a research career, what's required when scientists have funny hours sometimes." Because of his two children, he spends more time at home than he would otherwise. But he does not feel tension between his private and professional roles. His wife followed him several times to educational and job locations, so he thinks it only fair that his geographic mobility was curtailed by his wife's job when he was unemployed.

Fred considers himself more politically aware than the average person. His political views are liberal. In general, he is fairly satisfied with his life. Among the ingredients of a good life, he counts the following: "I have a reasonable income, I'm not starving, I have a house, have a car; the children are reasonably healthy and well adjusted."

Key points:
- Selected esoteric research problems
- Was hampered by lack of employment opportunities
- Had limited geographical mobility because of family considerations

At first Fred followed the career path that was predestined for him by his academic family background and his talent, but he did so without fervent conviction; he lacked ambition and drive. His selection of obscure and extremely difficult research problems might indicate that he did not devote much attention to strategic career planning.

There are several causes for his leaving science. His research was not, as he now acknowledges, top quality. After federal budget cuts eliminated his position, he could not find another science job because his family situation limited his geographic mobility and the demand for scientists in his subspecialty was low.

Fred's strong ego has not suffered from his somewhat erratic career path. Although he acknowledges some disappointment at having done less-than-brilliant research, his explanation of his exit from science stresses mainly external causes. He would probably have remained in research science if he had found employment. In his case, a strong dose of self-confidence, paired with the absence of large ambitions, has created such a stable personal outlook that even potentially traumatic career turns can hardly faze him.

George

George works as a manager in a science-related corporation. He is in his early forties and married, with one child.

George "was pretty committed towards science as a very, very young kid, and probably the biggest influence I had was my father who was kind of a frustrated man of science. He came from [a foreign country] and grew up during the Depression. He didn't have the necessary education, but always had a real interest in science." When George was in elementary school, he was already carrying out scientific experiments in his basement laboratory. His interest in science was boosted by society's enormous excitement about science during his childhood. "It was the great era of Sputnik and the great era of science fairs and 'Let's get a man on the moon' and all that sort of good stuff, which was very, very motivating." George joined a rocket club, whose projects included making rocket fuel and launching rockets. Those early science experiments caused occasional trouble with the police.

In high school, George tried to take as many advanced science courses as possible. "Several really good teachers were helpful to me, and in particular teachers that not only knew their subject matter but knew how to teach and would constantly challenge you with concepts and problems, not just deliver to you the rote message from the book." Such good experiences kept him on a straight path into science, which at that time was already "pretty well established." With his friends from the rocket club, he continued to carry out "just little pet projects that [we] would dream up for ourselves."

In college, George "spent equal time having fun and doing a lot of things other than science," but he still received "a pretty good education." He majored in a science and went on to study it in graduate school. After half a year, however, he "came to a dead end." It became clear to him that he did not want to continue with this science because he "wanted something more applied." Therefore, he dropped out of school. "I spent about a year doing odds and ends" in jobs that were not career related. Finally, he returned to graduate school to study a different science that offered an applied approach more to his liking. This time, George enjoyed graduate school. "I was not in graduate school so that I could eventually get out and make a specific amount of money or achieve a certain job—I had no idea at that time that I would be sitting here in this job today—I just did it because I liked it." His work as a research assistant provided a "very valuable learning experience." In addition to doing his thesis research, he was involved in several other research projects. One of them was at a research institution where he continued to do a post-doctoral fellowship after receiving his doctorate.

George's postdoctoral mentor was very helpful, and the work environment was excellent. "It was an international community of scientists working on a very active theme at that time, and really, you got to meet, interact with, work with, some of the top scientists in the world, which was absolutely super."

After his postdoctoral fellowship, however, George made a "radical departure" in his career. "Research was fun. I could spend my entire life at it, but I decided not to, and at that point I elected to see if all of this knowledge that I had accumulated and developed could be applied to something useful. So I switched and took an industrial position with the company that I'm with today." Another factor in his decision was that he found the low pay offered for academic positions "insulting."

George entered the company as a scientist but then moved "very rapidly into a semimanagement position as the laboratory head." After a few years of doing some research work of his own and managing the laboratory, he was promoted to a number of increasingly senior positions, which took him completely out of research science and into management. George yearns to change his work responsibilities to make room for some hands-on research. "My goal for myself right now [is] to get out and away from the paperwork that constantly consumes people—myself being a prime example as a victim of that—and hopefully being able to get back into the laboratory a little bit."

George has never been completely satisfied with his professional achievement or with his life as a whole. "I'm never there; I'm never satisfied. I'm never happy with my performance in any job, no matter how well I've done. And I just continually need to be challenged by something else, or challenged by further improvements in my own particular position. . . . I have the constant need to learn new things in different areas, and that's driven me somewhat erratically." George is at least as ambitious as his average colleague, if not more, and he will continue "to look at challenges and try to seize upon opportunities."

George did not have "a great vision of what my career should be and religiously [pursue] a path to that goal." Rather, he has focused on the next concrete step. Good luck, in terms of being at the right place at the right time, has, in his view, played an important part in his career. He considers himself fortunate to have worked with excellent people who served as role models. "I'll be the first to admit that I've learned by emulation." At his company, George had "a number of good mentors, people who were themselves scientists, or at least scientists at one point in their careers." They helped him with the transition from research science to management.

As personality traits that helped his career, George mentions that he has a "terribly inquisitive" nature and likes to challenge orthodox wisdom. He also has good social skills. "Somehow I got a compromise. [I am] certainly not the brightest person in the world or the most theoretical or the most scientific, and I'm probably not the best humanist or the best people person, but I got a very nice blending of the two skills. I literally can speak both languages, which was helpful in a career of this type."

A difficult period in his career occurred at the beginning of his graduate studies, when he discovered that he did not really like the science toward which his whole education had been oriented. "I went through this terrible period of self-examination and [was] literally down in the pits, and turned my eyeballs inward and started doing a hell of a lot of internal scrutiny, and spent a year floundering at odd jobs."

He feels that he did not make the most of his opportunities, mostly because he was "victimized by having maybe too many diverse interests," which led to a somewhat erratic career path. "I look back and I would say, God, you could now be a key guy in an academic organization or national laboratory or something like that, had you stayed on track, had you pursued your original work in [a particular research field], had you gone out, climbed up the tree, gone to the end of a branch, gone to a twig at the end of the branch, carved out your little niche and said, yes, I will be the expert in this. I didn't do that because it probably goes against my character and against my interests." In hindsight, he believes he should have made some decisions differently, but he thinks such errors are a necessary component of learning by mistake.

George considers himself self-confident. He is good at interacting with people and has not been afraid to offer up the results of his research "and have other people shoot at [them]." He also regards himself as resilient, owing to his "terminal optimism. I've never, ever felt like I've been so far down in the pits that I couldn't climb out." He is energetic and hardworking but "not as hardworking as I could be. I am not a workaholic."

In respect to gender differences in science, George says that he has not interacted with his male and female colleagues in different ways. He does not think there is any fundamental difference in the ways men and women do science. Women scientists do, however, have problems achieving recognition, in his opinion. "I think in the sciences, women probably have a greater difficulty achieving credibility. And it's strictly a perception problem, not a technical problem on their own part. A lot of times, credibility is how you present your ideas, your concepts, your plans or science, how you present your research, your results, whatever. And oftentimes women are not as forceful, maybe as confident, or don't appear to be, but that may be a cultural thing, it may be a perceptual thing."

George's working style as a scientist was "a little bit erratic. I would work in spurts." He thinks that other scientists he knew were more capable of long periods of intense work. High-quality science, in his opinion, is "innovativeness" that transcends existing theories and generates "totally new ideas. . . . Really good science involves taking a look at a problem from a different standpoint and developing an innovative, new approach to solving. It's higher-risk work rather than a relatively safe or low-risk variation on a theme." Bad science is characterized by, among other things, a "total disregard for scientific principles, such as the scientific method." Although George does not think that output as measured by the number of publications is an important part of being a good scientist, "I played that game for a while. I did publish some things that were variations on a theme, if you will. Here's a project, here's some results, spin that off into several publications. I think that's done quite a bit today. Unfortunately, we don't have a good yardstick to measure quality of publication. So we tend to do it by quantity."

George considers unrestricted exchange and discussion of ideas with colleagues—which he terms "peer expectation"—an important environmental factor conducive to good research. "You develop a rapport with these people; you look to them for advice; you look to them for ideas. They're people you're not afraid to bounce ideas off of, no matter how silly you might think they are initially." George chose research problems that were "somewhat off the track" and could be studied from a novel perspective by using an interdisciplinary approach. He enjoys collaborating with researchers and feels he can contribute "a whole host of different perspectives, including a management perspective from years spent in management."

Although George is no longer an active research scientist, he thinks he has fulfilled his original aspirations of being in science because he is still connected to it. His professional identity is more rooted in science than in business. "That will never change. I think like a scientist; I don't think like a businessman."

George's wife, a teacher, has been "a very good sounding board and very supportive." He appreciates that she is an equal partner rather than submissive. "One of the big things I enjoy with my wife is intellectual discussions on an equal basis." Her income also provided valuable financial support while George was in graduate school. He tries to keep his career and his private life in balance. "I probably am not willing to drive as hard as many of my other colleagues and friends, because I do keep a very big balance on that. My personal life is important." If he had been single, he might have been more inclined to take a lesser-paid academic or pure research position rather than go into industry.

George's idea of the good life is the "achievement of a certain amount of happiness." A bad life "is when you're constantly worried about the basic necessities that keep you alive, and you never have any time to pursue other things that make you happy."

Key points:
- Put off by low monetary rewards of academic science
- Had strong interest in applied science
- Was promoted out of industrial research science

George grew up in both a familial and a societal environment conducive to scientific pursuits, and his scientific inclinations were apparent from an early age. His later departure from research science was precipitated not by failure but by promotion. In a career path somewhat parallel to that of Florence, who rose through the ranks of academic administration, George was promoted to managerial positions in industrial science and had to leave actual research science behind. He yearns to do some actual research, a common feature in our group of people who left research science.

What were George's reasons for leaving basic science and entering industry? One reason was his personality. The very curiosity and inquisitiveness that was his driving impulse to become a scientist also deterred him from steadily focusing his interest on a narrow research topic, which he considers typical for a career in academic science. George is restless—never satisfied with his past achievements, always looking for a new challenge. Large measures of self-confidence, resilience, and optimism equip him well for adventuresome career moves. Another reason for going into industry was his interest in applied research. Finally, whereas in graduate school George "did not have a dollar figure in front of [himself]" when he considered career options, the higher salary level in industry, compared with that in academic science, later became an incentive.

Hank

Hank works at a university in an administrative position. He is in his late thirties and married, with no children.

Hank "determined at a very early age" that he wanted to be a scientist. The societal focus on space exploration profoundly inspired his interest. "I remember staying up to watch the landing on the moon and thinking about that. In fact, one of my hobbies was model rockets." The family's cat was named Yuri, after the pioneer Soviet cosmonaut Yuri Gagarin. One of Hank's childhood heroes was Albert Einstein. In Hank's eyes, Einstein was "someone that people initially didn't think much of, and yet he had this tremendous brilliance that impacted the scientific world so much. And as a kid, I guess I latched on to that, and it was something that I stuck with." Hank's father was an engineer, and his family reacted positively to his interest in science.

During his time at a small rural school Hank studied with one good science teacher, but "I don't remember anything particularly inspirational. I felt much more like I was motivated by other things that I saw outside of the school, not by things in school." Toward the end of his school years, a former student at his high school, who had become a science professor at a nearby university and taught an evening course at the high school, influenced Hank's later career path. This professor discussed Hank's college options with him and convinced him to go to prestigious X University.

"The first year [at the university] was very difficult because I had come from a small rural school into the big city school." Hank did not have as strong a background in mathematics and the sciences as many other freshmen did. He nevertheless struggled through his freshman year and, as a sophomore, received his first *A* in a science course. "That really gave me the encouragement to stick with it." The professor who taught the course was very supportive. Hank further acknowledges his undergraduate thesis advisor, for whom he was also a research assistant, as "a very great influence on me regarding my scientific career."

After graduating, Hank wanted to take a job so that he could pay off his student loans while deciding whether to go to graduate school. Owing to a recession, he had difficulties in finding a job and finally accepted the offer of a professor at X University to work as a research assistant. After a year, Hank entered graduate school at X University. He found his graduate research fascinating. Contrary to some friends' "horror stories" about advisors' exploitation of graduate students, Hank had a very positive experience with his advisor, who took care "to develop me as a researcher."

After completing his doctorate, Hank took a postdoctoral fellowship at Y University and worked on problems related to his graduate research. "And I guess that's where I started to get disenchanted." Several aspects of research led to his dissatisfaction. He felt that research "was a grind"— long hours of hard work. "You stuck yourself away in a back room and worked away on things, and you were expected to grind away on Saturdays as well." And the work was not rewarding. Hank had to spend most of his time on his advisor's research program and had little opportunity to do his own research. He viewed himself as a small contributor to a huge research project whose tangible impact he could not see. "I didn't want to be just a member of a publications factory; it just didn't seem like that's what science was all about. I wasn't sure that I saw what impact or results we were going to have."

Hank also felt socially isolated and uncomfortable. "Faculty members didn't know you. You were just sort of a cog in a wheel of one of the labs working there." He did not have much respect for "the way [some of the scientists] treated people, the way they acted with people."

The final drawback was the low pay. After enduring the lean years of being a poor undergraduate and graduate student, Hank found that the postdoctoral fellowship did not dramatically improve his finances. He grew tired of making "the sacrifices [that] were constantly expected for this path" in academic science.

Hank received another postdoctoral fellowship at the same university, but the situation did not get better. When the second fellowship came to an end, he "decided that I was tired of the sacrificial life. . . . I never felt that I couldn't do the work or what was necessary to succeed. What I felt was that it wasn't worth it. It wasn't something that was worth devoting my life to." Although he had an offer to do another postdoctoral fellowship at a different university, he switched to an administrative position at Y University.

This position immediately relieved him from his social isolation. "I can remember one of my first reactions after the first four weeks was, my God, I've met more people in the past month than I did in a year and a half here." In his new position, the work was more group-oriented. It was much different from the scientific work, in which there had been hardly any actual teamwork even though the individual research projects were connected. Hank found his new job exhilarating at first but subsequently got "very frustrated with the atmosphere" at Y University. After about three years, he moved back to X University to take another administrative position. Although this position did not require any research, Hank still kept his "fingers in the research area. . . . What I've found is that I do want to have some component of my job involve scientific research. And I do miss that a lot." At the time of this interview, Hank had just "worked out an arrangement to take six months to go back to [a professor] and work full time with him in research."

When Hank started out in science, "my aspiration was really to do something that would be remembered by my peers, not something that would necessarily change the world or whatever, but something that was significant and lasting" within the scientific community. During the final stages of his involvement in research science, he revised this original ambition. At that time, he "would rather do something significant and lasting outside of just the scientific world." He now regards himself as ambitious in terms of a management career but not in terms of a science career.

Hank considers it a career advantage that he went to X University for his education because it provided an environment conducive to research. Two internal characteristics that have helped him in his scientific work were a logical approach and "a fairly open problem-solving style"—a style that takes different, even far-fetched, possibilities into account. As an important mentor in his later career, Hank mentions a male colleague who also changed from scientist to administrator. This colleague was Hank's "management mentor" and helped him realize "that there's this whole other aspect of people that I hadn't been exposed to in a research environment." Good luck played an important role in his career. A particularly fortunate coincidence was his connection with his graduate advisor through a chat with another professor at X University. In sum, "things have worked out pretty smoothly." Hank thinks he faced smaller difficulties and obstacles in his science career than his cohorts, both women and men. An internal obstacle was that he lacked "patience with things that were screwed up" and would get angry about them too easily.

Although Hank is satisfied with the achievements of his career, he now thinks he should have handled his career switch differently. "I would have preferred, in looking back on things, not to have made such a dramatic shift in my career at the time, but rather looked more widely at the possibilities that might have taken me in a somewhat different direction, but still kept my ties in the research area, the research world. . . . Certainly there's something inside me that I'm still working on in terms of 'Why did I run away from the research environment?' And that's something that I often think about now, particularly since I'm trying to head back that way."

Hank feels overall confidence in his professional competence because he knows he has been doing a good job. He does not feel so self-confident outside work. In respect to his plan to become scientifically active again, "my feeling is I've been out of touch and that I have to do something in order to become credible in a research community again." He considers himself hardworking and energetic. "I have this underlying feeling that if you work hard, things will come to you."

Hank notes that women scientists experience greater difficulties than men.

> [Science] was a field that women were basically locked out of. And to get into the field, they had to overcome basically the attitude that women weren't meant to be scientists. And I think it's so ironic. I know that the attitude in science is one of competition. And I know that this is something that boys are taught at an early age. You have these games, and you have these rules, and you play with the rules, and you fight each other, and you compete, and someone wins and someone loses. And I think that's really how the scientific community's set up. In terms of grants, all that stuff, it's all competition. And yet the irony is that in today's world, what's important is to work with other people and to collaborate and work in a very different style, and that's what women are strong in.

He recalls that, at school, girls were not encouraged to become scientists as much as he and other boys were. There was also a lack of female role models; all the scientific heroes "like Einstein and the astronauts were men." Moreover, in the current social organization of science, "there's been no accommodation of some of the problems that women face, in terms of bearing children and things that take them out of their career for a while." Hank acknowledges differences in the way he interacts with male and female colleagues. "I tend to be much more sensitive to what I say to a woman. Sometimes I find myself putting on the men's role to deal with some [men]. I've got to talk about what men talk about. And there are things that I would talk to the women colleagues about that I wouldn't talk to the men colleagues about."

In terms of the general status of women, Hank feels "that there's been a number of positive things that have happened, but I've also realized how much more there is to go to reach some things." He notices that people who are only little older than he is hold totally different views about women's issues.

Hank's working style as a scientist was "pretty intense," but he worked "in spurts. I would really get involved with something for a period of time, push through on something, then ease up some, and go back to being intense again." Really good science, in his opinion, "arises out of a fairly simple model, something that can be communicated to people who are not directly in the field." It also "leads to other ideas and opens new doors" and stands the test of time. Bad science is characterized by "skipping over important holes" in the argument, using results selectively to support one's point, or behaving unethically. Hank considers his quality standards higher than the average standards in his field. Although he regards his publication output (when he was a working scientist) as "pretty good," he does not think that the quantity of publications is an important part of being a good scientist. The pervasive emphasis on publication productivity "is one thing that really turned me off from the postdoc." What he liked most about science were "these few periods where you'd be on a new track with something, and things would just come together, and you'd feel like you'd really come up into a new idea and a new area and see something different." He rates his ability as a scientist as about average, although he thinks others might rate it below average.

Science is not everything for Hank. "I just think that there's a lot more to life than one aspect. . . . I felt proud of the fact that I had outside interests, interests other than science." Earlier in his life, Hank's career had priority over his private life, but now he "would make tradeoffs." He got engaged when he was at the end of his stay at Y University and was looking for a new position. He moved with his future wife to the area of X University. Now he does not want to "upset what my wife is doing. I don't want to drag her to someplace new. I already did that to her once; I wouldn't do it to her again." He feels tension between the various roles in his life. "I want to have a balance, but I don't think that I've found the right combination yet." His marriage has had an impact on his career. If he were not married, he would be more likely to change jobs. Career considerations have somewhat influenced the decision not to have children up to this point. "I think there's always a concern, on my part at least, will I have time to do everything that I need to do? And I don't want to have children and ignore them."

Although Hank works actively for environmental causes, his degree of political awareness and engagement is, in his view, lower than that of his average colleague. His idea of the good life is "a balanced life" that is fulfilling. The bad life is one in which a person feels trapped. Hank says he is increasingly satisfied with his life in general.

Key points:
- Was attracted to science by space program
- Persisted through initial difficulties in college
- Felt alienated from the culture of science
- Voluntarily left science

Early in his life, Hank was touched by the euphoria of the space program. With the exception of a difficult freshman year in college, his science career path was relatively straight and smooth until he quit after completing his postdoctoral fellowships. Hank left research by his own choice, not because external circumstances forced him to leave. His reasons were rooted in the social organization and culture of science. Some of his complaints are, without doubt, shared by a great number of individuals who decide to leave science. They also correspond to society's negative stereotypes about science and scientists.

Hank resented being socially isolated, working long hours, being a cog in the wheel of someone else's research project, and receiving little money for his efforts. A key concern is achieving a balance between the various aspects of his life—a balance he considered unattainable in a research science career, which required too great a personal investment.

Hank may resent some aspects of science but, like most other respondents who left research science, he clearly still loves science and feels some regret about his departure. He has been working on an arrangement that would allow him to return to full-time research for a certain period of time.

Ian

Ian works as a scientific consultant for a big firm. Around forty years old, he is married for the second time and was expecting his first child at the time of the interview.

Ian remembers "quite clearly that I became interested in [science] at a pretty early age, early high school." His older brother, who had been interested in a particular science, gave Ian a great number of books on topics related to that science, "which I dove into and found very interesting." Ian was attracted to this science because "it was a body of knowledge that a large number of people didn't understand very well, and I grasped a lot of its basics very early on."

Except for the formative influence exerted by his older brother, Ian ventured into his career basically on his own. His father was an engineer, but he did not particularly stimulate Ian's interest in technology or science.

Rather, Ian grew up in an atmosphere of "benign neglect. I did not receive strong intellectual direction or encouragement, nor did I receive any discouragement. I got a general benign encouragement that pretty much whatever I wanted to do would be okay." In spite of this lack of encouragement, he "never really wavered. I knew that I wanted to study [this science] in college when I was still in high school. I did, I got a bachelor's degree and ultimately a doctorate, and never really questioned, until well after my education was completed, in any serious way, whether that was the right thing for me to do. . . . It was almost inertia. Nothing operated to push me off the course, so I just stayed on course."

Ian's college education was uneventful in terms of his career direction. When he entered college, he had already made a "general decision to pursue a doctorate in [his science]." After graduating he took one year off and worked in an unrelated job before entering graduate school. He had a choice among two top graduate schools and a less prestigious one. "For a mixture of money and personal reasons," Ian selected the less distinguished X University.

From his graduate experience, Ian recalls that the first year was "intensely challenging, but that's probably the way it should be." According to him, only a few individuals strongly influenced his education, although he acknowledges "a lot of fine teachers." One person who did have an impact was his dissertation advisor, who brought Ian's specialty fields and his dissertation topic into focus.

After receiving his doctorate, Ian did a postdoctoral fellowship at prestigious Y University and then worked in a "quasi-academic setting" for a nonprofit research institute. After about five years at that institute, he was offered a position on the Senate staff, which he eagerly accepted. He had felt demoralized at the institute because he was doing work "which didn't strike me as particularly important. I felt like I was becoming part of a system that fed on this world of grants and contracts because it was there, not because the underlying work was inherently valuable. . . . I particularly remember frustration and discouragement at what I felt was the low level of importance or quality of the work, and unhappiness with it."

Ian enjoyed his work for the Senate, which was much different from the research work that he had done before. After four years, however, he decided that this work, "though it was a lot of fun, was really not what I was trained to do." He then joined his present company, where he does scientific consulting.

As career advantages, Ian acknowledges scholarship assistance, both at the undergraduate and graduate levels. An internal advantage was that "I was always a bookish sort, and that seems to be probably a pretty important prerequisite for anybody who wants to pursue advanced academic training." Good luck, "being in the right place at the right time," played a key role in getting the Senate position. He learned about the job from a co-worker whose wife, a high-level Senate staffer, was looking for a scientist to fill this position.

Ian considers it bad luck that he entered the academic job market at a time when there was an oversupply of qualified scientists and intense competition. "I often felt like a number of people, who were tenured professors and only a few years older than I was, would not have been hired in the job market I was in." Compared with his average male or female cohorts, Ian believes that he, on the whole, faced smaller difficulties and obstacles. His obstacles were not at all unusual, "only the same obstacles that everyone confronts. You have to compete with many other very talented people. And if you want to stay in school for four years, or five years even, after graduating from college, you have to sacrifice to do that."

Ian now thinks his straight path into science resulted, to some degree, from his lack of reflection about his career goals and prospects. "To a certain extent, I muddled through rather than engaging myself at an earlier age in a very serious examination, what it was I wanted to be and do." Only after he had become a professional scientist did he reexamine his career. "Later, when I was an adult and into my career, I often wondered whether pursuing the Ph.D. in [this science] was in fact the best course I could have followed. There was a heavy measure of ignorance in my choice of career path. I think that had I to do it over again, and knowing what I know now, I would have done some things differently. In particular, I would probably not have pursued an academic career, and perhaps by extension, an academic degree, as long as I did."

The underlying causes for the revision of his initial career goal were, in addition to frustration about what he felt was meaningless work at the research institute, "a combination of my own innate skills, some educational and other choices that I had made, and the state of the academic market. I simply was not going to get a tenure-track job at a first-rank university." In hindsight, he considers it "not a wise decision, especially insofar as my goal was to pursue an academic or research [science] career," to have gone to X University for graduate studies rather than to one of the two prestigious universities that also accepted him. "It would have been better to have made whatever sacrifices were necessary" to receive graduate training at one of these renowned schools. On the other hand, he suspects he was not "really cut out for a research career" in this science. Thus, "it might very well have been the case that I would have been

more successful in pursuing the wrong goal had I gone to [a top school]."
During the phase when Ian reexamined his career path and abandoned
his goals in academia, he received support from his wife and one of his
colleagues.

Ian's self-confidence, resilience, and optimism stem, in his view, from
being successful and reassured from early on. "I was always a success at
everything that I tried, until I failed to achieve the goal that I thought I
wanted of being an academic researcher." Ian also describes himself as
hardworking and energetic, which he traces to his upbringing. His ambition is about average compared with all scientists in his discipline, and
below average when compared with his immediate colleagues.

On the average, Ian sees no difference in the ways male and female
scientists work. Neither does he think that being male affects the way he
does science, except in the area of professional behavior, where he thinks
gender influences how one interacts with people. The women's movement "generally influenced the way I deal with women, and that has certainly had a general influence on my life."

Ian was attracted to his particular field of science by its "intellectual
beauty. I was quite taken by the elegance of the system of thought." He
thinks his standards of good work are higher than the overall standards
in the field. In his opinion, really good scientific work is, first of all, "imagi-
native." Bad science is "careless, sloppy." He rates his scientific ability as
above average. Although his own publication productivity was small, he
considers a substantial publication output an important part of being a
good scientist. "A good scientist must produce a volume of work. If
Stradivarius had only made one violin he wouldn't have been a great
violin maker. He had to make hundreds." To do good science it is not
necessary, in his view, to identify completely with the scientific profession. In his scientific work, Ian has tried "to figure out what the question
is that needs to be answered, and then what constitutes evidence." His
favorite aspect of doing science is hypothesis testing, "rejecting possible
explanations on the basis of contradictory evidence and ultimately accepting whatever conclusions you accept as being the most consistent
with the facts."

When Ian started out, "I sought a conventional academic career in a
university, doing traditional [scientific] research, and I don't think the
particular subject matter of the research mattered to me so much as the
fact that I would be performing at a high level, [compared] with my peers."
He did not fulfill these original career aspirations. He is not particularly
pleased but is satisfied with the course and achievements of his career.

"It could be better, but it could be a whole lot worse, too. I see people of my age and with certainly no more than my talent, who have advanced further professionally than I have. And that's the result of a number of things, partly it's a result of my changing career paths several times." The importance attached to his career as compared with his private life is declining. Whereas a decade ago private life and career had about equal weight, currently his private life has clear priority. But being the primary wage earner in his family "keeps your attention focused."

Ian was married before he finished graduate school, but this marriage ended in divorce many years ago. He remarried recently. He thinks that being married had no effect on his career except that "for a man of my age, not to be married could have a deleterious effect on his career. Being married is a symbol of being responsible." His second wife was expecting their first baby at the time of the interview. Ian does not feel a tension between the various roles in his life and does not foresee a major increase in such tensions after the baby's birth because his career "does not keep me slaving away every night and weekend, anyway."

Ian characterizes his idea of the good life as "pretty bourgeois: secure home and family, good health, enough to eat, sufficiently stimulating intellectual activity, and companionship. I don't derive my sense of meaning in life by appeal to abstract philosophical principles. I derive them out of my concrete day-to-day life with my family involved. And if I did not have those things, I would probably have a deep-seated sense of meaninglessness in life, because I haven't created anything else that's going to last for eternity." Ian is very satisfied with his life in general.

Key points:
- Worked toward career goal with little reflection
- Was dissatisfied with research job
- Experienced bad job market

Ian decided at an early age to become an academic scientist in a particular discipline. He proceeded on this track without much outside encouragement and without much further reflection on his career goals and opportunities—almost as if he were on autopilot. Only when he recognized that the career he was taking for granted was resembling a dead-end street did he thoroughly re-evaluate his plans. Disappointed with what he considered work of low importance and quality, he left research science and has since shifted his focus from his professional career to his private life as he has become more of a family man.

He shows some regret at his previous naïveté, which prevented him from making a career switch earlier, but he nonetheless has a positive outlook and is very satisfied with his life. His self-confidence has not suffered from the fact that his career trajectory fell short of his original aspirations.

In Ian's case, the laws of the labor market have been of paramount importance. His career path is typical for a job market in which too many scientists compete for the available positions. If the scientific labor market improves, people like Ian will have a better chance of staying in research science.

John

John and his wife owned a company, which they recently sold. He is about fifty years old and has two children.

John's family background was academic; his father was a science professor. Nonetheless, John did not show much academic promise in his early youth. He was "a fairly immature kid, not a very serious student" through most of high school. A significant change occurred when his father transferred him from a public to a private school to complete the last year of high school. "I was, at the time, very unhappy with that [transfer], but I did go there, and that really made a substantial difference in my orientation to academic study. I went from an environment where a concern for studies was almost irrelevant to one where it was normative to be concerned and interested in studies." John took schoolwork more seriously and did well enough to be accepted into prestigious X University for college.

During his sophomore year, he took a part-time job with a research company where he was introduced to a burgeoning new subfield of science "and just absolutely fell in love with it. I got so interested in that [field] that I stopped studying and was working long hours for the corporation. I did that to such an extreme that I was asked by [X University] to take a year's leave after my sophomore year, because of very crummy grades at that point." During this year of leave, John continued working for the company. He then reentered X University and completed his college education.

After graduating, John worked as a researcher in his field of interest, first at renowned Y University and then at a private company. While at Y University, he met his wife, who majored in the same field. His research work was so exciting that after two years he decided to go on to graduate school in this field. The problem was that "it was too early." At that time, this field was just developing and there were few graduate programs. Thus, he entered graduate school at prestigious Z University in a related discipline where he could do the type of research in which he was really interested.

Having obtained his doctorate, John went back to Y University for a year to do a postdoctoral fellowship. He then returned to Z University as an assistant professor and taught full time for a year. By that time, he had grown disenchanted with pursuing a tenure-track academic career. He switched to part-time teaching at Z University but soon left teaching altogether. His decision to abandon his academic career was informed by an increasing awareness of the negative tradeoffs that come with the lifestyle of an academic: "the very long hours, the time away from the family, the need to raise our children in a location that we really weren't very excited about, and also a feeling that there was perhaps something that was more important or significant that I could be doing with the abilities and the talents that I had." Thus, John's decision to leave academic science had a "spiritual, moral dimension, as well as a social dimension."

John worked for a public agency for a while, and then he and his wife founded a company whose work is connected with his general field of interest but does not involve actual research. Recently, John and his wife sold their company. He still works there during the transitional period but will be leaving soon. He has no firm plans for his future yet, but he envisages some teaching. He is interested in "working in environments for which the compensation isn't money."

John's early career aspirations were to become an academic scientist and establish "an interesting line of research work at a reasonably good institution." This goal "was certainly endorsed by my parents, although they weren't particularly vocal about that." In the course of his somewhat circuitous career path, his "career goals changed quite a bit." He did not fulfill his original career aspirations, but he is reasonably satisfied with his career. "Looking retrospectively at the career decisions, I don't think I would have done much differently."

John thinks he has had "a very fortunate career path, and probably in that sense, [the career] had less problems" than the careers of comparable scientists. He asserts that good luck played a major role. As a student, John happened to become involved in an expanding field. And later, his own company was "in a growing business at the right time in terms of the marketplace. I guess I'd be hard put to distinguish what part of that was due to great insight and what part was due to just serendipity."

As one of his major career advantages, John acknowledges his jobs at the research company while he was an undergraduate and at Y University immediately after graduating. At both places, his work was at the cutting edge of a developing field, and he was very excited about participating in pioneering research. Another advantage was "having enough money to be able to go to graduate school, be able to devote full time to studies, and my wife not having to work. That was a bit unusual. Most of my married graduate student friends were struggling very hard to make ends meet."

A setback during the early years in business was a decline in the stock market. "What I took to be my financial independence evaporated, and we had to become rather more concerned about that in the years following than I had anticipated." His wife was very supportive during that phase. When their company hit difficult times, "there were decisions made then in terms of how to deal with the financial problems that I think were both surprising and difficult to deal with. The company was not as compassionate as it should have been, nor as sensitive to the people involved." In general, John considers the environment at their own company to be somewhat more social than at the other companies and academic institutions where he used to work. Their company, for example, "has got a softball team and people that go out and play volleyball. There's a bunch of us that go out and run regularly together. And there are social things that go a little bit beyond work."

John considers himself self-confident, a trait he traces back to his upbringing. "I had parents who were basically optimistic in outlook. And I was mainly successful at the things I did as a boy growing up." He also describes himself as resilient, hardworking, and energetic. "My father was a very competitive person, and I have acquired that from him to the point of going beyond the boundaries of what I might wish it to be. But I have always been very competitive and very goal-oriented." As an internal disadvantage, John notes that he "might have wished to have been a little bit more of a risk taker."

He does not believe being male influenced the way he did science. His discipline was "fairly free of gender bias," in his opinion. At their own company, John does not interact differently with male and female employees. "My relationship has been in terms of the position, not gender-related." But he also says that "from the perspective of being an entrepreneur and starting a business, it's probably been advantageous—this is somewhat speculative—to have been a male. I think there's probably an easier acceptance. I think back to the people I've had business dealings with, in terms of the company here and the company we sold our business to; they were all males."

John thinks that, in the academic world, good scientific work requires complete identification with one's profession. Because of family obligations, women scientists are, in his opinion, less likely than men scientists to make that identification. He considers honesty the main characteristic of really good scientific work—that is, "the ability to deal with the facts as they come up, irrespective of your wants and philosophical and theoretical orientation." A second characteristic is "the ability to think globally"—in other words, to question the overall theoretical framework of a scientific discipline rather than accept it as a given. By contrast, bad scientific work is dishonest. It "is done knowingly from the viewpoint of only getting something for publication, with full knowledge that it really doesn't contribute anything to an understanding of the field or any important questions." John rates his own ability as a scientist as above average. In his scientific work, he was active in an expanding subfield for which at that time "there was almost a disdain among many of the top [scientists]" in the discipline. Moreover, his subfield was still very small, "so the topics that I could choose for dissertation research, for example, were fairly limited at the time." John was attracted to this research field precisely because it pushed the limits of existing disciplines and opened up a whole new area. What he likes best about science is the "freedom to choose your own research topics." He dislikes "that power/prestige business that I looked at with great dismay when I was at [Z University]. It was not very appealing."

Currently, career and private life have equal weights, but earlier in his life, the career had priority. Being married has had a great impact on John's career—family issues played a large part in his decision to quit academic science. John and his wife had the "desire to be involved together in something that we felt was important, the desire to have a place [where] we wanted to raise our children." These goals, they thought, were incompatible with John's academic career.

His wife worked for a while after graduating from college but stopped when she was pregnant with their first child. Two years after the first, the second child was born; and John's wife stayed home for about nine years until both children went to school. When she wanted to work again, "it was really rather difficult getting back into [the science], having been out. People looked at her with a jaundiced eye and wondered how skilled she still was after that time." John's wife eventually obtained a position at another company, where she worked for about three years. Then she joined their own company until her recent retirement. Thus, John and his wife, who are both in the same field, "almost always worked very closely together."

John rates his political engagement as above average; his political views are moderately liberal. He is active in community volunteer work and environmental organizations. His religious beliefs are "quite important" and also influence his professional life. They encompass "holding in fairly high regard the need for honesty in work, tempered with compassion for the people I work with, have dealings with. They are values that are sometimes a little bit antithetical to the business environment."

The good life is "one that has the right relationship with God, as evidenced in the way I live, the way I interact with others, the way I spend my energies and time and money." A bad life would be oriented toward a "false God," which could be "the pursuit of prestige within one's discipline for its own sake or the pursuit of wealth beyond the point of what's necessary to deal with what your family needs." John is quite satisfied with his life in general.

Key points:
- May not have entered science if not for influence of private school
- Put off by high intensity of academic science
- Left science to start business with his wife
- Felt his idealism could not be expressed in science

John's early years sharply contrast with those of the majority of our scientists, whose academic and scientific inclinations were already conspicuous early in their lives. Had John's father not transferred his somewhat immature son to a good private school, John might not have entered higher education at all. Thus, he benefited from having a family that emphasized the value of education and had the financial means to send him to a good school.

One of the early members of a scientific subfield at the moment of its takeoff, John was a maverick scientist with a penchant for pioneering research. Although he loves the actual pursuit of science, he voluntarily quit his academic career. He had little interest in success in terms of promotions, prestige, and influence within a conventional academic career. He also disliked the total commitment he felt was needed to pursue academic science, which would leave him little time for a family life. From a moral aspect, he felt he could make a more important contribution outside of science. John might have been retained in academic science if there were positions or career tracks requiring less time and energy than the usual academic job.

John's career, although it has parted from academic science, was certainly a success from a business point of view. It has also allowed him to devote time to goals he considered worthwhile. There was a simple, if somewhat unique, solution for the common two-body problem of finding jobs for two spouses in the same field: John and his wife founded their own company and worked in it together. Finally, John has had the opportunity to do a considerable amount of volunteer work for good causes.

John's idealism, one of the reasons for his dissatisfaction with academic science, may have played a role in the decision to sell the company. He acknowledges that his values were sometimes overridden by the cold realities of the business world. He is now in search of fulfilling and socially important work and appears to have earned the freedom to choose such work regardless of its financial rewards. His career and life choices have been strongly influenced by his religious beliefs, a somewhat unusual finding among our respondents.

The ten people profiled in this chapter abandoned research science for a variety of reasons. Some had to leave for lack of a job; others quit voluntarily; still others found themselves, by way of promotion, gradually distanced from research science. Although a number of the interviewees were frustrated and disillusioned with certain aspects of the field, they typically retained a high regard for science and their science education. Quite a few would love to return to some form of research.

CHAPTER 4

▼ ▼ ▼

Pieces of the Puzzle: Toward a Bigger Picture

The twenty biographies in chapters 2 and 3 gave you a chance to make your own interpretations, come to your own insights, and, above all, note patterns and details that help you understand your own circumstances. But such anecdotal information gains considerably in value when you know to what extent individual experiences are widespread or unique. Therefore, we now connect the profiles with results from our 699 questionnaire responses and 200 interviews.

The profiles highlight the fact that the individual career paths of scientists—men and women—are intensely idiosyncratic and cannot be easily categorized according to simple gender dichotomies. Some of the women, for instance, had careers that may seem "typically male," while some of the men followed career paths that may seem "typically female." When we speak of the "typical" or "average" male and female scientist, we must not forget that such typicalities or averages convey only a small part of the whole story. They are apt to conceal the many differences within each gender group as well as the many similarities across genders. Nonetheless, men's and women's career paths are not entirely indistinguishable; and the profiles do illustrate some basic gender disparities in the experiences of male and female scientists, which the questionnaire responses and interviews allowed us to quantify.

There is no question that the women we studied are exceptional. Because they continued through the science pipeline to a doctorate and a prestigious postdoctoral fellowship, they clearly did not fill traditional gender roles. But their success in reaching that point does not necessarily prove that there are no obstacles to women's careers in the sciences. Rather, in most cases, their success was a matter of perseverance in the face of major impediments and both skill and luck in responding to opportunities. Our group of comparable men scientists allows us to gauge the degree to which these obstacles and advantages were gender specific. We look first at issues within the world of science and then turn to those raised by marriage and parenthood.

HOW WOMEN AND MEN ARE TREATED IN SCIENCE

The deficit model of gender disparities holds that external obstacles explain women's relative lack of career success in science—for example, that the most successful quartile of our interviewees working in academic science (as determined by our composite success measure) includes only 29 percent women, whereas the bottom quartile contains 50 percent women. The obstacles may be formal barriers, such as a policy of not hiring women for certain positions. Or they may be quite informal: rather than placing an outright ban on women from a laboratory, for example, a laboratory director may give an important project to a young man on his staff while assigning some less consequential task to a young woman. In the deficit model, we are most often talking about what is commonly called gender discrimination.

Discrimination

Gender discrimination appears to be far from eradicated, according to reports from the women we interviewed. Almost three out of four women (73 percent) said that they had experienced sex discrimination in their careers, while 13 percent of the men mentioned reverse discrimination. When asked about incidents that made them feel uncomfortable or surprised, 40 percent of the women mentioned episodes of sex discrimination, sexism, or sexual harassment. Thus, although outright gender discrimination may be on the decline, it remains so pervasive within science that a woman entering the field now should be aware that at some point in her career she might encounter behavior that she will consider gender discrimination.

The notion of discrimination includes various levels of seriousness, ranging from offhand sexist remarks to career-destroying incidents. Jane, for instance, reported that she was denied a job because the hiring committee felt they should protect her marriage. Two successful scientists, Barbara and Elizabeth, noted discriminatory episodes of lesser consequence. Serious incidents of discrimination reported by our interviewees included denials of jobs, promotions, or tenure when the women felt they were well qualified for a positive decision. One woman scientist related that her university "nominated me for the nontenured women's faculty fellowship as the outstanding female researcher who does not have tenure, and, less than a year later, denied me tenure on the basis that my research was terrible. No, there is no logic to that, but it happened."

Serious incidents of discrimination were less frequent than cases of insignificant slights, but one-fifth of the women interviewees (22 percent) said that discrimination had been a career obstacle: 17 percent mentioned discrimination by superiors, and 5 percent noted discrimination by peers. As one might expect, women who had left science were much more likely (39 percent) than academic scientists (19 percent) and women scientists outside academe (19 percent) to mention discrimination as a career obstacle. A few men reported that reverse discrimination had hampered their careers. One man, for instance, noted, "I am all for affirmative action for blacks and other minorities, but not for women. Being a white male is one reason why I am at a teaching college despite over thirty publications and $180,000 in grant money."

Because gender discrimination is now illegal and violations can result in costly litigation and fines for the institution, women are never told that they are being rejected because of their gender, if that is the reason. Thus, they are apt to guess at the motives behind a negative decision. This situation is very different from past days when gender discrimination was much more overt. A scientist in her late fifties described an incident that happened in the 1960s when she had two small children. "I had been promised a fellowship in the department of medicine at [X University], and I hired a housekeeper and got everything all together in my household. After a month, I went and presented myself to the man who had offered me the fellowship. And he looked at me and said: 'I have no place for housewives in my department.' It was quite a performance—the kind of thing that would never happen in this day and age." Several older women, acknowledging sweeping changes in the situation of women in the sciences, expressed regret that they were not born later.

Sexual harassment was reported by 12 percent of the women interviewed. The following is a classic example. The thesis work of one woman graduate student was evaluated by a renowned expert outside her own university. When they finally met face to face at a conference, he initiated an affair with her. "Although I participated fully, I think it was a real abuse of power, and it was unethical of him." Another woman mentioned a more bizarre case: "The day I was to be voted on for tenure here, one of the associate professors walked into my office at ten o'clock in the morning and said, 'Either you go to bed with me at noon, or I'm voting no for you at four.'" She added that she threw him out and received tenure nonetheless.

It is important to keep in mind that in less self-evident cases the same event may be perceived as discriminatory by one person and not by someone else. Two patterns appeared to influence the women respondents' perception of discrimination. One is a general trend within American society: the increasing awareness of gender discrimination and harassment. The other pattern links individual career outcomes to the awareness of discrimination. Several women reported that in hindsight they consider some experiences discriminatory but did not judge them to be so when they happened. Recall Jane's words: "I don't think I could have described well enough what I was experiencing when it was happening to get help with it." She credits the women's movement with clearly articulating, or naming, experiences of discrimination that previously were not acknowledged as such. In these cases, the women's movement provided the conceptual tools for reinterpreting an experience as discriminatory.

The interviews elicited two quite different kinds of stories about personal experiences with gender discrimination. In one, discriminations were minimized; in the other, they were maximized. The great majority of women volunteered hardly any mention of discrimination. Details came to light only in response to a specific question about gender discrimination. Other interviews, however, prominently featured a protracted list of discriminatory incidents. Women whose careers floundered were more likely to relate accounts that contained a whole series of mistreatments. To some degree, a career failure may provoke feelings of bitterness and anger and heighten a woman's awareness of discriminatory episodes. On the other hand, however, the predominance of discrimination in these career stories may well indicate a real process in which discrimination somehow begets further discrimination. For instance, if a woman unsuccessfully fights a discriminatory tenure denial, she might gain the reputation of being a troublemaker, which may then lead to the denial of other employment opportunities. An adverse snowball effect of this kind fits the more general theory of the accumulation of advantages and disadvantages in scientific careers (Merton 1973; Zuckerman 1989).

Informal Obstacles

In the interviews, women also talked about more informal obstacles. Many reported being excluded from informal social events with their colleagues, such as playing sports together or going out for drinks. In the old days, women might have been explicitly told not to participate in such gatherings, as one woman scientist reported. More recently, explicit exclusion has become rarer, but there remain some cultural factors that make women feel out of place in a predominantly male group of colleagues. As one woman said, "there's always a sense, especially in a group that does not include many women, that you're not one of the guys, and that works against you, and that is impossible to fight, of course." At this level of subtle, informal gender segregation, the deficit and difference models converge. Men's informal exclusion of women can have its complement in women's reluctance to participate in types of social activities that do not appeal to them.

Interactions between colleagues are colored by the gender of the participants according to a substantial number of the men and women we interviewed, although more women than men thought they have, at least sometimes, interacted differently with male and female colleagues (men: 40 percent; women: 54 percent). Of those, a majority of women, as well as some of the men, noted that their interactions with women were better than those with men (men: 12 percent; women: 66 percent). As Barbara observed, men "talk to each other in a way that is slightly different in terms of sharing problems and stuff like that, from what one's able to do if you're of the opposite sex; and if you don't have people to talk to about these things, you have to be fiercely independent."

The sexual dimension can be a complicating factor in collegial relationships. Of the men who felt they interacted differently with men and women colleagues, one in five referred to sexual tension in interactions with colleagues of the opposite sex; only one in fifteen of the women raised this issue. Deborah described how she curtailed her social interactions with colleagues to avoid any possibility of sexual misinterpretation. Another female scientist noted that it is just impossible for a woman scientist at a conference to invite a male colleague to her room for an informal discussion about research over drinks, whereas this is very common among male scientists.

Social interactions with colleagues may affect scientific careers. About half of the people we interviewed (with no difference between men and women on this part) thought that their social interactions with their peers had an impact on the progress of their career. Some women felt that their exclusion from informal contacts hindered their career because important information is exchanged and decisions are made at casual meetings among colleagues. Thus, women's absence from these occasions may render them invisible. As Jane poignantly put it, "certain things were clearly closed to me. There were little social hours and stuff that involved male camaraderie that I really didn't feel like busting in on. But I knew that those were the places where hiring decisions got worked on." Even if bans on outright discrimination are energetically enforced, the effects of unofficial decision making (which is much more difficult to police) may ensure the same end as an overtly discriminatory act would.

Some women also reiterated the often-noted double standard for male and female behavior: behavior that is acceptable in men may be unacceptable in women. For instance, an assertive woman is likely to be seen as bitchy, whereas a man with the same temperament might not be so judged. In a vivid description of the double standard, a woman talked about a male scientist who did a postdoctoral fellowship simultaneously with her in the same research group. This man "was always running around screaming, and very temperamental and just impossible. A woman could never have gotten away with acting like that. We'd always have to be more conciliatory, more mainstream, more normal. And this person was absolutely paranormal, but he was viewed as a brilliant scientist." In this respect, it is interesting that, when asked about gender differences among scientists in general, a few of the men (6 percent)—and none of the women—thought women scientists were *more* aggressive, competitive, or risk taking. These men may adhere to a traditional standard of female pliability. By contrast, about one in eight of the men, and one in ten of the women, said that women were *less* aggressive and likely to take risks.

Possibly one of the most important social interactions occurs between mentor and student or junior scientist. We often heard about the great impact (positive or negative) that the relationship with a mentor had on the further course of a young scientist's career. Barbara was blatantly rejected by a professor as a graduate advisee because she was female, but such outright rejections were rare. What appears more typical is Jane's experience: her male graduate advisor, although supportive in general, "wasn't tapping into his network for me the way he did for his male grad students. There didn't seem to be, in his mind, the push to have my career be a success." Of course, not all male scientists benefited from their mentors either. Fortunately, however, good mentors appeared to outnumber bad mentors by far. Many people we interviewed, both men and women, praised their mentors for affording them valuable assistance.

Women's informal marginalization within the social system of science may also be fostered by what some women perceive as heightened risks of collaborating with colleagues—that is, typically with male colleagues who have predominated in the pool of potential collaborators in most disciplines. Some women we interviewed, such as Gail, found col-laborations with other women preferable and less risky than those with men; and with increasing numbers of women scientists, collaborations among women may become more frequent.

More women than men said they liked working alone when asked whether their gender influenced their working style as a scientist (men: 6 percent; women: 16 percent). Some women noted that their reluctance to collaborate stems from the fear that their work would be misappropri-ated by collaborators. One woman, for instance, expressed a sense "that things would be taken away from me if working with others." Often this fear was based on past experiences with collaboration, when women did not receive the credit they felt they deserved.

Some women scientists are becoming more open to collaboration at later career stages when they feel more established and self-confident. As one woman said, however, her greater openness to collaboration is not always matched by men's willingness to collaborate.

> As far as my male colleagues are concerned, at this stage I would be very much more willing to work with men on projects, and I don't find them very accepting of my participation in some of the things that they do. In the earliest part of my career, I was very much an isolationist, in terms of my work. And it's a habit that's kind of hard to break, and I had a very specific reason for being that way: there were no women to collaborate with anyway, and my very strong feel-ing was that any work a woman did as a coauthor or a coprincipal investigator was always credited to the male, and I damn well wanted credit for what I was doing. So I wasn't going to dilute that by letting five guys have their names on what I was doing, and it was a tough decision to maintain, and it's probably the only reason I survived as long as I did as a recognizable researcher in the field.

The danger that women's contributions to collaborative efforts may not receive due credit would be considered an informal structural ob-stacle within the deficit model. In the next section, on the difference model, we will explore socialization differences that might also make some women scientists reluctant to enter collaborative enterprises even if there is no threat of exploitation.

HOW WOMEN AND MEN ACT IN SCIENCE

The difference model of gender disparities claims that women have career paths different from men's because they *are* different from men. In our interviews, we asked men and women to rate themselves on personality traits and socialization patterns—which, according to many other studies, show strong gender differences and could affect the way scientists approach their work. As we look at the former fellows' answers, we should keep in mind the point often made by proponents of the difference model: the typically male pattern has no compelling superiority over the typically female pattern, and women's distinct attributes ought to be rewarded both for the sake of fairness and the good of science.

Socialization Differences

Simply by becoming doctoral-level scientists, the women in our group do not fit the typical female pattern. Nonetheless, they differed from their male cohorts in their own estimation of self-confidence, ambition, and related traits. Substantially more men than women reported that they considered their scientific ability to be above average (men: 70 percent; women: 52 percent), whereas more women than men considered theirs to be average (men: 18 percent; women: 35 percent). Similar results were found on self-evaluations of technical skills. In addition, more men than women thought others rated their scientific ability above average (men: 70 percent; women: 53 percent); slightly more women than men thought it was rated as average (men: 18 percent; women: 24 percent). Somewhat more men than women considered themselves self-confident (58 percent versus 49 percent). When asked whether they should have handled their career obstacles in a different way, many more women than men thought they should have had more confidence or been more assertive (25 percent versus 5 percent).

On the whole, women were more likely than men to have entered their science career gingerly, taking a step-by-step approach rather than having clear overall career goals at the outset. About four times as many women as men (16 percent versus 4 percent) said they had vague or unclear career aspirations when they started out in science. Even now, only 34 percent of the women, as compared with 44 percent of the men, said they were more ambitious than the average colleague.

In a difference model approach, one would consider such gender differences among the causes that make women scientists, on average, less successful than men. Indeed, within the group of men and women currently working in academe, their ambition ($r = 0.30$), their estimation of how their colleagues rate their scientific ability ($r = 0.30$), and their own evaluation of their ability ($r = 0.27$) correlated considerably with actual attainment of success in the university setting. Weaker correlations were found for self-confidence ($r = 0.15$) and interviewees' rating of their technical skills ($r = 0.09$). We should emphasize, however, that these correlations do not indicate a direction of causality. Ambitious scientists, for instance, may become more successful; or successful scientists may become more ambitious. Thus, rather than being the cause of the women's average lag in career success, the gender differences in these traits might be the end result of women's greater career obstacles and ensuing relative lack of success—a view proponents of the deficit model might take. Again, there may be some reinforcing combination of both processes that intricately links elements of both the difference and the deficit model in real career paths in science.

As to internal obstacles, more women than men interviewees mentioned their personality (60 percent versus 42 percent), but more men than women referred to bad work habits (22 percent versus 7 percent). Apparently, men tend to fault specifics, whereas women tend to blame more global features of their personality, thus making it harder for women to address a particular problem that may hold them back and to initiate change.

In the pursuit of their careers, men appear to be more independent of their social surroundings. As a woman scientist said, "male scientists are very internally directed, and they don't listen to what people are saying around them." Twice as many men as women asserted that nobody helped them deal with their obstacles (21 percent versus 9 percent). By contrast, more women than men acknowledged the support of family and significant others (63 percent versus 43 percent), colleagues (50 percent versus 35 percent), and friends (31 percent versus 15 percent). Thus, women scientists evidenced a relatively great need for support, which stemmed from two sources. First, more women than men respondents reported that they had encountered obstacles on their career paths (77 percent versus 68 percent), and second, women seemed more dependent on social support systems in overcoming obstacles. This latter result corresponds with theories that propose a greater social connectedness among women, which, of course, makes us wonder if women receive this much-needed support within the current system of science.

We found other evidence of the existence of—and the need for—greater connectedness among women. In her interactions with her co-workers, Deborah observed that "the currency of conversation tends to be slightly different" from the way her male colleagues interact with their co-workers; that is, she emphasizes a more personal interaction style. Similarly, another woman said that the members of her graduate-student research groups were more on "family terms" than was usual for male-led groups. The family imagery was expressed even more vividly by a third woman scientist: "I've tried to create families out of my collaborations with people. The relationship is equally important to me as the work itself. I pick people that I like working with, and then we do projects that I consider to be really fun."

By themselves, these few statements may not suffice to postulate a general trend among women scientists to consider family relations the prototype of human relations to be emulated in the science domain. They do, however, exemplify what has been termed the "historical allegiance of women to the family model as an ideal form of organization" (Nowotny 1991, 155). Residues of this allegiance may partly explain a certain uneasiness some women feel with the common type of scientific collaboration, which is more fleeting and superficial than they might prefer (even when, as is fashionable, the word *family* is used by groups of collaborators). Because these women scientists make heavier emotional investments in their collaborative relationships, they might choose fewer and closer collaborations. In turn, this collaboration style may contribute to the marginalization of some women in the social system of science. Christine, for instance, notes that the trend in her field to do research in larger and larger collaborations might restrict her in the future because she is "not a very good joiner" and prefers to work with a small number of other people and her students.

Family-style collaborative relationships may be more rewarding, but they can also be more disastrous because they intensify both positive and negative emotions toward colleagues. After all, if the failure of a collaboration were also seen in family terms, it would be the equivalent of divorce, bereavement, or abandonment. A broken family causes more problems than the disbanding of what is viewed as a temporary business arrangement.

Styles of Doing Science

Somewhat more women than men saw gender differences in the work of scientists in general (men: 49 percent; women: 61 percent). When asked about the influence of their gender on the way they themselves do science, substantially more women than men thought there was such an influence, particularly in professional conduct (men: 26 percent; women:

51 percent). Although fewer thought there were gender influences on aspects more closely related to the substance of scientific work, women were much more apt to think that gender affected their choice of a research subject (men: 16 percent; women: 40 percent) and ways of thinking in science (men: 20 percent; women: 36 percent). The lowest proportions were found in respect to methods adopted, but there the male-female difference was particularly striking (men: 10 percent; women: 35 percent). Thus, women appear to be much more convinced than men that gender influences activity in science. Men, however, are more prone to associate themselves with the traditional gender-neutral doctrine of science. Of course, we are dealing here with scientists' perceptions and self-reports that are not necessarily based in reality (that is, in measurable gender differences in actual scientific behavior). Nonetheless, if, in the minds of a sizable proportion of scientists, gender has become a relevant variable for interpreting scientific behavior, this fact in itself is bound to have some repercussions for the notion of gender-blind science. We should add that, contrary to what one might expect, the various aspects of the belief in gender differences are generally unrelated to outcome measures of scientific success (both among men and women).

The following sections concentrate on the perceived gender differences in scientific style, but we have to keep in mind that a large majority of the men we interviewed and a majority of women in some respects (and a substantial minority in others) did not believe their gender influenced their way of doing science.

Women's Professional Conduct: Less Careerist

Gender differences in interaction styles may have a considerable impact on men's and women's career progress in science. A common observation among both men and women we interviewed is that men scientists have more "entrepreneurial spunk," as Gail called it. They are, in this view, more aggressive, combative, and self-promoting in their pursuit of career success; so they achieve higher visibility. In short, they are better at playing the political game of career advancement. Men's heightened careerist fervor may, to some degree, also be connected with the fact that, among our married interviewees, 80 percent of the men but only 34 percent of the women were primary wage earners. Differences in professional conduct, although noted here among the difference-model obstacles, may of course be structurally reinforced and then also assume the character of deficit-model obstacles.

Furthermore, some women interviewees reported that men have a way of showing off at conferences that alienates women. One woman vividly described the behavior as well as the cultural rules discouraging women scientists from initiating professional discussions with men:

> A lot of the connections that people make at meetings and so on, I couldn't do, because what men did is they stood in the hallways and found the great men and went over and shook their hands or asked them to have a drink with them or something, and women couldn't do that in my day. So you couldn't initiate anything. . . . but if you were in a group of people who managed to connect with that person, then you could try to talk to him. But more often than not, when you were in a group like that, the men showed off for each other, they took themselves terribly seriously and they said any kind of thing that came to their head. I call it "professor talk," and I can do it very well. To me it's a big joke, but it's something that men do all the time with each other, and it's a kind of stroking behavior, makes them all feel good, even though they're really not talking about anything and they're really not communicating very much. And I found that a waste of my time.

Professor talk may indeed be a total waste of time in terms of exchanging research information or gaining scientific insights. Nevertheless, it may be anything but wasteful in terms of its hidden agenda. Professor talk—or a bull session, as Ann called it—appears to have the important social subtext of a bonding ritual. The bonds thus forged may have some beneficial impact on a scientist's research and career. This again may reflect gender differences in interaction styles. Men's greater independence in their career pursuits finds its complement in what some women consider superficial and hollow rituals of establishing social contact with colleagues.

Individuals set their own career goals and define what success means for them. Certainly, some of the women we interviewed are as ambitious as the men (if not more so) in terms of career success. Typically, however, the women tend to set their goals somewhat lower than the men do, which may be connected with women's less aggressive conduct. In other words, the women scientists appear to be the "purer scientists"—they are somewhat less concerned with the political aspects of science, such as influence and power.

Judging by their responses, few of our scientists, men or women, are hungry for scientific power. A large majority appeared to be burdened rather than elated by their opportunities to make decisions affecting other scientists' careers, and nobody confessed to relishing administrative tasks. When asked about the aspect of science they like best, their staple replies mentioned the actual scientific work, doing the experiments, or tackling difficult problems. There was a slight gender difference, however. Women scientists, even the most successful, said they were less interested in influence and power than their male counterparts were. Ann thinks it is typically male to aspire to chairmanships or deanships, and she says she does not harbor such aspirations. Nor have the other successful women scientists profiled in this book set their sights on achievements of this type. The successful women scientists could be described as reluctant leaders. They recognize that having an elevated position in their fields has given them a substantial amount of power—some of them seem to think maybe too much power—and they intend to be very scrupulous in exercising this power fairly. These women either fulfilled most of their aspirations already or see their yet-unfulfilled ambitions in terms of greater recognition for scientific achievements: for example, election to the National Academy of Sciences.

Although most of the men share a similar attitude to power, two of the successful men scientists we profiled are quite comfortable with it. Allan, who served a term as department chairman, acutely appreciates the division of labor in science; he defines his role as directing and managing a large-scale research operation rather than mainly interesting himself in his own experiments and supervising a group of researchers on the side. With great ease, Charles acknowledges that he is a leader in his field with a large amount of power. Moreover, among the cases of former fellows who left research science, Fred, who now works in the government grant administration, has no qualms about rejecting most of the proposals he receives.

Except for a small number of respondents who were disaffected with the culture and social conditions of scientific labor, most of the people we interviewed expressed their strong enthusiasm for doing research. Many felt privileged that they had the opportunity to be employed to do what they enjoyed most. As Allan put it: "So much fun, and you get paid for it, too." A large majority (men: 80 percent; women: 78 percent) said they were satisfied with their life in general. The most popular responses to a question about the favorite aspect of doing science referred to the actual process of problem solving in scientific research (men: 52 percent; women: 60 percent) and to gaining new knowledge and insight (men: 58 percent; women: 50 percent). Thus, men seemed to be somewhat more interested in obtaining the end result of research than in the process, whereas women slightly emphasized the intellectually stimulating process of scientific research. This might slow women's careers at various junctures when scientists' track records are assessed.

Women's Problem Selection: Niche Approach

In respect to choosing subfields and problems, a number of men and women agreed with a woman who noticed "fewer women in highly theoretical/mathematical subfields (including myself—I am not much of a mathematician, compared with many of my male colleagues)." But gender differences appeared to go beyond differences in mathematics interest or training. In terms of problem selection, many women followed a niche approach—creating their own area of research expertise. A good example is Jane, who liked "to sense that I had my own area, that I wasn't just a cog." Similarly, Barbara is predisposed to select research problems that are completely her own: "I very much dislike working on problems that I know other people are working on." Rather than competing with other researchers and research groups in a race toward the solution of a problem, she carves out a niche for herself. Deborah, who said she did not follow this strategy herself, nonetheless considered the phenomenon widespread among her female colleagues.

A woman observed: "Although men and women may do similar research, women tend toward long-term problems which involve a lot of detail, while men want to do dramatic things which bring grand results quickly." Men seemed more likely to join the fray in hot fields and breakthrough topics. Allan, for instance, said he consciously seeks out problems that command a great deal of interest in the scientific community. Another man remarked that "as a male, it's easier to pick a more ambitious topic, say you're a graduate student and you're working on a doctoral dissertation." According to this scientist, men are better able to be "maverickish or nonconformist," whereas women stick more to established rules and procedures. Although these mavericks operate somewhat outside established science, they often do not choose that approach to create a quiet niche for themselves. Rather, they hope to bring about major changes in science, thus moving their field to the forefront. Brad typifies such a maverick. From early in his career, he was among the founders of a new field of scientific research despite some hostility from scientists in the neighboring traditional disciplines.

Women's niche approach is also reflected in the focus of their professional identity. In the interviews, fewer women than men identified themselves by the broad label of *researcher, scientist,* or *academic* (men: 59 percent; women: 44 percent); but twice as many women as men focused their professional identity on a subdiscipline (men: 9 percent; women: 20 percent).

Both the difference model and the deficit model offer explanations for women's greater propensity toward a niche approach. On the one hand, some women may be predisposed to avoid areas of potential conflict and take fewer risks than men would. On the other hand, it may be structurally necessary for women operating in fields dominated by men to carve out niches in order to maintain a sense of autonomy and control.

Women's Methodology: Perfectionism

When the people we interviewed remarked on a specifically female methodological approach and way of thinking, they usually did not refer to some alternative approach, such as a nonandrocentric science, that is occasionally discussed in the literature (see chapter 1). Among the rare exceptions was a woman geologist who described herself as having an increasing feeling of oneness with a mountain the more she analyzes it. Another woman noted: "There very likely is a difference in the degree of holistic versus logical/sequential thinking that is innate."

The responses in this area emphasized that women are more cautious and careful in their methods and pay more attention to details. A woman stated that "women are often more careful in their research and more hesitant to make statements until they feel they can really 'prove' them." In the words of another woman, "women are more thorough, less likely to shoot from the hip." Yet another woman observed that women tend "to wait until some piece of work is 'perfect' before we publicize it." Like Ann, numerous women acknowledged a tendency to be perfectionists in their scientific work. Some said they were perfectionists because they wanted to avoid failure or criticism. Another woman scientist stressed women's attention to detail: "Women are more meticulous; they tend to deal in details. And so I think that does affect how you do science. I don't know why that is; it just seems that for me, and the other women scientists I've dealt with, we tend more to deal in the minute details, fine points."

According to the people we talked to, women on the whole also aim to see the broader picture and do more comprehensive work. Ann, for instance, described her predisposition to produce complete and synthetic papers. Another woman observed: "Women tend to work longer on individual projects and take on projects that are broader in scope than do men. Women seem to find it more difficult to break projects into small parts, and consequently obtain fewer publications per project." In the words of a third woman scientist, "women tend to do more integrated work, maybe a little more big-picture stuff, and something that relates back to something that's relevant."

These findings suggest a reassessment of the often-observed publication productivity gap between the genders (for example, Cole and Zuckerman 1984; Fox 1983; Long 1992)—which we also found in our sample. The tendencies we have mentioned about thoroughness and comprehensiveness may combine to reduce women's quantitative publication output. If women scientists are more thorough and perfectionist than men, on average, and if they favor more comprehensive and synthetic work, the quantity of their publications per annum will tend to be lower.

Several woman (but hardly any man) agreed that for women scientists, a higher quality of the individual paper counterbalanced the lower quantity of publications. "Publications by women appear to be of higher quality with more data, more replications, more cautious interpretations and extension beyond data, and with greater depth into the question," commented one woman respondent. And another woman said: "I have observed men who do not do careful work and will report erroneous work. I have observed men who will publish, slightly rework a problem, and publish again. I have observed women who also publish nearly the same work in several articles. I personally do not publish work unless it is complete and I am very confident of the results."

One should emphasize that a perception, even if it is widespread, is not necessarily true—the low-quantity-but-high-quality claim may just be a self-serving justification for low productivity. Nevertheless, some indirect quantitative evidence for the women scientists' tendency to publish articles that contain more substantial or comprehensive work emerged from a small study we made of the citations in the scientific literature to articles written by biologists (Sonnert, in press, b). (We chose biology because our group of former fellows contained a high percentage of women in this field.) Among the study's subsample of twenty-five former NSF fellows in biology who are now academic scientists, women's articles received significantly more citations per article, on average, than men's articles did (24.4 versus 14.4 citations; $p = 0.0337$). This greater impact might indicate that the women's articles tended to contain more noteworthy contents on the whole. A gender difference in citations per article in the same direction was also found by Long (1992) in a much larger sample of biochemists, as well as by Garfield (1993) in a study of the one thousand most-cited scientists.

This casts doubt on the appropriateness of the traditional indicator of a scientist's performance—publication productivity—which can be of great importance when decisions about scientists' careers are made. A long publication list appeared indeed to be the most powerful determinant of quality judgments among peers, especially for a first impression, as our study among biologists confirmed (Sonnert, in press, b). If women, as a group, tend to have a slightly different publication behavior—less quantity but more quality—a performance measure based chiefly on publication counts may be biased against women.

Interestingly, similar proportions of men and women do not consider a high quantity of publications an important part of being a good scientist (men: 55 percent; women: 59 percent). This belief is only weakly related to their actual publication output, but the direction of this relationship differs between the genders. Among the women in academe, there is a small positive correlation ($r = 0.16$) between believing that a high production output is important and the quantity of publications they produced. Among the men, however, there is a small negative correlation ($r = -0.19$). The more publications the men interviewees produced, the less they tended to believe that a high publication productivity was an important part of being a good scientist. One might speculate that men, even if they reject the quantitative quality standard, are nonetheless more prepared to abide by this standard for strategic reasons. Women, by contrast, may tend to be less willing to play the game of publication maximization if they consider it irrelevant to true quality—and this may contribute to the gender differential in average publication rates.

In another result on gender differences in the general area of methodology, more men than women described their overall scientific approach as creative (men: 27 percent; women: 12 percent). The gender gap in the weight given to creativity is particularly intriguing because it runs counter to the common stereotype of women as more creative and men as more logical and analytical. Both our scientists' self-reports and their observations of others oppose this stereotype. Allan, a senior male scientist, for example, asserted that, owing to some deep-rooted gender differential, females were less creative and intuitive than males, which made them less suitable for high-quality work in his subspecialty. The responses in our group may, of course, reflect another stereotype about creativity—that men are the creative geniuses in all fields. Perhaps the comparatively strong emphasis on creativity among the men we interviewed reflects a powerful identification with the heroes of science, who are overwhelmingly male.

Standards of Good Science

Gender differences in the normative concept of good science may be an important element in bringing about different ways of doing science. We wondered if our women interviewees, as a group, had a different idea about what constitutes good science. Women and men equally agreed that addressing an important problem was a major characteristic of really good scientific work (men: 35 percent; women: 33 percent); but men emphasized creativity (men: 43 percent; women: 30 percent) and good presentation of research (men: 11 percent; women: 4 percent), whereas women stressed comprehensiveness (men: 20 percent; women: 36 percent) and integrity (men: 5 percent; women: 14 percent). In regard to the last aspect, a male scientist observed that women have "certainly kept their scientific integrity a lot more intact than some of their male counterparts. Few, if any, of the bozos involved in scientific fraud have been women, and hurrah for them, say I!"

When asked what distinguished top-quality from average work, women again emphasized comprehensiveness more than men did (men: 15 percent; women: 31 percent). In characterizing bad science, more women than men mentioned lack of comprehensiveness (men: 21 percent; women: 29 percent) and dishonesty (men: 9 percent; women: 24 percent). Men were somewhat more likely than women to consider attention to an unimportant problem as an indicator of bad science (men: 28 percent; women: 20 percent).

These findings do not indicate the existence of radical gender differences. The women and men we interviewed do not mention completely different sets of quality criteria. But certainly there are gender differences in emphasis that appear to reflect the gender differences in perceived scientific styles and perhaps also in actual scientific behavior—as indicated by the difference in citation rates. For instance, the trend for women to do broader, more comprehensive work is echoed in a greater normative emphasis on comprehensiveness. The emphasis on integrity may be connected with their tendency to be more thorough and perfectionist, to spurn "quick and dirty" work. It may also relate to women's less careerist approach to science or their unwillingness to cut corners for career success. Thus, these observations on the normative level bolster our comments on the causes for the productivity gap and for the higher citation rate of women's publications.

We conclude that the differences between how women and men scientists act lie less in the epistemological and methodological than in the social aspects of science: for instance, collaboration with peers, competitiveness, problem selection, and professional conduct. The methodology is essentially the same for men and women, but women tend to be more meticulous and perfectionist in its use. Rather than being iconoclasts, women appear to uphold, to a particularly high degree, the traditional standards of science, such as carefulness, replicability, objectivity, and connection to fundamentals. The women scientists in our sample seem to have internalized the conventional epistemological rules of science more thoroughly than the social ones.

Thus, we found little evidence that women in science follow or believe in a radically divergent epistemology or methodology that some feminist theorists of science have suggested. It may, of course, be proposed that women (and men) with alternative methodological and epistemological approaches do not flourish or survive in the science pipeline for very long, so that the scientists who are reasonably successful under the current system of science are predisposed to it, or at least have learned to accept it. Our sample of former postdoctoral fellows, however, does not lend itself to testing such a proposition.

Conformity with the formal rules of science and distance from the more informal ways of doing science appear to be two sides of the same coin—the social marginalization of women scientists. Perhaps somewhat ironically, women's status as newcomers to science tends to make them conservative to a particularly high degree, whether predisposed to following accepted ways or not. They conform with the traditional scientific core rules because their work is often under heightened critical scrutiny. Whereas the epistemological and methodological standards are relatively explicit, there are also many implicit and informal aspects of a science career. Women scientists may be at a particular disadvantage in these more intangible aspects.

Faint echoes of marginalization are found even among the women whose success stories we related in chapter 2. Christine said she is not a good joiner of large collaborative teams. Barbara and Ann report a feeling of isolation in respect to social interactions with their male peers. Similarly, Deborah is very conscious of her conduct around male scientists to prevent any suspicion of impropriety. Elizabeth suffers from an unsupportive and highly competitive atmosphere at her institution. In other words, all five of these successful women are to some extent isolated or estranged from the predominantly male collegial network. This is one of the significant gender differences that will demand attention when we come to make policy recommendations. The successful men reported no such problems for themselves, but their accounts mirror and support the women's observations of gender differences in social interactions. Allan, for instance, notes that a woman in his place might not be as well connected with his mostly male colleagues.

Personal sociability does not sufficiently explain the degree of a scientist's marginalization. Even men who regarded themselves as nonsociable successfully operated within the collegial network, whereas women scientists who regarded themselves as social persons remained somehow isolated. Barbara enjoys the social aspects of doing science with collaborators in the laboratory, and Christine also thinks she is good at relating with people; but they both still report some isolation from the collegial network. David, by contrast, although confessing to a certain lack of social skills, still managed to make contacts and connections with other scientists that proved crucial for his career success.

Thus, social marginalization is clearly a problem for many women scientists, even for some of the most successful ones. Added to potential obstacles outside science (above all, family obligations) this marginalization makes it harder for women scientists to reach the very top of their professions. Our successful women scientists may provide some explanation for the finding from the larger sample of 699 former fellows that women were particularly underrepresented in the top positions of the scientific hierarchy: among the older scientists now working at top academic institutions, 88 percent of the men but only 40 percent of the women held the position of full professor. Conceptually, this obstacle of marginalization is a combination of informal structural obstacles (those noted in the deficit model) and attitudinal obstacles (the focus here of the difference model). For instance, insofar as men scientists tend to exclude their women colleagues from collegial networks or subject their work to extra critical scrutiny, the women face informal structural obstacles. Insofar as women's general socialization patterns favor certain ways of doing science that are disadvantageous for career advancement, they face attitudinal obstacles in themselves.

SYNCHRONIZING THREE CLOCKS: THE TRIALS AND REWARDS OF MARRIAGE AND PARENTHOOD

So far we have primarily focused on elements in scientific career paths that belong to the world of science. We now turn to an aspect of life outside science that has a crucial impact on women's science careers in particular—marriage and parenthood. In family life, women are often faced with structural obstacles that men escape; and in family matters, distinctive cultural and socialization patterns internalized by women show themselves most clearly. In other words, both the deficit model and the difference model are needed to understand gender differences in science careers resulting from the experience of marriage and parenthood.

Most of the women we interviewed have been married at one point in their lives, and the proportion of married men is even higher (men: 93 percent; women: 87 percent). The majority of these women also have children, at about the same proportion as the men do (men: 71 percent; women: 70 percent). In contrast with earlier decades, when a larger proportion of women scientists were single, the problem of combining marriage and family with a career has been a key issue facing most of the women we interviewed.

Among the small group of unmarried people, a sizable minority of both women and men said that their decision not to marry was influenced by career demands (men: 27 percent; women: 35 percent). Career considerations appeared to be more prevalent for married women than for married men in their decision not to have any children (men: 46 percent; women: 78 percent).

When asked about gender differences among scientists, a few men thought that men were more focused on their careers than women were (men: 10 percent; women: 3 percent). But when asked to assign percentages to the amount of priority given to science versus private lives, men and women scientists attached similar weights: both ranked science higher in importance than their private lives (men: 61 percent; women: 64 percent). The women, however, were somewhat more likely to report feeling at least some tension between the various roles in their lives (men: 66 percent; women 73 percent). Thus, this group of women, on the average, kept their focus on their science career—while facing some extra strain from the domestic sphere.

A considerably larger percentage of the female questionnaire respondents mentioned family demands as a career obstacle: 21 percent compared with only 3 percent of the men. Although similar proportions of the men and women we interviewed had contemplated abandoning science (men: 40 percent; women: 43 percent), their reasons were somewhat different. More women than men mentioned family and spouse considerations (men: 7 percent; women: 17 percent), whereas the lack of recognition, success, or money was more prevalent among men (men: 32 percent; women: 17 percent).

When we asked those who were married if their marriage had affected their careers, almost everyone said yes (men: 91 percent; women:

92 percent). Contrary to our intuitive sense that marriage may be a career obstacle for women, many women reported career advantages instead that derived from being married. The effect of marriage on their career was considered positive by almost half of the married respondents (men: 46 percent; women: 49 percent). Only a small group mentioned an explicitly negative impact (men: 15 percent; women: 18 percent). Both men and women mentioned as a key advantage the emotional support and security that marriage provides. Deborah, for instance, noted that marriage "made me more secure; it let me devote myself to my work in ways I might not otherwise have, because my attention would have been diverted to finding a mate, or finding a companion, and being married helped me be settled."

A likely scenario for women scientists is to be married to another scientist, often in the same field (see Fava and Deierlein 1988; Pycior, Slack, and Abir-Am, in press). In our questionnaire sample 62 percent of the married women but only 19 percent of the married men had a spouse with a doctorate. Spouses who are also scientists were often described as understanding and supportive of the time-consuming and irregular lifestyle of scientists. Allan recounted how his first marriage floundered largely because of his rigorous work schedule. In his second marriage, to a scientist in his field, "it's okay if I work ten hours a day. I'm married to someone now who also likes to work ten hours a day, so it's not a problem." A spouse in the same field is also a sounding board for ideas, a source of inspiration and criticism. Spouses often collaborate, but the potential pitfall for the woman is that she might be perceived as her husband's assistant and junior partner in their collaborative efforts.

The negative aspects of marriage include restrictions in mobility. Because women scientists are much more likely than men to live in two-scientist marriages, the problem is more prevalent among women scientists. More women than men thought that geographic issues were a factor in their careers (men: 63 percent; women: 76 percent). In addition, these issues are typically solved at the wife's expense when it comes to the crunch. Many women compromised their careers by following a husband to his job location or staying in a place unfavorable for their own careers because the husband was not geographically mobile. A few of the people we interviewed have resorted to some form of long-distance marriage. Gail and her scientist husband, for instance, work in different cities a few hours apart and lead a commuter marriage. In an extreme case, one woman reported that she and her husband, a scientist in the same field, live on different continents and see each other mostly at conferences.

Single people noted the obvious advantages of their status—more time to work and optimal career choices unrestricted by spouse or family considerations. On the negative side, there is the lack of emotional and even practical support in managing the chores of everyday life. As Florence said, "it is very clear, as my other single friends and I agree, everybody needs a spouse, somebody to do things for them, if only to take the cat to the vet."

Whereas those corollaries of unmarried life apply to both men and women, single women also face a set of unique disadvantages within the social system of science. A single female scientist can have a particularly awkward standing in a predominantly male environment (Kaufman 1978). She might be considered "available" and thus be more likely to attract unwanted sexual attention from colleagues as well as hostility from colleagues' wives. A man observed "enormous pressure on an unattached woman scientist to date her colleagues, and no pressure for a comparable male scientist." A single woman might also deter male colleagues from socially interacting with her for fear of a misinterpretation of their relationship. A divorced woman noted that by "having a man anywhere in the picture instead of always standing on my own, I would have had substantially more clout. Because then at those departmental parties or whatever, when the scientists were bringing their wives, I would have brought my husband." Finally, single women scientists might be viewed as wives- and mothers-to-be and thus be unable to escape any potential prejudice against married women scientists.

Gender differences are substantial when it comes to the perceived effects of parenthood. Almost all the women with children said that being a parent had somehow influenced their careers, but only two-thirds of the men felt this way (men: 65 percent; women: 93 percent). While some parents noted a positive influence of children on their careers (men: 18 percent; women: 19 percent), a slightly higher percentage noted negative influences (men: 25 percent; women: 32 percent). The largest group stated conflicting or unclear effects (men: 55 percent; women: 48 percent).

A major problem with parenthood, as most women agreed, was that children take time and energy away from scientific pursuits. And the years of raising a family typically coincide with the crucial early career phase of establishing scientific credentials. Some men also reported negative career effects of parenthood. Allan, for instance, who found himself in the somewhat uncommon role of a single father with four young children, noted that his scientific career went into a dip during that time.

Another male interviewee said he was "starting to turn things down because I hate to see my older boy disappointed when I'm not there to tuck him in." On the other hand, parents also noted that children provide an intense emotional satisfaction that puts their career in perspective and even helps them to function as scientists, as this woman frankly professed: "I think that if I had to look at myself in terms of my accomplishments entirely in terms of my career, I would be a sad cookie. And that these setbacks and stupid remarks, and the crap that gets thrown at you would bother me a shitload more if I had also sacrificed the experience of having a child."

The career disadvantages of marriage and parenthood appear to be straightforward and intuitively plausible—restricted mobility for dual-career couples, for example, or the effort of child rearing. The advantages, by contrast, are more indirect and subtle; it is hard to gauge the impact of the social and emotional support that a spouse provides. Thus, it appears easier to name the negative effects of marriage and childhood than the positive ones, which may be a source for the common view of marriage and family as career obstacles for women.

It seems impossible to summarize our results into one simple statement about the effects of marriage and parenthood. First of all, the style of marriage is important. If, in a traditional mode of marriage, the wife has to take care of the domestic chores, then the husband is an extra burden. One woman who divorced her husband and raised her child by herself commented: "When I left my husband, it was as if I had two children less." A more cooperative mode of marriage, by contrast, eases the wife's burdens and provides her with additional support. The second style of marriage is becoming more widespread, although the reality of housework arrangements may sometimes lag behind the professed ideal of a cooperative marriage.

Moreover, the profession and seniority of the spouse are crucial factors. Even in our group of married women, many of whom were distinguished scientists, the majority had husbands who were the primary wage earners. Of the married women, only 34 percent reported to be the primary wage earner, but 80 percent of the married men did. A general marriage pattern in our culture is for women to marry men who are older and professionally senior and who earn more money than themselves, which encourages the couple to give the husband's career priority. It is not surprising that an advantageous marriage choice for women is to follow a nontraditional pattern by marrying a junior or equal-status scientist or a "trailing spouse" whose job makes him geographically mobile (CSWP 1992, 12). Being the main breadwinner has both financial and psychological effects. As Deborah said, it "helped reinforce my being determined" to pursue career success.

Rather than thinking of marriage and parenthood as having a fixed effect on women scientists' careers, we should see them as a set of problems and opportunities. Women scientists are faced with the dilemma of "synchronizing" the often conflicting demands of three clocks: their biological clock, their career clock (such as their tenure clock), and their spouses' career clock. On the other hand, a husband and a family can provide emotional security and financial stability as well as scientific support if the husband is a scientist in the same field. Largely depending on how the problems are resolved and the opportunities used, the effect of marriage and children on women scientists' careers may be positive or negative.

There are women among those interviewed who "have it all," combining a family with a successful career; but there are also those who have had both a troubled career and difficulties in private life. One woman, for instance, made several career sacrifices to accommodate her husband; he eventually terminated their marriage anyway, and she was left in an insecure job. The constraints of family obligations and the availability of a wide scope of options (ranging from family- to career-orientation) are not mutually exclusive explanations for women's choices in balancing family and career. Rather, they often seem to combine and reinforce each other. In some cases, family obligations create difficulties for a woman's career that then make her opt to focus on her family. For instance, when Elizabeth's marriage limited her career chances, she tried to make the best of it by scaling back the priority of her profession and starting a family while working part time. Other women we interviewed also responded to difficulties in one area by concentrating on the other. For some, like Elizabeth, disappointment in a career led to a greater focus on family; but this mechanism also works the other way around. Never-married Florence describes how she became a career woman by default. If she had met a suitable husband, she indicated she would have willingly reduced her career aspirations.

A man is still widely expected to have a successful career and be the breadwinner of his family, so "going home" to be a house husband is an unconventional and rare option. Nonetheless, some among our male interviewees expressed a desire, if not to become house husbands, at least to be more involved with their families. John, for instance, quit his academic position to have more time for his family. The trend widening the range of women's options in terms of family life or career has facilitated their participation in all kinds of professional careers. This trend may eventually widen the range of options for men and allow them to focus more strongly on their family life.

CHAPTER 5
▼ ▼ ▼

Mapping Scientists' Careers

No one becomes a scientist overnight. Rather, scientists are made in an arduous process of many years. From our sample of hundreds of men and women, all of whom had been well on their way toward a successful career in research science, we solicited information about every stage of this long process—and about the points of divergence between the career paths of those who became successful academic scientists and those who left research science. It was precisely this divergence that we wanted to study most.

FROM HIGH CHAIR TO DEPARTMENT CHAIR: STAGES AND STRATEGIES IN SCIENTISTS' LIVES

Early Inclinations

Almost all of the twenty profiled women and men displayed an early inclination for science or for learning in general. They typically began their narration by stating that they had always—or at least from a very early age—wanted to be a scientist. In this, they agree with the great majority (over 80 percent) of the scientists and engineers in a large-scale NASA study, who related that they had decided on a science career before completing high school (reported in Tobias 1990, 10). This is not surprising given the fact that the science pipeline has many leakage points but hardly any influx at later stages. Changes in career plans are almost always switches away from science. Not simply choosing science, the people we interviewed spoke as though science had chosen them. A fair number of men and women reported that by nature they conformed to the popular stereotype of the young scientist: shy, bookish, and unsociable—the personality type described in Roe's (1952) classic study of (male) scientists.

Family Background

In our large questionnaire sample, 43 percent of the men said that neither of their parents had any college degree; this was the case for only 30 percent of the women. For 32 percent of the men as compared to 41 percent of the women, both parents had at least bachelor's degrees. A relatively high educational level among parents appears to counteract the cultural pressures that generally discourage girls from aspiring to the sciences. On the other hand, although socioeconomic background may influence the odds of becoming a scientist, it does not control fate. Contemporary science is a relatively open profession for talented people; note, for instance, that four of the five successful women scientists we described came from relatively humble backgrounds.

The familial microenvironment of parental attitudes and behavior rather than the macroenvironment determined by broad educational criteria appears to influence a child's choice of a science career. Men and women from lower socioeconomic groups described experiences that may be somewhat unusual among children of poor or working-class parents. Irene, for instance, pointed out how strongly her family's positive attitudes toward scholarly achievement contrasted with the prevailing outlook in her small-town environment. In some cases (Barbara, Erik, and George), a parent's own wish for a college education had remained unfulfilled, sometimes thwarted by the economic gloom of the Depression, and the children were groomed to realize the parent's missed opportunity. Barbara clearly expressed this situation, noting some paternal transference in her desire for a science career. Some of the people we interviewed came from ethnic or immigrant subcultures that valued learning, even if the parents were not educated themselves. Growing up among people with a high regard for the life of the mind encouraged budding scientists' interests and somewhat insulated them from the antiscience elements in mainstream society.

Nevertheless, if John had come from an uneducated or poor family, he probably would not have made it into a prestigious college. He described himself as a "fairly immature kid" who had no interest in academics. Only his father's intervention (sending John to a good private high school) set him on the academic track. This example shows that a privileged background sometimes gives children a second chance, an opportunity not available to those from different backgrounds. Children from poor and uneducated families have to rely on the public schools. If they do not resist the flow of the prevailing culture in many of these schools, they might be swept off the path leading toward higher education.

Children from less privileged backgrounds lack the normality of the route into science. Allan, coming from a blue-collar family, discovered only after high school that people could actually earn money as basic scientists. Contrast his experience with that of the children of a college professor; sometimes people from academic backgrounds end up on the science route almost by default. Just as something extraordinary has to happen to derail these children from the science track, something extraordinary has to happen to get less privileged children on course. They may need exceptional enthusiasm and talent or a special source of inspiration—be it encouraging parents, teachers, or a memorable visit at a science institution—but our cases clearly show that it is possible to become a successful scientist from relatively humble origins.

Encouragement from mothers has been identified as a powerful predictor of the number of science courses female undergraduates take (Rayman 1993). In accordance with this finding, women in our interview sample mentioned various positive influences from other women in their families. As in Deborah's case, several women felt their career paths were particularly facilitated by the example of mothers or other women in the family who worked outside the home. Some women pointed out that, because they came from all-female families where women had to do everything, they learned firsthand just what women can do. One woman thought that having no brothers, only sisters, along with attending all-female schools, were crucial factors in shaping her interest in a science career. Gail similarly considered having gone to an all-girl high school a plus.

Educational Experience

From what the men and women we interviewed told us about their educational experiences through graduate school, we can distinguish several major components that made a difference—positive or negative: the quality of regular science instruction, peers' attitudes toward scientific or academic excellence, fellowships and financial support, mentors and role models, and special educational environments.

Many counted good science instruction and good teachers among their crucial career advantages. By contrast, Elizabeth and Irene felt that their high school science education was deplorable. Elizabeth recounted that the lack of a solid foundation in the sciences greatly handicapped her later. Brad and Hank also reported initial difficulties in college resulting from poor preparation in science and mathematics. Remedial courses appear to be critical in this respect. Brad remembered how important it was to have been graded on a pass-fail basis in his initial science and mathematics courses, a system that gave him time to catch up and develop self-confidence. Thus, the first contact with science at college level can be crucial for a first-year student's decision to pursue science. Introductory courses designed to winnow out and discourage weaker students may turn away a great number of potentially talented scientists and thus deal the final blow to those young people already handicapped by a poor high school science education (see Tobias 1990).

Although both men and women mentioned the quality of high school science education as an important influence, some women recalled having to contend with social ostracism directed against girls who excelled academically. Two successful women scientists, Ann and Deborah, were outstanding students but were (or were caused to be) loners who clearly had social adjustment problems in school. In response to the hostility of her peers, Ann became socially withdrawn and developed a hard shell to protect herself from teasing. Deborah's behavior was not affected, but she suffered from feelings of loneliness and misery. Reactions like these seem to be widespread among aspiring women scientists. Helson (1973) found a strong degree of introversion and rejection of outside influence among creative women mathematicians.

Jealousy of model pupils may be a very general phenomenon among students, whether the teacher's pet is a boy or a girl. Compounding the problem is the social ineptitude of many "nerds"—male or female—which may contribute to feelings of isolation. But the difficulties faced by budding female scientists are to some extent amplified by gender; boys with scientific inclinations have a larger number of like-minded cohorts, and their scientific interests seem somehow more excusable in their peers' eyes. In the heyday of space exploration, Hank developed a childhood interest in rockets; and a rocket club proved to be an important stimulus for George's science career. We do not know how many girls this rocket club contained, but we suspect there were few, if any.

Exposed to strong peer hostility in high school, Deborah considered the elite university where she spent her undergraduate years to be a cultural haven for nerds; she enjoyed the prevailing proscience culture. Similarly, Irene found it liberating to be at a college where intellectual pursuits were not considered a social drawback, as they had been at her rural high school.

Almost all our respondents received generous fellowships during their undergraduate, graduate, and postdoctoral years; and many mentioned them as advantages in their science careers. Although women on the national average receive less financial aid than men, the women in our sample (who were considered particularly promising scientists) generally did get ample financial support. An exception was Elizabeth, who was denied a graduate fellowship, apparently in an act of gender discrimination. While David emphasized that fellowships were crucial in providing the funding to complete his research, Deborah emphasized the nonmonetary effect of a prestigious fellowship: it boosts self-confidence because it shows that one's performance is valued highly. This illustrates the general finding that financial support tends to increase women's intellectual self-esteem and persistence (Matyas 1991, 21).

Many of the people we interviewed gratefully remember the help they received from supportive mentors. Mentors are important aids in explaining the politics of science, as Erik and Deborah emphasized. Some women mentioned that a distinct lack of mentorship had adverse effects on their careers—Florence's career is a prime example. There are, of course, those young scientists who do not seem to need mentors because they are already on course. Christine, for instance, said she was set in her career track from an early stage; she felt that mentors did not have a great effect on her career, although she, too, acknowledged the support of senior scientists. In general, men scientists appeared to be more independent and self-motivated (or felt more inclined to present themselves as independent in the interview). One-fifth (21 percent) of the men we interviewed but only 9 percent of the women said there was no one who had helped them with their career obstacles.

In the public discussion of gender issues in science, it is often assumed that the key problem for female students is the dearth of women role models. But the problem may not be simply numerical. The few senior women scientists available as potential role models were not necessarily considered good examples by the younger women (see also Yentsch and Sindermann 1992, 157–159). On the one hand, Elizabeth and Gail acknowledged the inspiring influence of women scientists on their careers. On the other hand, Jane did not regard her female undergraduate advisor as a role model because the advisor had sacrificed all other aspects of life for her career; this tradeoff did not appeal to Jane. Ann presents the advisor's side of this problem. She reports having difficulties with some of her women graduate students because, she says, they do not quite understand that a serious commitment to science requires sacrifices in other areas of one's life. Ann is married but decided not to have children because of career considerations. Christine, who has never been married, acknowledged that she may not be an ideal role model for those young women who want to have careers *and* families. Among the few women scientists of earlier cohorts, a large proportion were single. But the great majority of the women we interviewed (87 percent) have been married; and among the young women who currently contemplate a science career, many, we expect, also wish for a family. Thus, what makes women scientists attractive as role models for younger women may not be their scientific success as much as their ability to combine personal satisfaction and professional success.

Some women interviewees believed that attending an all-women educational environment was a great plus. Elizabeth, for instance, who attended a women's college, doubted that she would have chosen a science career in a coeducational setting. Her case illustrates the findings that women's colleges turn out a disproportionately high number of concentrators in fields that are not traditional for women, including science (Tidball and Kistiakowsky 1976).

One particular type of experience was apparently very powerful in counteracting the forces that deter students from choosing science. Early encounters with "real science" had an enormous impact on the formation of career goals, especially for budding women scientists. While the men pursued a more "normal" career path and may not have needed such inspirational special events, hands-on experience was pivotal for many women. Four of the five successful women scientists we profiled, as compared with only one successful man, mention their early exposure to the possibilities of research as key influences on their outlook about their careers (although one cannot be sure whether that importance has become a factor only in hindsight). The essential opportunity implied a change of locale—be it a summer course, a co-op work-study program at a major research university, or a laboratory visit—that provided intellectual as well as social experiences. Several attended one particular summer school; this program was apparently highly successful in stimulating young scientists. During these encounters, the young scientists went from their ordinary environment, which may not have been an ideal science training ground or a source of particular encouragement, to places where "real science" happened. The glimpse of this different world was a strong motivational force for many, especially for women. Such hands-on experience shows a student the difference between science as a repository of well-known facts (as it usually is taught) and science as the process of venturing into the realm of the unknown.

Factors in Leaving Science

The great majority of our former postdoctoral fellows have become active research scientists in academic or other settings; the proportion of those who left science is small (men: 9 percent; women: 10 percent [questionnaire respondents]). Nonetheless, this small group should provide valuable insights into factors and obstacles that may cause even highly trained and motivated individuals to abandon research science.

A few former fellows who left science experienced a severe illness, had to respond to the illness of close relatives, or became involved in some other kind of personal tragedy. We did not choose these sad life stories for the biographical chapters because instances of blind fate do not have the wider policy and strategy implications we wish to examine.

A number of career paths can be considered gradual promotions out of science. As individuals rise in the hierarchies of academic institutions or industrial organizations, they take on administrative and managerial duties that reduce the time available for actual research. At a certain point, such tasks completely distance these persons from research. Florence's career is a good example of how involvement in high-level academic administration can lead a person out of research science, and George's career exemplifies the road into science management within an industrial company. They belong to a group for whom leaving active research science was not a radical reorientation or a case of dropping out. By most standards, their careers are very successful.

A different category includes those who were forced out of science by not finding a job, being denied tenure, or being discriminated against or subjected to a hostile, harassing environment. Fred lost his research job and was unemployed for a while. His research in an esoteric field failed to produce breakthrough results, and not being in a hot subfield in his discipline reduced his chances of employment. Irene's tenure denial sent her career into a tailspin. In Jane's case, the lack of a job position and discrimination combined to shut her out.

A third group consists of those who decided to quit science voluntarily. Holly left an assistant professorship, as did John. Hank departed from research science, although he had an offer of another postdoctoral fellowship; and Ian left his research job on his own volition. These people were convinced to change their careers to a different track even though they did not have to do so. A frequent cause mentioned by both men and women was rooted in the culture of science: they felt their science jobs required too many hours of hard work, the work itself was too fragmented and meaningless, and the results lacked applicability and relevance. Men also mentioned low pay. Another cause was related to family considerations. Holly quit her assistant professorship to move to her husband's area, and John's decision was also influenced by his desire to have more time with his family.

Often the causes for leaving science were multiple and complex, and the boundary between forced and voluntary exit blurred. Typically, one cause compounds with another to make a more convincing case—for instance, if individuals were not really satisfied with their work, they were more likely to leave science once they encountered difficulties in the job market. For women in particular, the combination of bad job prospects and good prospects in the family sphere might precipitate the decision to exit science, as Jane's case showed.

Some causes are gender-neutral, as we have seen, but other causes apply more specifically to women. Notable gender differences occurred in two types of obstacles: discrimination and family issues. Episodes of gender discrimination and sexism forced several women out of science. Jane was denied a job in favor of a man whom she considers less qualified. Another woman who had left science related a classic horror story of discrimination, sexism, and sexual harassment during her graduate training. At a much subtler level, Florence and Jane reported a lack of mentorship.

Family considerations were often a handicap for women who left science. One typical form was the two-body problem, in which one spouse's career moves (almost always the wife's) were severely restricted because the other spouse's (usually the husband's) job was given priority. Holly, for instance, gave up her professorship to move to her husband's area. Another typical problem was connected with child rearing. One woman who left science graphically illustrated both the great time demands and the psychological feelings of inadequacy and guilt that sometimes arise in the attempt to combine the roles of scientist and mother.

> [Working in research science] was wonderful but then there was this feeling, "Well, I can't start this reaction because I have to leave in forty-five minutes and it takes an hour and a half. Maybe I can get somebody to come in and look at it for me." You don't want to do that because then people start resenting you for leaving them with your work and you don't want to let someone look after your precious experiment. It was that kind of thing constantly—trying to squeeze in and plan and be very efficient and very organized and getting it right, and I'd come home and I'd be here and happy to be here, but then I'd have to pick up and leave the kids, drop them at day care, if they were sick get some help—there was always a crisis.

And there was always the feeling—and this was what really undid me in the end—there was always the feeling that I was never doing either job as well as it should be done. I was never really a mother, heart and soul, to my kids; I was never a scientist, heart and soul. I remember quite clearly in August of [year], realizing that in fact this was never going to change. I had always thought it would get better, I'd figure this out, I'd figure out how to manage career and family; the kids would get older and it would be easier. And it hit me like a cement block falling on my head that it was never going to be any different, that there would always be that tension between the family and the work. And that I had to choose whether I wanted a life filled with that tension—and that I would choose that because the rewards were worth it—or choose a life of, in a word, peace. And I chose the peace. In a way I think that choice had been coming for several years, but it was very, very hard, as I saw it, to give up everything that I had worked for.

Of those individuals who left research science, most—not surprisingly—found jobs connected to their science training. Some became science writers or editors; some went into science policy, consulting, or university administration. One thing almost everyone had in common was a certain amount of regret. Typically, they felt that the long years of scientific training should not go unused: they would love to be involved again in research science, at least to a moderate degree.

Factors in Successful Career Paths into Academic Science

The experiences of the women and men who became successful academic research scientists allow us to identify situations and strategies that contributed to success in science. Nevertheless, we should not forget that these people, too, encountered some obstacles during their professional careers. The most common obstacles were a bad job market and scarce funds for research projects. In addition, the successful women were also apt to have encountered the more typically female obstacles that we described in previous sections.

To a large extent, two pivotal events after the postdoctoral fellowship determine a career path into academic science (or out of it): securing an assistant professorship or equivalent and then getting tenure. An assistant professorship puts the young scientist on the professorial track. The caliber of the academic institution (whether it is a major research university or a college concentrating on teaching undergraduates) influences the balance between a professor's research and teaching activities and consequently his or her standing in the scientific community (which clearly values research over teaching). Tenure affords the academic scientist a high degree of job security for the rest of his or her career.

For junior faculty members, there is a tradeoff between the prestige of the institution and the probability of receiving tenure. While most academic institutions have tenure tracks, several very renowned universities promote their own junior faculty members to tenure status only if they win out in a competitive search over the whole field. People who are denied tenure at these eminent universities have fewer problems in receiving tenure at another university than people who fall off the tenure track at less prestigious institutions. For instance, Ann found a professorship at another university after not receiving tenure at a very prestigious university, but Irene's tenure denial at a less renowned college effectively terminated her academic career.

Elements of Success for Men and Women

A host of factors contribute to career success, many of which cannot be planned but depend on luck. Among the men and women interviewed, securing material support (fellowships, research grants, and job positions) was the most frequently mentioned career advantage (men: 58 percent; women: 53 percent). But a close second was good luck (men: 46 percent; women: 39 percent). Luck's impact on science careers appears so important that we will discuss it in greater detail later in the chapter.

Here we note some specific elements that tend to lead to success for both men and women and therefore might be pondered by aspiring scientists. They include choices about scientific work as well as strategies for handling the politics of science, internal characteristics as well as social opportunities and advantages.

Choice of Institution

In the highly stratified American system of higher education, it might be advantageous to select renowned institutions at various educational stages (college, graduate school, postdoctoral study). For the women in our questionnaire sample, attending a prestigious postdoctoral institution had a beneficial effect in terms of later academic rank. A top graduate school may also be an asset for one's future science career. Ian, for instance, considered choosing a less distinguished graduate school an eventual career handicap. At the college level, the pro-achievement and pro-science atmosphere that pervades many high-caliber institutions might fortify a budding scientist's aspirations, as in Deborah's and Irene's cases. Antiscience peer pressure, by contrast, might become an obstacle in less achievement-oriented colleges.

Choice of Research Topics and Fields

One element in Allan's success is his conscious focus on hot research topics. John's career, which led out of science for other reasons, greatly benefited from his pioneering work in a growing field. David took an unusually large risk in his graduate research that paid off in a big way. Of course, the flip side of taking great risks is an increased chance of failure. Although David successfully completed his high-risk research, Fred, who worked on difficult, esoteric problems, failed to make the breakthrough that could have catapulted his little-known specialty area to prominence. In an age of extreme scientific specialization, a clearly focused research program in a well-defined research area is commonly considered more advantageous to a career than undertaking disjointed projects.

Publication of Research Results

David clearly understood the importance of publishing his graduate research findings, which ultimately secured him an assistant professorship at a prestigious university. There is generally no better way to bring oneself to the notice of one's colleagues than through publications. A strong publication record tends to boost a scientist's standing: our small study among biologists shows that the publication rate predicted peers' quality judgments more strongly than anything else did (Sonnert, in press b).

Mentors

Several scientists counted a mentor among their most crucial career advantages. Allan would not have ended up in academe without his mentor's prodding. A good mentor will discuss the politics of science with a student or junior scientist, make contacts and connections, and help with job positions. If Ann's mentor had not hired her as an assistant professor at a prestigious university, her career would have taken a much different trajectory. She would have probably ended up in a teaching career at a college, but her assistant professorship opened the door to a distinguished career in research science.

Somewhat counterintuitively, we found that for the former fellows who answered our questionnaire, association with a postdoctoral advisor of junior rank correlated with a high current academic rank of the former advisee. Thus, a good mentor does not necessarily have to be an established senior scientist. Affiliation with a junior mentor may hold a strategic advantage, especially if this mentor is one of the rising scientific stars in a discipline. Junior mentors might also allow their advisees more freedom in the choice of research direction or empathize more with the situations their advisees face.

The Political Game

Mentors are often helpful in teaching political savvy. Crucial tenure decisions do not always depend on merit alone but also on relationships with the decision makers. Erik attributed his success in the tenure process at a prestigious university partly to his knowing how to play the game. Scientists who are able to form alliances with their colleagues are at an advantage. Brad's successful confrontation with a former department chairman also illustrates the importance of building good relationships with departmental colleagues.

Networking

Achieving visibility among the wider group of colleagues working in a research field and becoming part of the informal network of contacts and information flows also enhances a scientist's chances of success. Deborah clearly understood the importance of "getting one's name on the map." As a postdoctoral fellow, she paid her own way to visit several universities and gave talks—a prudent investment that led to an excellent job.

Hard Work

What seems to be even more important than intelligence is the ability to work hard—that is, the ability to transfer intellectual excitement into long hours of routine work and attention to detail. The people we interviewed work, on the average, with great intensity: 74 percent of the men and 85 percent of the women considered themselves hardworking. Most of the successful scientists are extremely focused on their careers—to the point of calling themselves workaholics, as Ann, Allan, and Charles did. Some individuals, such as George, Hank, and Deborah, noted cycles in their working style. Periods of high-intensity work alternate with times when they are in what Deborah called "maintenance mode."

Elements of Success for Women

While the topics we have just discussed apply to both men and women scientists, those that follow are mostly associated with women.

Solving the Two-body Problem of Marriage

For married women scientists, especially those married to other scientists, a successful solution to the two-body problem is crucial. Ann and Barbara were able to get positions for both themselves and their husbands in the same departments. It should be noted that, in these cases, the husband scientist held either similar or slightly lower seniority. Contrast these examples with Elizabeth's marriage to a much senior scientist, which had effects that stunted her career development. Deborah's career benefited from the fact that her husband was not a scientist and geographically mobile.

Affirmative Action

A particular advantage for women of a certain age group was evidently the introduction of affirmative action. Barbara attributed a large part of her career success to the rise of the women's movement; but among the successful women scientists we presented, she was the only one to do so. In the interview sample, only 4 percent of the women mentioned affirmative action as a career advantage. Christine reports she got to her current position mainly on her own merits. Ann is suspicious about "women doing things as women" in science. She takes a strictly meritocratic view, saying everybody must be judged according to the quality of his or her work.

These successful women scientists are certainly not feminist activists. In their deeply meritocratic and individualist attitude, they resemble successful women academics studied in Israel (Toren 1988). The women who might have greatly benefited from the women's movement apparently give it little acknowledgment, but those who had to yield to exactly the obstacles against which the women's movement has fought tend to acknowledge it as a crucial help in understanding their situation.

Persistence

We found a marked gender difference in internal qualities in respect to persistence or perseverance. Of the women we interviewed, 45 percent named these qualities as an advantageous internal factor, compared with only 20 percent of the men. Persistence in the face of obstacles may be more important for women than for men because the typical career path of women scientists contains more obstacles and difficulties.

How to React to Gender Discrimination

A uniquely female area of strategies is how to react to gender discrimination. Because a large proportion of the women we interviewed reported discriminatory experiences, we surveyed their reactions to discrimination in some detail.

Many thought that they were not aggressive enough in the face of discrimination. Gail, for instance, declared that she "should have fought back" when she felt pushed around in graduate school; Jane also wished she had taken a more resolute stance when she encountered job discrimination. In general, a quarter of the women we interviewed believed that they should have been more self-confident or assertive in handling their career obstacles.

On the other hand, women volunteered some pragmatic strategies for dealing with discriminatory incidents, especially less serious ones. The following tactics were reported to have worked for some of them, under the stated conditions.

Ignoring some incidents. During social interactions with other scientists, women are bound to encounter "fifty-year-old men who don't know how to talk to you or call you 'sweetie' or 'honey.' But I get around it, or I just ignore it. No, they shouldn't treat me any different than their male counterparts; but what are you going to do, make an issue out of it, or just go on and get what you want and be done with it? And that's the way I've approached things." A number of women felt that having a thick skin was among their best advantages. A certain stubbornness and lack of oversensitivity allowed them to ignore and overcome subtle or not-so-subtle hostilities in environments that do not actively welcome women.

Humor. Several women said they tried to defuse and circumvent potential discrimination of the lesser sort by reacting in a cordial way rather than confronting it and battling it out. They see this as a more productive approach. As Florence said, "it is clear to me there are difficulties, and there are certainly prejudiced men. However, I find it is easier, and I think one is more effective, if one finds a nice, joking way of conveying that, rather than being hostile."

Compliance. In some instances, women just complied with what they considered trivial requests rather than fought about points of principle. For example, the male supervisor of a woman scientist in industry wanted her to change her appearance to look more like a management consultant, which meant wearing suits and pinning up her pigtail. Although she would probably have had grounds to protest this request, she complied because "if you can make your boss happy with four oversize bobby pins, you're an idiot not to do it."

De-emphasizing femininity. In an effort to avoid gender-related problems, some women said they de-emphasize their femininity and emphasize their professional identity as a scientist. As one woman put it, "I think to make it as a female scientist, you have to be a scientist and truly downplay the female." This strategy, of course, is hardly available for a pregnant woman. In another woman's words, "being a pregnant woman is the most awful of all. You're not treated with the deference that a cute young thing is treated with. And never are you more loudly proclaiming your womanliness, so the comments get made about the seriousness of your pursuits. Everybody thinks it's fair game to ask an obviously pregnant woman exactly what her plans are, or things like that."

Avoidance. One woman said that she had been able to detect potentially discriminatory situations from the outset and then immediately avoid them. "The times that I sensed that there could be a problem [with gender discrimination], I was always in control from the standpoint of finding a new advisor or getting allegiance with someone else who didn't feel that way. I never stayed in a situation that I thought was going to be detrimental. I always got out of it at the first hint."

By reporting these pragmatic strategies, we do not intend to advocate a general pacifist attitude for women scientists or dissuade them from vigorously fighting discriminatory acts, as some in our sample have had to do. The tenure issue in particular has triggered tough confrontations for several women respondents. We do emphasize the importance of a flexible repertoire of strategies, a broad scope of responses to potentially discriminatory encounters ranging from circumvention to confrontation. Someone who is able to choose her battles may do better than someone who always withdraws in the face of potential conflict or always comes out fighting. The successful women among our interviewees tended to choose their responses and battles carefully, navigating around the less severe types of discrimination instead of confronting every slight head on.

Under some circumstances, the choice of strategy may entail a tradeoff between the benefits for the individual woman scientist and for the collective situation of women scientists in her institution or even in a wider constituency. One woman, for instance, noted that, in their totality, small sexist comments and remarks can create an institutional atmosphere inhospitable to women. She believes that such an atmosphere perpetuates itself if the small comments go unchallenged. A heated, highly visible fight, even one that is a lost cause for the individual, may raise consciousness and lead to policy changes benefiting women scientists as a group.

By contrast, a conciliatory strategy may help the individual surmount an obstacle but do nothing to remove similar barriers for other women scientists. The majority of the women we interviewed appeared to follow a very pragmatic, individualistic approach in their science careers.

KICKS AND KICKING BACK: THE DYNAMICS OF A CAREER PATH

The data collected in our 700 questionnaires and two hundred interviews enabled us to distill those points that illuminate the similarities and differences in the careers of men and women scientists. Now it is time to change perspective: to shift our focus from particular career stages and events to scientists' career paths as a whole—in other words, to view career paths as dynamic systems.

Arrows and Spirals

Two metaphors, *arrow* and *spiral,* describe the career paths of scientists. At one extreme are those scientists who have flown through the stages of a science career without any detours or breaks, moving from one triumph to the next. At the other extreme are those whose routes have been circuitous, with detours, stops, and perhaps some backsliding along the way. Most scientists' careers contain, in various proportions, both arrows and spirals.

With the exception of Christine, who made arrowlike progress into academic science, it would have taken very little for the careers of these successful female scientists to be deflected toward completely different directions early in their careers. All four entertained and pursued alternative career options with various degrees of seriousness. They transferred their early interest in science to related fields that were, according to traditional cultural stereotypes, more "feminine"—notably the helping professions of medicine and veterinary medicine. Ann played with the idea of becoming a veterinarian. Elizabeth changed her major at college away from science but eventually changed it back. Both Barbara and Deborah were accepted into medical school but did not go—Barbara because of an exciting summer job in science, Deborah because of personal problems with her boyfriend. Ann also had the lingering ideal of a family life that might take precedence over her career aspirations. Only after her divorce did she change priorities and focus her energies on her career.

For these women, there was a critical difference between a generalized interest and talent in science, which they all had from early on, and the concrete career goal of becoming a scientist, which only Christine had from the start. Once the successful women made their career choices, however, their progress became more arrowlike. The exception was Elizabeth, whose career was somewhat hampered by her marital situation, which restricted her mobility.

Although straight career paths may be more frequent among men (as in the cases of Brad and Charles), winding career paths can also be found even among very successful men. Allan, for instance, took two years off between college and graduate school to work in unrelated jobs, and David took time off twice—between his bachelor's and master's, and between his master's and doctorate degrees.

The Kick-Reaction Model

Describing the overall trajectory of a career is only a preliminary step toward understanding it. To delve into the problem more deeply, we must examine the internal dynamics of career paths. Cole and Singer (1991) have developed a highly formalized kick-reaction model of scientific publication productivity that will help us here. We use this model not in its mathematical rigor but as a basic concept; and we apply it to scientific career paths in general, not only to publication productivity.

According to Cole and Singer, the course of a career in science can be described as a sequence of kicks from the environment and the scientist's reactions to those kicks. A kick is any event in the environment that has a potential effect on the individual's career, be it positive or negative. Likewise, the individual's reaction to a kick can be positive or negative. Over the course of a career, the pattern of kicks and reactions changes. Positive kicks tend to increase the likelihood of further positive kicks in the future; likewise, negative kicks are bound to spawn further negative kicks. There is, in other words, an accumulation of advantages and disadvantages over time.

Probably the best examples of the accumulation of advantages and disadvantages are the divergent career paths of Irene and her husband. While Irene's husband went from good jobs to better jobs and ended up as a full professor, Irene had a sequence of less elevated jobs, was denied tenure, and occupied increasingly marginal science positions until she had to drop out completely. Then there is Brad, who has had a charmed career in which one positive event led to another—an exemplar for the accumulation of positive kicks. Toward the later stages of a career, feedback mechanisms of kicks tend to stabilize an arrowlike career on its straight path or impede a spiral-like career from becoming highly successful.

There appears to be an analogous change in reaction patterns. Success, for instance, typically increased both ambition and self-confidence through a process of reinforcement, which may increase positive reactions and lead to further success. About three-fifths of the men and women referred in their interviews to previous experiences as the cause of their current level of self-confidence. But this process of reinforcement did not apply to every successful scientist. There were also a few whose self-confidence decreased with increasing success. Allan, for example, was full of self-confidence during the early stages of his career but now fears he may at some point no longer be able to produce landmark research and thus slide from his elevated position among his peers.

Some people—for instance, Brad and Christine—have been propelled in their careers by a strong motivation from the beginning. Their careers, intrinsically driven and arrow-straight, seem to follow a predestined, almost inevitable path. Those with persistently strong motivation will, in the language of the kick-reaction model, tend to have more positive reactions to kicks (especially more resilient reactions to adverse kinds of kicks) than those who lack this sort of motivation from the start of their careers. A considerable number of the scientists we profiled belong to this second category. Some of those who came from academic families entered their science careers by default: they conformed to vague family expectations without feeling a real desire to become scientists. Others, such as Ian and Irene, just took the next step without devoting much reflection to the direction of their career. After high school, they went to college, graduate school, a postdoctoral fellowship, and a job—not in accordance with an overall plan but because it seemed to be time to move on to a new stage after each prior one was completed.

A strong motivation from the start is not a necessary ingredient for an arrowlike career. We found that people can, for instance, stumble forward in a straight line, taking step-by-step advantage of positive kicks. Even someone who finds success by accident is then likely to increase both ambition and self-confidence through a process of reinforcement. This process helps to transform spiral-like beginnings into arrowlike endings. Most of the successful women scientists entered their science careers step by step; they had relatively low ambitions and little self-confidence at the beginning, but they revised these attitudes as their successes multiplied. It seems truly remarkable how accidental the beginning careers of four of the five successful women scientists were. This may shed light on how many talented women have been lost to science in the early stages of the pipeline.

A characteristic pattern for those whose spiral-like careers led them out of science was to reduce or revise their ambitions to maintain a high level of self-confidence. Again, variability within genders is large; but the contrast between Florence and Fred might be instructive. Florence felt guilt and self-blame over her successful career because it led her out of science. By contrast, Fred's big ego and self-confidence were not affected by his realization that his research was not particularly good and by his somewhat erratic career, which included a prolonged period of unemployment and employment in a totally unrelated field. While Florence blames her own personality, Fred blames a slump in the labor market for his exit from research science.

Luck, Good or Bad: A Difference That Can Make a Difference

In this global perspective on science careers we must reiterate the paramount role of luck. Many of the people we questioned mentioned good luck and serendipity as career advantages. In response to specific interview questions about luck in their careers, an overwhelming majority acknowledged that good luck had affected their careers (men: 89 percent; women: 85 percent). Bad luck was acknowledged by a higher proportion of women than men (men: 34 percent; women: 49 percent).

Luck in a science career can come in different shapes. First, creativity, that crucial element of scientific progress, eludes planning; and nobody knows from the outset if a creative idea is really true or successful. Both conceiving a creative hypothesis and having that hypothesis quickly corroborated by experiments depend to some degree on luck. This type of good luck in actual research was, however, mentioned less frequently (men: 11 percent; women: 9 percent) than a second type—luck that takes the form of serendipity, as many called it in the interviews (men: 91 percent; women: 88 percent). These respondents acknowledged they were in the right place at the right time. Research programs and whole scientific fields may on short order turn hot or cold; promising ones may stagnate, while long shots may produce a breakthrough that catapults researchers from the margins to the center of attention. John's case illustrates the truism that being in a field at the time of its takeoff can be a great bonus, whereas Fred's focus on a somewhat marginal subfield was a career handicap.

At the concrete level, serendipity was often described as meeting the right people. The right person can be a leading scholar who inspires the young researcher scientifically. It can be a powerful figure in the science establishment who makes the right introductions and connections for the aspiring scientist. It can be someone whose personal integrity and kindness are impressive. It can be someone who teaches the scientist how to play the political game of furthering one's career in science. Or someone who combines several of these aspects. But meeting the right people in one's field does not have to happen by sheer luck; it is one of the few externalities a scientist can make more probable by taking the initiative.

More women than men explicitly mentioned their fellowships among good-luck career events (19 percent versus 9 percent). This appears to reflect the fact that, on the national average, women receive less fellowship support than men (Hornig 1987; Matyas 1991, 21). The women in our sample may be aware that they were among the relatively few women afforded such opportunities, whereas a larger number of men may have taken their fellowships for granted.

Reverse serendipity—being in the wrong place at the wrong time—was the most common version of bad luck, although fewer people (men: 62 percent; women: 57 percent) reported bad luck than mentioned good luck. Bad luck in actual research was a somewhat more frequent response among the men (24 percent) than among the women (7 percent).

In sum, the vast majority of men and women acknowledge that luck—good or bad—was a decisive force in shaping their careers. This emphasis may be due to the fact that science careers are influenced by luck to a particularly large degree compared with other professional fields. Science, by its very nature, probes into the unknown; and it is difficult to prearrange breakthrough discoveries or position oneself on the particular part of the science frontier where the next major advance will occur. Using the terminology of the kick-reaction model, one would say that in spite of the tendency for advantages or disadvantages to accumulate, one's kicks often arrive quite unpredictably.

A key problem for the scientist, then, is to recognize and take advantage of serendipitous situations once they arise. The scientist has to realize the potential effects of a kick and respond with a proper reaction. In Erik's words, "the way people really succeed is being able to recognize when a good thing has happened and take advantage of it." And Charles would concur: "All the things that are significant that occur in one's research career result from some kind of lucky break, on the one hand, and on the other hand, from what the individual is able to do with it."

Resilience and Flexibility, or Knowing How to Kick Back

Flexibility and resilience are two somewhat contradictory ingredients in successful science careers—the flexibility of taking advantage of new opportunities and the resilience of persisting in one's research project in the face of difficulties. Too much flexibility may lead one astray and prevent the completion of research projects when disappointments arise, as they do in almost every project. Too much resilience may also be a trap; there is no advantage to plodding on with a project that has clearly shown that it is going nowhere. But it is sometimes difficult to distinguish one situation from the other. In most cases, risks have to be taken. Thus, a key characteristic of successful scientists must be a high tolerance of uncertainty and a disciplined work habit in the face of potential failure. A basic optimism that, despite temporary setbacks, things will work out eventually (as mentioned by Charles and Brad, for example) may be an essential quality for a successful scientist.

The appropriate strategy to counter negative kicks is resilience and hard work—gritting one's teeth in the face of obstacles and persisting. The appropriate strategy for taking advantage of positive kicks is different—being flexible in adjusting one's research in light of opportunities and taking adantage of novel ideas, projects, or new jobs. Women scientists, on average, experience more negative kicks and fewer positive kicks. This may explain why more women than men in their interviews emphasized the virtues of resilience and hard work and why more women tended toward "safe science." The women who survived in the science pipeline have, on average, been exposed to a relatively greater number of negative kicks and have learned from experience the value of resilience and hard work. Conversely, men's greater average rate of exposure to positive kicks may have taught them the value of following ideas that challenge conventional wisdom and have given them the confidence to be more daring.

The kick-reaction model also offers at least a partial explanation for the glass ceiling that keeps women out of the top positions in the sciences. To become a well-known scientist, it might be even more essential to take advantage of positive kicks rather than overcome negative ones. But owing to their career paths (and perhaps to their prior dispositions), women scientists are more conditioned to making the kinds of responses that overcome negative kicks. They may have come to expect that, in an environment that is less favorable to them, they run a greater risk of being thwarted. As a result, the more defensive approach—remaining in a relatively safe niche and not rocking the boat too obviously—seems more appealing.

If, because of lack of mentorship, marginalization within the social system of science, or family demands, the probability of encountering potentially serendipitous opportunities is somewhat lower for women, then they would have to make up for this handicap by being more astute in taking advantage of the opportunities that do come along. Unfortunately, women may again be disadvantaged in this respect because they appear less likely than men to pursue opportunities vigorously. Thus, what we have described as a double handicap for women as a group—the combination of informal structural obstacles, according to the deficit model, and attitudinal and behavioral obstacles, according to the difference model—can easily be translated into an interpretation based on the kick-reaction model. Women scientists experience a slightly lower rate of positive kicks as well as a slightly lower probability of positive reactions to them.

CHAPTER 6
▼ ▼ ▼

What Can Be Done?
Advice for Novices and
Policymakers

"Make your mistakes as rapidly as possible!" was the career advice that distinguished physicist John Wheeler reportedly gave his students—a humorous remark meant to be taken with a grain of salt. We now give aspiring scientists a few more tangible pointers that we hope will help to avoid some mistakes entirely. At the end of the chapter we offer policy suggestions that may be useful to policymakers who wish to facilitate scientists' careers, especially women's careers, and to enhance the well-being of science institutions.

THE SOCIAL SYSTEM OF SCIENCE: NOW AND FOREVER?

As we mentioned earlier in the book, we have found great variations among career paths within the genders as well as substantial overlap between the genders. Not all gender differences and gender-related obstacles applied to every individual scientist, of course. Rather, they are tendencies and trends.

For young women and men embarking on a career in science, the established social system of science is primarily a given. New voices are not completely ignored, but their opportunities of affecting the system are restricted. Nonetheless, knowledge of this social system gives newcomers a sound basis and a clear focus for any changes they might propose. Moreover, the better they know how the system works, the better they can take advantage of it for career advancement and scientific excellence. A prime objective of this book, then, is to help scientists make informed career decisions within the established setting at a time when they cannot expect to modify the system.

For policymakers, however, the social system of science is a target for intervention. For instance, the level of funding for particular programs and areas or the availability of jobs and grants for particular groups of persons are things that policymakers can affect. Depending on their position, policymakers may try to influence the situation in a department, a university, a company, or nationwide. But even the most powerful national policymakers are far from omnipotent; they have to wrestle with budget and authority limitations as well as economic and demographic factors beyond their control. But if they are aware of the kinds of problems that arise in actual careers, they may be able to make appropriate interventions to enhance the system's ability to yield desirable results.

LESSONS FOR ASPIRING SCIENTISTS

What is the bottom line of our analysis for aspiring scientists? If one had to draw up a short list of helpful strategies, it might look like this:

- Attend high-caliber educational institutions
- Carefully assess the potential benefits and risks when choosing a research topic
- Keep your research program clear and well defined
- Expect setbacks and be resilient
- Be ready to change research topics if the promise of success has clearly faded
- Expect serendipity and take advantage of it quickly
- Put priority on publishing your research results
- Find supportive mentors and avoid or leave those who are not supportive
- Become versed in the politics of science
- Aim at achieving high visibility in your field
- Work hard and do the best you can

For women scientists in particular:

- Plan carefully how to coordinate career, marriage, and motherhood
- Choose your battles when facing discrimination
- Respond promptly and appropriately to positive or negative kicks

A warning: don't put excessive faith in these suggestions. Although aspiring scientists who understand the trends presented in this book may be more likely to fulfill their career goals, we are not offering a recipe for guaranteed career success. People who follow our list might still fail, and most of our profiled scientists achieved success even though they violated one or several of these strategies.

More important than following individual suggestions is understanding two basic influences on science careers. First, being a scientist has crucial social components on which most scientists do not like to concentrate. But a career can rise and fall in relation to the attention scientists pay to career-enhancing factors. Here, the genders appear to differ in two respects. Women may be taught these informal social skills to a lesser extent than men are. And some of these skills—for instance, "professor talk"—may seem more repugnant to women than men. For young women just starting out in science, it might help to examine the biographies of our female scientists who succeeded in the social system of science, sometimes under conditions more adverse than today's.

A second key element is the importance of luck. Of course, careers in every walk of life entail elements of luck; but career decisions in science involve a particularly high degree of uncertainty, and outcomes depend on luck to an unusually high extent. Although you cannot plan luck, you might be able to make serendipitous luck more likely by exposing yourself to opportunities and situations in which it might occur. Scientists who lock themselves into their own research project and have only minimal contact with colleagues do not give luck a chance to happen. By contrast, communicating and networking with other scientists, inside and outside your own discipline, increases your chance of a serendipitous connection or of picking up a novel idea that will greatly stimulate and advance your own work.

There is no single right way to become a successful scientist. The idiosyncratic career profiles in this book illustrate that many roads may at first seem promising but eventually lead out of science. Likewise, a great number of different routes lead to success in science. The fact that even some highly successful scientists have gone through rough spots and detours along the way shows that there *can* be second chances. It is not impossible to rectify unfortunate decisions and bad luck.

One final point: the women and men we interviewed typically found research science exciting and fascinating, but nobody said it was easy. Although talent enabled some of them to breeze through the early stages of science education, this was not possible later on. The biographies of both the successful scientists and those who left research science illustrate that research science as it is today is a tough, aggressive, competitive enterprise that requires almost single-minded devotion. Considering the joys and the demands of research science, the excitement and the exhaustion, *you* must set your goals within or outside science and define your own notion of success.

RECOMMENDATIONS FOR POLICYMAKERS

What suggestions can our study provide for policymakers who wish to improve the representation of women in science and engineering? The United States has already passed the first stage of policy intervention—the legal prohibition of gender discrimination. Once the decision was made, the implementation was relatively fast, cheap, and easy. But these legal changes were not enough to secure women's equal participation in science; "full access [to science and engineering careers] goes far beyond just opening the doors of educational institutions and the workplace" (Wilson 1992, 4–5). Today's obstacles are more subtle, and interventions are more difficult. Therefore, change will happen more slowly.

A great variety of policies have been tried, and an even greater variety of programs have been proposed. Typically, policy measures are classified according to which stage in the science pipeline they target. Wilson (1992) and Matyas (1992), however, have proposed more sophisticated frameworks for ordering the multitude of interventions. Following their approaches, we note that important distinctions among policy interventions include duration (single events versus ongoing programs), institutional level (department versus national science), degree of formalization (informal volunteer efforts versus programs with paid staff), and amount and type of money required ("soft" versus "hard"). In addition, we suggest to distinguish whether a policy measure is rooted more in the deficit model of women's career achievement (aims at helping women become more successful under the current rules of the game) or in the difference model (aims at changing the rules themselves). On the one end of the spectrum, there are programs that raise women's awareness about career-enhancing strategies or give them compensatory support, such as special mentoring, fellowships and grants, that enable them to offset past disadvantages and compete successfully within the current social system of science. On the other end, there are interventions that change working conditions or the criteria of performance, hiring, or promotion.

The amount of pay is certainly one of the most obvious factors in job and career choice, in general. More people will want to be scientists if salaries in science are higher. But money is not the only important factor, and it seems to be a less decisive factor for women than for men. In the profiles, only men mentioned the low salaries in academic science as a reason to take other types of jobs. This appears connected with the fact that, among the people we interviewed, men were more likely than women to be the main breadwinners in their families. To increase the attractiveness of a science career for women, changing work conditions may be as important as offering higher salaries: reducing long work hours when necessary, providing high-quality child care, and improving the social atmosphere.

Moreover, wider cultural issues, such as the definition of gender roles or the image and prestige of science, play a role in recruitment patterns. The division of labor within the household may be beyond the reach of the science administrator, but national and local policy could help many women scientists by providing child care and facilitating dual appointments for husbands and wives in a given geographical area. (As noted, 62 percent of the married women in our large questionnaire sample had a husband with a doctorate.) As to the societal image of science, more young people are attracted to a science career when scientists are considered the heroes of society than when they are the villains. The space euphoria of the 1950s and 1960s inspired George and Hank—and many others (mostly males) in their age group. Currently, the image of science in the mass media tends to emphasize failure or anger, expense and fraud, rather than success and progress. Nonetheless, societal attitudes are not immobile; they could, if a concerted effort were made, swing toward a fairer image of science. This time, however, women should be included in the picture of scientists who make valuable contributions to society. The implementation of concrete policies has also indirect effects: it is a signal that leading segments of our society care about women scientists. And this might influence wider social attitudes. Our policy suggestions were informed by the insights we gained about scientists' actual working lives. Some of these recommendations advocate the expansion of existing programs, while others call for new initiatives. Although the suggestions primarily focus on academic science, they are also applicable to nonacademic science. By concentrating on the career stages after the postdoctoral fellowship award, we do not deny the importance of reforms in earlier stages. Change is needed from grade school to graduate school in order to attract more women into science and keep them there. (For a detailed discussion of intervention programs in various segments of the pipeline, see Matyas and Dix 1992). Yet those relatively few women who have persisted in science to the postdoctoral level constitute a skilled human resource that is available in the short term. It would be a severe loss to both science and society if a significant proportion of these women left science or were prevented from realizing their full potential.

Policies Within Science

One key factor within science itself may obstruct the career paths of even very successful women: their relative isolation from the collegial network. Whether it results from subtle exclusion or is their own predisposition, this isolation decreases women's visibility and may prevent them from achieving prominence in their fields. Most of the following policy proposals aim at integrating women into the collegial network (providing more positive kicks) and educating them about the mechanics of successful careers (leading to more positive reactions). We also discuss a modification in the stratification mechanisms in science (that is, in the criteria for scientific performance).

1. Voluntary conferences and workshops for interested women scientists should be organized at the institutional, regional, and national levels. These meetings should include explicit discussions of strategies that lead to successful science careers and raise women's knowledge and consciousness about these issues. Many women in our study have approached crucial career issues with glaring ignorance, naïveté, or reluctance regarding the politics of science. Conferences (or equivalent counseling) for airing these issues in a factual way might induce women to take them more seriously. Once women scientists recognize certain tendencies— in their own behavior and that of others—that might set back their careers, they will be in a better position to decide how to respond to them.

2. To become visible in the scientific community and enter collegial networks and collaborations, partcipation in conferences is crucial for young scientists. Special conference travel funds would encourage emerging women scientists to attend. This kind of material help would be most useful for exposing participants to potential employers. NSF already considers the absence of women at NSF-funded conferences to be prima-facie evidence of one form of gender discrimination (Etzkowitz et al. 1994).

3. Newly available means of electronic communication, such as the Internet, give women scientists added opportunity to counteract isolation. In its various forms (for example, bulletin boards, mailing lists, instantaneous one-on-one communication), electronic networks can facilitate the exchange of information and support (Etzkowitz et al. 1994).

4. Fellowship administrators should pay more attention to follow-up.

Their current approach focuses on the award process rather than recognizing any long-term investment in a scientist. All agencies awarding such fellowships—for example, NSF—should keep in touch with former recipients and maintain an updated data base concerning them. The costs would be small and the benefits significant, particularly for women scientists. In the most prestigious departments, where the underrepresentation of senior women scientists is severe, one can often hear the lament that there are just not enough qualified women in the applicant pool. This is not surprising; as our study shows, women scientists find it relatively harder to achieve visibility and prominence. An updated data base of former postdoctoral fellows could supplement the information available through a department's own network by providing current CVs of those former fellows interested in new science jobs—among them a fair number of women. Employers, organizers of research symposia, and so on might discover that qualified women already exist, even if they are hidden in the wings. (Needless to say, we do not wish to imply that only former recipients of prestigious postdoctoral fellowships should be considered as qualified applicants.)

5. NSF has already instituted a program called Visiting Professorships for Women (Sposito 1992), and our research underlines the importance of such initiatives. More short-term visiting professorships for women scientists should be instituted at major departments. This would benefit both the scientists, who would increase their visibility in the scientific community, and women students at participating universities.

6. Another NSF program, Faculty Awards for Women, also seems on target (Sposito 1992). It is intended to provide support for women scientists with outstanding potential, making it easier for them to break through the glass ceiling and achieve prominence in their fields. Even in our sample of particularly promising scientists, women as a group were less likely to achieve top positions in the scientific hierarchy. Therefore, rectifying this disparity should be a prime focus for policy intervention.

7. Women as a group produce fewer publications than men, but their publications tend to be more substantial according to the self-described working style of the women we interviewed. (In studies by Project Access and others, women's papers are, on the average, cited more often than men's, a finding that supports women's own comments.) When evaluating a scientist's performance, institutions

should be encouraged to look at a reasonably small number of publications that include what evaluees consider to be their best work rather than judge productivity chiefly by quantity. Some institutions, among them NSF, have already implemented this strategy.

Family-related Policies

Family-related problems loom large among women who left science and those who stayed. As we noted, women scientists must often synchronize three clocks: their biological clock, their career clock, and their spouses' career clock. Ultimately, the individuals (women and men) must devise viable solutions for these problems and find a successful balance between career and family; but institutional support that alleviates family-related burdens could help enormously.

1. Institutions should support scientists in the task of raising a family. At this time, important issues include child-care facilities, parental-leave policies, and the stopping or slowing of the tenure clock as needed.
2. Conscious efforts should be made to accommodate two-career couples in the same geographic area despite the obvious problems this may entail. Fehrs and Czujko (1992) have discussed some possibilities. For instance, if two full appointments are not possible, one position could be split between the spouses without reducing the status of the part-time appointments. Both half positions would be on tenure track if the original position was tenure track. According to Fehrs and Czujko, other initiatives have already been implemented at some institutions: arranging a sabbatical position for the spouse (not necessarily at the hiring institution) and offering the spouse one or two years of salary—presumably to give him or her time to find a suitable position. The collaboration of two or more academic institutions in the same area is at last becoming another way to solve the problems of two-career couples.

Policies for Re-recruiting the Dropouts

Finally, the door to science should be kept open for people who have dropped out of research science. Typically, such individuals regret leaving to some extent, even if they have successful careers in other fields. Because the social system of science has become accustomed to an oversupply of scientific personnel, scientists have sometimes been considered expendable; and there has been little concern about dropout rates. (By contrast, the military understands the value of trained personnel and the importance of keeping their skills honed after leaving—witness the reserves.)

If the number of women scientists is to be increased in the near future, it may be advantageous to treat trained women scientists who now have left the field as a kind of science reserve. Apart from reentry programs (see Lantz 1980), science agencies such as NRC and NSF might provide contact programs that would offer interested doctoral-level women scientists who have left research the opportunity to become involved with research groups. Thus, these women could keep their skills and interests active so that eventual reentry would be easier and more likely.

Generally speaking, while policies based on the deficit model can expect wide approval, those based on the difference model are likely to be highly controversial. Such policies may, for instance, aim at reducing the high levels of work intensity, competitiveness, and aggressiveness, which have alienated a number of women scientists in our study. (In various professions, low-intensity "mommy tracks" have been discussed. But such an option also appeals to some men—and not necessarily for parental reasons.) Proposals for a less competitive environment are bound to evoke stiff resistance from those who believe that performance, as defined in the conventional sense, should be the only or chief criterion by which scarce resources are allocated in science. To these people, a core ideal of the scientific community is at stake, one defined roughly by the term *meritocracy* (positions and funding awarded according to the quality of scientific performance).

In stark contrast with the near-universal allegiance to the meritocratic ideal, the actual determination and measurement of scientific performance has remained elusive. For lack of a simple quantitative criterion, the scientific community has in practice frequently turned to publication output or publication rate as a proxy. Using this measure alone, however, may on average be biased against women for two reasons. First, as several studies have found, it may not do justice to their publication habits. Second, it may not take into account the interpenetration of work and domestic obligations they might experience at the decision point. Acknowledging that these circumstances might apply to the individual case at hand would be a step toward evaluating a scientist's quality against the background of the person's total life obligations and responsibilities.

Therefore, it has been suggested that, in decisions about hiring, tenure, and promotion, quality of performance should be broadened into a multidimensional concept. Wilson (1992, 9) advocates a "shift from a *singular* strategy of 'survival of the fittest' to a *broader portfolio* of strategies to develop human potential to its fullest." If such changes were made, they would benefit persons not because of their gender but because of their particular circumstances. Thus, these changes could also benefit men with unconventional publications habits or family responsibilities.

The measurement of scientific quality, difficult enough as it is now, would become much more complex through policies of this sort. Nonetheless, this may be the price one has to pay. We foresee that, in the coming decades, the debate about the standards of current scientific performance—and about predicting its future quality in a career—will become as central as it is difficult.

The Big Picture

Concrete policy programs and interventions do not take place in a vacuum. They operate within the framework of two fundamental factors that have an enormous impact on women's representation in science: the scientific job market and the critical mass of women already in science. The situation is a "bad news–good news" story.

One of the most important determinants for policy is the scientific labor market. The bad news is that forecasts of an impending shortfall of scientific personnel are now doubtful. In addition, a reduction of federal support for science and technology is already in progress. If there is indeed an oversupply of scientific personnel, policymakers concerned with equitable gender representation may lose their human-resource allies. In this case, the push toward increasing the proportion of women scientists must rely solely on the equity argument, perhaps augmented by the argument that the participation of scientists with nontraditional backgrounds and experience may stimulate scientific progress (Wilson 1992). Among all professions, science has one of the highest proportions of people with an all-powerful intrinsic motivation—they love nothing more than science and enjoy spending almost all their waking hours doing it, even with less-than-ideal working conditions and external rewards. If there are enough available "workaholics" to fill science positions, there may be little incentive, from a human-resource perspective, for making science more hospitable to more people. Moreover, when there is an oversupply of scientific personnel, policies that aim at raising the representation of women in science may encounter increased resistance and resentment from men who feel unfairly shut out of a science career.

The good news is that women scientists may already have gained a critical mass in many departments and fields. The critical-mass argument contends that change sometimes comes about by sheer numbers. Project Access questionnaire data show no gender difference in the ranks achieved among academic biologists, where there is a relatively high proportion of women. But a marked gender difference exists among physical scientists, mathematicians, and engineers, where there is a relatively low proportion of women. Such findings make it plausible to expect that, once a critical mass of women is achieved, the disparity problem will be eased. When a department or a field has a sufficient number of women scientists, women lose their status as oddities or tokens (Kanter 1977). Dresselhaus (1986), for instance, observed that isolated women in physics classes used to be very taciturn; but once the proportion of women reached a critical mass of 10 percent to 15 percent of the class, women's level of participation became indistinguishable from men's. Although women scientists' attitudes also make a difference, as Etzkowitz and collaborators (1994) pointed out, a substantial numerical presence of women that transforms science into a mixed-gender environment is likely to change the social conditions of science in a variety of ways—from the style of day-to-day interactions, to implementing policies on day care, to tenure decisions.

To conclude, we offer policymakers the same caveat we directed to aspiring scientists. Career paths are enormously idiosyncratic and to some extent shaped by luck. No single recipe for career success emerged from the interviews, and that result was to be expected. Policymakers should keep this in mind when trying to influence the social system of science. Of course, they must try to identify key areas of possible intervention, such as those we have mentioned, and monitor the success of their programs. But given the nature of scientists' career paths, no single policy program can expect general success. Hence, we need a large number of varied, even parallel, programs that expose a wide variety of budding scientists to different opportunities and thus increase the chances that an aspiring scientist will take advantage of one of them. Such diversity in policy programs follows the model that has worked well in American society. In order to improve the representation of women in science, a great variety of targeted programs may be more advantageous than one neat master plan. Our overall strategy should be to accommodate the idiosyncrasies of our diverse population in the social system of tomorrow's science. Thus, we shall maximize the humane use of those human beings whose chief aspiration is to advance science in this nation.

APPENDIX
▼ ▼ ▼

QUESTIONNAIRE AND INTERVIEW SAMPLES AND METHODS

Questionnaire Sample

Our set of 699 former postdoctoral fellows comprises men and women who received a National Science Foundation (NSF) fellowship from the inception of the program in 1952 through 1985 or a National Research Council (NRC) associateship from its start in 1959 through 1986 (see Table A.1). The respondents include 460 former NSF postdoctoral fellows (99 women and 361 men) and 239 former NRC postdoctoral associates (92 women and 147 men).

This was the most extensive sample of former NSF and NRC post-doctoral fellows that we could reasonably obtain. The NRC, which keeps an address data base of its former associates, made available the addresses of all former associates who indicated their willingness to participate. The NSF gave us the names of all their former fellows, whom we then had to locate, chiefly by contacting the alumni offices of their colleges or graduate schools.

Before 1975, men outnumbered women among NSF postdoctoral fellows roughly 20 to 1. Therefore, we modified the selection procedure for this group. We attempted to contact all women who were fellows before 1975 in the usual manner. Then we matched the women respondents with the men of the same academic field and year of fellowship and attempted to contact only these men.

Our data were collected between 1987 and 1990 through a lengthy questionnaire that was sent out to the former fellows we located. If the first mailing did not result in a response, we repeated our attempts. Of the postdoctoral fellows who were contacted, the response rate was 60.6 percent for former NSF fellows (62.1 percent for men and 55.6 percent for women), and 82.1 percent for former NRC associates (81.7 percent for men and 82.9 percent for women).

Our respondents' mean year of receiving the doctorate was 1975 (men: 1975; women: 1976). The mean birth year of the respondents was 1946 (men: 1946; women: 1946).

Among our respondents, slightly fewer men than women were U.S. natives (87.6 percent versus 90.5 percent); and fewer men than women were naturalized American citizens (3.6 percent versus 6.3 percent). Information about racial and ethnic heritage was available only for NSF respondents. All of these women and 97.5 percent of these men were white, eight men (2.2 percent) were Asians or Pacific Islanders and one man was black (0.3 percent). Among the white former NSF fellows, two women and fifteen men were of Hispanic heritage. Thus, Hispanics form the largest minority (4.7 percent) in our sample; but fourteen (82.4 percent) of the seventeen Hispanic fellows traced their ancestry to Spain, not to countries of Central or South America.

Reflecting a general pattern among scientists, more women than men respondents work in the biological (46.1 percent versus 29.7 percent) or social sciences (17.8 percent versus 8.1 percent), while fewer women work in the physical sciences, mathematics, and engineering (36.1 percent versus 62.2 percent).

To form a general impression of the representativeness of our sample, we compared the distributions of three key variables in the active population, in the contacted sample, and among our respondents. Those variables were gender, year of fellowship, and academic field. Information on these variables was available from NSF records regardless of whether or not a person responded. The active population included all those former fellows who fell within the scope of our study. The contacted sample was those former fellows who were considered to have been contacted by mail (all those who were sent a questionnaire minus the relatively few whose mailings were returned by the post office as undeliverable). Inspection of the three variables indicated no major bias among our respondents as compared with the active population or contacted sample.

Interview Sample

After a period of developing, testing, and revising an open-ended interviewing procedure, one interviewer traveled extensively from summer 1989 through fall 1990 to conduct two hundred face-to-face interviews with former postdoctoral fellows across the United States (see Table A.2).

Table A.1. The Questionnaire Sample

	Men			Women		
	Biology	*PSME*	*Social sciences*	*Biology*	*PSME*	*Social sciences*
Active scientists	136	293	35	80	64	26
Left science	15	24	6	8	5	8
	151	316	41	88	69	34

NOTE: PSME stands for physical sciences, mathematics, and engineering.

The interviews typically lasted between two and three hours each and were usually conducted in the interviewees' institutions or homes. The interviewees were first asked to narrate their whole career path in their own words and were then asked the open-ended questions one by one.

A subset of twenty-four interview transcripts (twelve males and twelve females) were thoroughly studied to distill themes of typical responses and develop a coding scheme. Thus, the categories in the coding scheme emerged from the interviews themselves rather than being superimposed from some prior information or theory. All interview transcripts were coded according to this scheme, and five coders participated in the coding. The average proportion of agreement between the coders was 93.7 percent; Cohen's kappa was 0.698.

The interviewees included 108 women and 92 men who had been NSF postdoctoral fellows (114), NRC postdoctoral associates (51), Bunting postdoctoral fellows in the sciences or engineering (28), or Bunting finalists in these fields (7). Whereas the NSF and NRC fellowships are open to both men and women, the Bunting fellowship is for women only. Different considerations entered the selection of interviewees from our larger sample of former recipients of these prestigious postdoctoral fellowships. On the one hand, we attempted to contact as many former fellows as possible within a limited budget. On the other hand, we wanted to match men and women in the sample by type of current position, academic age, and academic fields. The resulting sample is a tradeoff: a larger sample that is not perfectly matched but is matched to a substantial degree.

Of the respondents, 58.0 percent (men: 57.6 percent; women: 58.3 percent) currently work in academic science; 30.5 percent (men: 31.5 percent; women: 29.6 percent) work as scientists outside of academia;

Table A.2. The Interview Sample

	Men			Women		
	Biology	PSME	Social sciences	Biology	PSME	Social sciences
Active scientists	30	44	8	37	33	25
Left science	5	2	3	3	2	8
	35	46	11	40	35	33

NOTE: PSME stands for physical sciences, mathematics, and engineering.

and 11.5 percent (men: 10.9 percent; women 12.0 percent) have left research science. The mean year of receiving the doctorate was 1974 for men and 1971 for women. More than a third (37.5 percent) of the respondents work in the biological sciences (men: 38.0 percent; women 37.0 percent). Men are overrepresented in the physical sciences, mathematics, and engineering (men: 50.0 percent; women: 32.4 percent) and, conversely, underrepresented in the social sciences (men: 12.0 percent; women: 30.6 percent). A great number of interviews (sixty-eight) were conducted in New England, reflecting both a geographical concentration of former postdoctoral fellows in northeastern states and easy accessibility for Massachusetts-based Project Access. In the state of New York, thirteen interviews were conducted, and forty-seven took place in the Mid-Atlantic region. Another geographical focus was the West Coast region, with forty-one interviewees. The remaining interviewees lived in the Midwest (eighteen), the South (seven) and the Mountain States (six).

The ten extraordinarily successful scientists whom we featured in chapter 2 were chosen from the interview subjects currently working in academia. Through regression analysis, the three success criteria of academic rank, departmental prestige, and publication productivity were controlled for fields, and academic rank was additionally controlled for years since doctorate. The weighted average (first principal component) of the resulting residual variables was used as the composite measure of success that ranked the academic scientists. The most successful female scientists were matched with highly successful male scientists of similar ages and fields.

In selecting the ten cases from the small group of former fellows who subsequently left science (chapter 3), we followed no formal algorithm. We did not, however, present any of the few cases in which a severe illness or some other personal tragedy forced the former fellow out of science.

In our twenty descriptions, we let the former postdoctoral fellows speak to a large extent in their own words. When transposing the spoken language of the interviews into written text, we lightly edited the original transcripts (for example, by removing false starts, word repetitions, major grammatical inconsistencies, and most of the stalling words such as *well, you know,* and *I mean* that creep into almost everyone's speech). Moreover, we indicated only major ellipses in the text. We believe that this approach, while maintaining the flavor of the spoken word, will make the quotations more readable.

To protect the anonymity of the selected respondents, we gave them pseudonyms, did not mention the names of other persons or institutions, and did not identify the respondents' scientific disciplines. Drafts of the case profiles were submitted to the described respondents to give them the opportunity to raise concerns or objections. One of the originally selected twenty respondents had major objections; her profile was replaced by an alternate's. Four respondents (Barbara, Christine, Erik, and Fred) requested minor changes that were implemented accordingly.

The descriptions reflect the respondents' situation at the time of the interview—that is, in 1989 or 1990. A few interviewees notified us of more recent changes in their situation; but for the sake of uniformity among the set of twenty biographies, we did not include these recent changes in our descriptions.

Both questionnaire and interview data have been archived and can be used for scholarly research at the Henry A. Murray Research Center of Radcliffe College. For a more detailed statistical analysis, we again refer the reader to Sonnert, with the assistance of Holton, *Gender Differences in Science Careers: The Project Access Study,* ASA Rose Book Series (New Brunswick, N.J.: Rutgers University Press, in press).

KEY RESULTS OF THE QUESTIONNAIRE SURVEY

Table A.3. Average Rank of Former Postdoctoral Fellows Currently in Academic Science

	Men			Women		
	Biology	PSME	Social sciences	Biology	PSME	Social sciences
Ph.D.						
Pre-1978	3.4	3.6	3.8	3.2	2.9	3.3
	N = 57	N = 105	N = 24	N = 23	N = 19	N = 14
1978 and after	1.9	2.6	2.9	2.1	1.7	2.1
	N = 52	N = 89	N = 9	N = 28	N = 16	N = 8

NOTE: Rank is a scale from 1 to 4. 1 = nonprofessorial positions, such as lecturer and research associate; 2 = assistant professor; 3 = associate professor; 4 = full professor. PSME stands for physical sciences, mathematics, and engineering.

Table A.4. Proportion of Full Professors among Former Postdoctoral Fellows in Academic Science

	Men			Women		
	Biology	PSME	Social sciences	Biology	PSME	Social sciences
Ph.D.						
Pre-1978	0.57	0.70	0.83	0.43	0.37	0.50
	N = 56	N = 105	N = 24	N = 23	N = 19	N = 14
1978 and after	0.03	0.10	0.33	0.04	0.00	0.00
	N = 52	N = 89	N = 9	N = 28	N = 16	N = 8

NOTE: PSME stands for physical sciences, mathematics, and engineering.

Table A.5. Proportion of Full Professors among Older Former Postdoctoral Fellows Currently in Academic Science

	Women	Men
Top institutions	0.40 N = 15	0.88 N = 34
Non-top institutions	0.47 N = 30	0.68 N = 109

NOTE: Older fellows are those receiving a doctorate before 1978. Top institutions are defined as being rated higher than 60 by Jones et al. (1982), correspondent to roughly the top 15 percent of the rated institutions. Non-top institutions are those with lower ratings. Unrated institutions are missing values.

Table A.6. Average Annual Productivity of Academic Scientists

	Biology	*PSME*	*Social sciences*
Men	2.77 N = 83	3.06 N = 140	2.46 N = 26
Women	2.47 N = 46	2.18 N = 29	1.39 N = 16

NOTE: Average annual productivity is number of publications of all kinds (except abstracts) divided by years since doctorate. PSME stands for physical sciences, mathematics, and engineering.

Table A.7. Average Academic Rank by Gender and Productivity

	Women	*Men*
High producers	2.6 N = 36	3.3 N = 133
Low producers	2.5 N = 55	2.9 N = 116

NOTE: Because productivity varies by field, the group of high producers consists of three subgroups: the high-producing halves of biologists, PSME scientists, and social scientists. The group of low producers was formed analogously.

Table A.8. Research Style at Different Career Stages by Gender

	Before fellowship	During fellowship	After fellowship
Women	2.17	2.32	2.67
	N = 189	N = 190	N = 184
Men	2.10	2.55	2.89
	N = 500	N = 500	N = 492

NOTE: The numbers are averages on a five-point rating scale, ranging from 1 ("I usually worked alone on my scientific problems") to 5 ("my research was performed almost exclusively in collaboration with other scientists").

Table A.9. Academic Rank by Gender and Postdoctoral Collaboration

	Women	Men
Low collaboration	2.6	2.9
	N = 69	N = 161
High collaboration	2.4	3.1
	N = 29	N = 144

NOTE: If the residual of a regression of collaboration style on type of fellowship, year of fellowship, and fields during fellowship was 0 or positive, the respondent was made part of the high collaboration group. Those with negative residuals form the low collaboration group.

Table A.10. Part-time Employment by Gender and Marital Status

	Women	Men
Unmarried	0.020	0.024
	N = 50	N = 84
Married	0.099	0.020
	N = 131	N = 400

Table A.11. Part-time Employment by Gender and Parental Status

	Women	Men
No children	0.036	0.025
	N = 84	N = 157
Children	0.112	0.018
	N = 98	N = 332

Table A.12. Current Academic Rank by Gender and Motivation for Postdoctoral Fellowship

	Women	Men
Took fellowship to be with spouse	2.4	2.7
	N = 28 (28.6%)	N = 25 (7.9%)
Did not take fellowship to be with spouse	2.6	3.0
	N = 70 (71.4%)	N = 291 (92.1%)

REFERENCES

Allison, P. D., and J. A. Stewart. 1974. "Productivity Differences among Scientists: Evidence for Accumulative Advantage." *American Sociological Review* 39:596–606.

Astin, H. S. 1978. "Factors Affecting Women's Scholarly Productivity." In *The Higher Education of Women: Essays in Honor of Rosemary Park*, ed. H. S. Astin, and W. Z. Hirsch, 133–157. New York: Praeger.

Bayer, A. E., and J. Folger. 1966. "Some Correlates of a Citation Measure of Productivity in Science." *Sociology of Education* 39:381–390.

Belenky, M. F., B. M. Clinchy, N. R. Goldberger, and J. M. Tarule. 1986. *Women's Ways of Knowing: The Development of Self, Voice, and Mind*. New York: Basic Books.

Benbow, C. P., and J. C. Stanley. 1980. "Sex Differences in Mathematical Ability: Fact or Artifact." *Science* 210: 1262–1264.

Briscoe, A. M. 1984. "Scientific Sexism: The World of Chemistry." In *Women in Scientific and Engineering Professions*, ed. V. B. Haas and C. C. Perrucci, 147–159. Ann Arbor: University of Michigan Press.

Brush, S. G. 1991. "Women in Science and Engineering." *American Scientist* 79: 404–419.

Campbell, P. F., and S. C. Geller. 1984. "Early Socialization: Causes and Cures of Mathematics Anxiety." In *Women in Scientific and Engineering Professions*, ed. V. B. Haas and C. C. Perrucci, 173–180. Ann Arbor: University of Michigan Press.

Chodorow, N. 1974. "Family Structure and Feminine Personality." In *Women, Culture and Society*, ed. M. Z. Rosaldo and L. Lamphere, 43–66. Stanford: Stanford University Press.

Cole, J. R. 1979. *Fair Science: Women in the Scientific Community.* New York: Free Press.

Cole, J. R. 1987. "Women in Science." In *Scientific Excellence: Origins and Assessment*, ed. D. N. Jackson and J. P. Rushton, 359–375. Newbury Park, Calif.: Sage.

Cole, J. R., and S. Cole. 1973. *Social Stratification in Science.* Chicago: University of Chicago Press.

Cole, J. R., and B. Singer. 1991. "A Theory of Limited Differences: Explaining the Productivity Puzzle in Science." In *The Outer Circle: Women in the Scientific Community,* ed. H. Zuckerman, J. R. Cole, and J. T. Bruer, 277–310. New York: Norton.

Cole, J. R., and H. Zuckerman. 1984. "The Productivity Puzzle: Persistence and Change in Patterns of Publication of Men and Women Scientists." In *Advances in Motivation and Achievement,* ed. M. W. Steinkamp and M. L. Maehr, 2:217–256. Greenwich, Conn.: JAI.

Cole, J. R., and H. Zuckerman, H. 1987. "Marriage, Motherhood, and Research Performance in Science." *Scientific American* 255(2):119–125.

Cole, S., and R. Fiorentine. 1991. "Discrimination against Women in Science: The Confusion of Outcome and Process." In *The Outer Circle: Women in the Scientific Community*, ed. H. Zuckerman, J. R. Cole, and J. T. Bruer, 205–226. New York: Norton.

Committee on the Status of Women in Physics (CSWP). 1992. "CSWP Grapples with Climate, Dual Career Issues. *APS News* 1(7):9–15.

Dresselhaus, M. S. 1986. "Women Graduate Students." *Physics Today,* 39 (June):74–75.

Eccles, J. S. 1987. "Gender Roles and Women's Achievement-related Decisions." *Psychology of Women Quarterly* 11:135–172.

Eccles, J. S., and J. E. Jacobs. 1986. "Social Forces Shape Math Attitudes and Performance." *Signs* 11:367–380.

Eccles, J. S., J. E. Jacobs, and R. D. Harold. 1990. "Gender Role Stereotypes, Expectancy Effects, and Parents' Socialization of Gender Differences." *Journal of Social Issues* 46(2):183–201.

Eccles-Parsons, J., T. F. Adler, and C. M. Kaczala. 1982. "Socialization of Achievement Attitudes and Beliefs: Parental Influences." *Child Development* 53:310–321.

Eisenstein, H. 1983. *Contemporary Feminist Thought.* Boston: Hall.

Entwisle, D. R., and L. A. Hayduk. 1988. "Lasting Effects of Elementary School." *Sociology of Education* 6:147–159.

Epstein, C. F. 1970. *Woman's Place: Options and Limits in Professional Careers.* Berkeley: University of California Press.

Etzkowitz, H., C. Kemelgor, M. Neuschatz, B. Uzzi, and J. Alonzo. 1994. "The Paradox of Critical Mass for Women in Science." *Science* 266 (7 October):51–54.

Fava, S. F., and K. Deierlein. 1988. "Women Physicists in the U.S.: The Career Influence of Marital Status." *Gazette: A Newsletter of the Committee on the Status of Women in Physics of the American Physical Society* 8(2):1–3.

Fehrs, M., and R. Czujko. 1992. "Women in Physics. Reversing the Exclusion." *Physics Today* (August):part 1, 33–40.

Ferber, M., and J. Huber. 1979. "Husbands, Wives, and Careers." *Journal of Marriage and the Family* 41:315–325.

Folger, J. K., H. S. Astin, and A. E. Bayer. 1970. *Human Resources and Higher Education: Staff Report of the Commission on Human Resources and Advanced Education.* New York: Russell Sage.

Fox, M. F. 1983. "Publication Productivity among Scientists: A Critical Review." *Social Studies of Science* 13:285–305.

Garfield, E. 1993. "Women in Science. Part 1: The Productivity Puzzle—J. Scott Long on Why Women Biochemists Publish Less Than Men." *Current Comments* 9 (1 March):3–5.

Griliches, Z. 1987. "R&D and Productivity: Measurement Issues and Econometric Results." *Science* 237:31–35.

Haack, S. 1993. "Knowledge and Propaganda: Reflections of an Old Feminist." *Partisan Review* 60:556–564.

Hahn, O. 1966. *Otto Hahn: A Scientific Autobiography,* trans. and ed. W. Ley. New York: Scribner's.

Hall, R. M. 1982. *The Classroom Climate: A Chilly One for Women?* (Project on the Status and Education of Women). Washington, D.C.: Association of American Colleges.

Harding, S. 1986. *The Science Question in Feminism.* Ithaca: Cornell University Press.

Harding, S. 1989. "Feminist Justificatory Strategies." In *Women, Knowledge, and Reality: Explorations in Feminist Philosophy,* ed. A. Garry and M. Pearsall, 189–201. Boston: Unwin Hyman.

Hargens, L. L., J. C. McCann, and B. F. Reskin. 1978. "Productivity and Reproductivity: Professional Achievement among Research Scientists." *Social Forces* 57:154–163.

Heikkinen, H. 1978. "Sex Bias in Chemistry Texts: Where Is Women's Place?" *The Science Teacher* 45:16–21.

Helson, R. 1973. "Women Mathematicians and the Creative Personality." In *Science As a Career Choice: Theoretical and Empirical Studies,* ed. B. T. Eiduson and L. Beckman, 563–574. New York: Sage.

Hoben, T. 1985. "A Theory of High Mathematical Aptitude." *Journal of Mathematical Psychology* 29 (June):231–242.

Hochschild, A. R. 1989. *The Second Shift: Working Parents and the Revolution at Home.* New York: Viking.

Hornig, L. S. 1987. "Women Graduate Students." In *Women: Their Underrepresentation and Career Differentials in Science and Engineering,* ed. L. S. Dix, 103–122. Washington, D.C.: National Academy Press.

Huston-Stein, A., and A. Higgins-Trenk. 1978. "Development of Females from Childhood through Adulthood: Careers and Feminine Role Orientations." *Life Span Development and Behavior* 1:257–296.

Jones, L. V., G. Lindzey, and P. E. Coggeshall, eds. 1982. *An Assessment of Research-Doctorate Programs in the United States.* 5 vols. Washington, D.C.: National Academy Press.

Kanter, R. M. 1977. "Some Effects of Proportions on Group Life: Skewed Sex Ratios and Responses to Token Women." *American Journal of Sociology* 82:965–990.

Kaufman, D. R. 1978. "Associational Ties in Academe: Some Male and Female Differences." *Sex Roles* 4:9–21.

Keller, E. F. 1983. *A Feeling for the Organism: The Life and Work of Barbara McClintock.* New York: Freeman.

Keller, E. F. 1985. *Reflections on Gender and Science.* New Haven: Yale University Press.

Keller, E. F. 1989. "Feminism and Science." In *Women, Knowledge, and Reality: Explorations in Feminist Philosophy,* ed. A. Garry and M. Pearsall, 175–188. Boston: Unwin Hyman.

Kelly, A. 1985. "The Construction of Masculine Science." *British Journal of Sociology of Education* 6:133–154.

Kerr, P. 1988. "A Conceptualization of Learning, Teaching and Research Experiences of Women Scientists and Its Implications for Science." Ph.D. diss., Cornell University, Ithaca.

Kistiakowsky, V. 1980. "Women in Physics: Unnecessary, Injurious and Out of Place?" *Physics Today* 33 (February):32–40.

Kjerulff, K. H., and M. R. Blood. 1973. "A Comparison of Communication Patterns in Male and Female Graduate Students." *Journal of Higher Education* 44(8):623–632.

Koshland, D. E. 1988. "Women in Science." *Science* 239:1473.

Lantz, A. E. 1980. *Reentry Programs for Female Scientists.* New York: Praeger.

Levin, M. 1988. "Caring New World: Feminism and Science. *The American Scholar* (Winter):100–106.

Lewis, G. L. 1986. "Career Interruptions and Gender Differences in Salaries of Scientists and Engineers." (Working Paper for the Office of Scientific and Engineering Personnel, National Research Council). Washington, D.C.: National Academy Press.

Lipman-Blumen, J. 1972. "How Ideology Shapes Women's Lives." *Scientific American* 226(1):34–42.

Long, J. S. 1992. "Measures of Sex Differences in Scientific Productivity. *Social Forces* 71:159–178.

McBay, S. M. 1987. "Science for Women and Minorities." *The Scientist* (30 November):29.

Maccoby, E. E., and C. N. Jacklin. 1974. *The Psychology of Sex Differences.* Stanford: Stanford University Press.

Matyas, M. L. 1991. "Women, Minorities and Persons with Physical Disabilities in Science and Engineering: Contributing Factors and Study Methodology." In *Investing in Human Potential: Science and Engineering at the Crossroads,* ed. M. L. Matyas and S. M. Malcom, 13–36. Washington, D.C.: American Association for the Advancement of Science.

Matyas, M. L. 1992. "Promoting Undergraduate Studies in Science and Engineering." In *Science and Engineering Programs: On Target for Women?* ed. M. L. Matyas and L. S. Dix, 43–65. Washington, D.C.: National Academy Press.

Matyas, M. L., and L. S. Dix. eds. 1992. *Science and Engineering Programs: On Target for Women?* Washington, D.C.: National Academy Press.

Merton, R. K. 1973. *The Sociology of Science: Theoretical and Empirical Investigations.* Chicago: University of Chicago Press.

Moen, P. 1988. "Women As a Human Resource." Sociology Program, Division of Social and Economic Science, National Science Foundation. Manuscript NSB/EHR 89–05. Washington, D.C.

National Research Council. 1981. *Postdoctoral Appointments and Disappointments.* A report of the Committee on a Study of Postdoctorals in Science and Engineering in the United States, Commission on Human Resources. Washington, D.C.: National Academy Press.

National Science Foundation. 1990. *Future Scarcities of Scientists and Engineers: Problems and Solutions.* Directorate for Scientific, Technological, and International Affairs, Division of Policy Research and Analysis. (Working Draft, Summer 1990). Washington, D.C.: National Science Foundation.

Nowotny, H. 1991. "Mixed Feelings: Women Interacting with the Institution of Science." In *Social Roles and Social Institutions: Essays in Honor of Rose Laub Coser,* ed. J. R. Blau and N. Goodman, 149–165. Boulder, Colo.: Westview Press.

Primack, R. B., and V. O'Leary. 1993. "Cumulative Disadvantages in the Careers of Women Ecologists." *BioScience* 43(3):158–165.

Pycior, H., N. Slack, and P. Abir-Am. In press. *Creative Couples in the Sciences.* New Brunswick, N.J.: Rutgers University Press.

Rayman, P. 1993. "Pathways for Women in the Sciences." Paper presented at AAAS annual meeting, 11–16 February, Boston.

Reskin, B. F. 1978. "Sex Differentiation and the Social Organization of Science." In *Sociology of Science,* ed. J. Gaston, 6–37. San Francisco: Jossey-Bass.

Roe, A. 1952. *The Making of a Scientist.* New York: Dodd, Mead.

Rosenfeld, R. A. 1984. "Academic Career Mobility for Women and Men Psychologists." In *Women in Scientific and Engineering Professions,* ed. V. B. Haas and C. C. Perrucci, 89–127. Ann Arbor: University of Michigan Press.

Salk, J. E. 1989. "How Did I Get There? Agents, Events, and Kin in the Mobility Accounts of Elite Young Business Professionals." Paper presented at the American Sociological Association annual meeting, 9–13 August, San Francisco.

Shamos, M. H. In press. *The Myth of Scientific Literacy.* New Brunswick, N.J.: Rutgers University Press.

Sonnert, G., with the assistance of G. Holton. In press, a. *Gender Differences in Science Careers: The Project Access Study.* ASA Rose Book Series. New Brunswick, N.J.: Rutgers University Press.

Sonnert, G. In press, b. "What Makes a Good Scientist? Determinants of Peer Evaluation among Biologists." *Social Studies of Science.*

Sposito, G. 1992. "Promoting Science and Engineering Careers in Academe." In

Science and Engineering Programs: On Target for Women? ed. M. L. Matyas and L. S. Dix, 101–118. Washington, D.C.: National Academy Press.

Stein, A. H., and M. M. Bailey. 1973. "The Socialization of Achievement Orientation in Females." *Psychological Bulletin* 80:345–366.

Tangri, S. S. 1972. "Determinants of Occupational Role Innovation Among College Women." *Journal of Social Issues* 28:177–199.

Tannen, D. 1990. *You Just Don't Understand: Women and Men in Conversation.* New York: Ballantine.

Tidball, M. E., and V. Kistiakowsky. 1976. "Baccalaureate Origins of American Scientists and Scholars." *Science* 193 (20 August):646–652.

Tobias, S. 1990. *They're Not Dumb, They're Different: Stalking the Second Tier.* Tuscon: Research Corporation.

Toren, N. 1988. "Women at the Top: Female Full Professors in Higher Education in Israel. *Higher Education* 17:525–544.

Vijh, A. K. 1987. "Spectrum of Creative Output of Scientists: Some Psycho-social Factors." *Physics in Canada* 43(1):9–13.

Weitzman, L. J. 1984. "Sex-role Socialization: A Focus on Women." In *Women: A Feminist Perspective,* 3d ed., ed. J. Freeman, 157–237. Palo Alto, Calif.: Mayfield.

Widnall, S. E. 1988. "Voices from the Pipeline" (AAAS Presidential Lecture). *Science* 241:1740–1745.

Wilson, L. S. 1992. "The Benefits of Diversity in the Science and Engineering Work Force." In *Science and Engineering Programs: On Target for Women?* ed. M. L. Matyas and L. S. Dix, 1–14. Washington, D.C.: National Academy Press.

Yentsch, C. M., and C. J. Sindermann. 1992. *The Woman Scientist: Meeting the Challenges for a Successful Career.* New York: Plenum.

Zuckerman, H. 1989. "Accumulation of Advantage and Disadvantage: The Theory and Its Intellectual Biography." In *L'Opera di R. K. Merton e la Sociologia contemporeana,* ed. C. Mongardini and S. Tabboni, 153–176. Genoa: Edizioni Culturali Internationali Genova.

Zuckerman, H., J. R. Cole, and J. T. Bruer. eds. 1991. *The Outer Circle: Women in the Scientific Community.* New York: Norton.

INDEX

▼ ▼ ▼

abilities, 3
access: to educational opportunities, 2;
to social networks, 2, 9, 157, 175,
191
accumulation of advantages and
disadvantages, 11, 141, 180, 183
advisors. *See* mentors
affirmative action, 176
aggressiveness, 3, 149, 177
androcentrism, 5, 6
androgyny, 7
attrition, 12, 14; and discrimination,
171; factors in, 169–172; for family
reasons, 158, 171; voluntary, 170–
171

bonding, 149

career(s): choice of institution as success
factor, 173–174; early aspirations,
145, 164–169; effect of mentors on,
143; effect of personality on, 146;
effect of social interactions on, 142;
factors in success, 172–179;
geographical restrictions on, 11, 13;
hints for success, 187; kick-reaction
model, 180–182; and marriage,
157–163; obstacles in, 10;
opportunities, 2; paths, 179–185;
persistence in, 176; positive
reinforcement in, 181; priority to
husband's, 11, 161; restriction of
opportunities, 2; success patterns in,
179–185; and "two-body" problem,
11, 159, 171, 176

collaboration, 12, 143–144, 147
creativity, 3, 154, 155, 182
cultural: patterns, 14, 158; stereotypes,
179; values, 4

deficit model, 1–3, 7, 139, 142, 144,
148, 157, 158
difference model, 1, 3–7, 142, 148, 157,
158
discrimination: and affirmative action,
176; articulation of, 141; and
attrition, 170, 171; avoidance in,
178; compliance with, 177; and de-
emphasis of femininity, 178; and
emphasis of professional identity,
178; in entry-level employment, 2;
gender, 139–141, 177–179; in hiring,
10; by peers, 140, 141–142;
perceptions of, 141; in promotions,
139; reacting to, 177–179; in
research funding, 2; reverse, 139,
140; by superiors, 140; in tenure, 2,
10, 139

flexibility, 183–185

gender: discrimination, 139–141, 177–
179; and division of labor, 4; effect
on interactions, 142; equity, 2;
polarization, 7; role socialization, 3,
6; segregation, 142; specific
differences, 3; stereotypes, 5
gender disparities/differences, 12, 139;
in academic-rank achievement, 12;
awareness of, 141; in career patterns,

4; decrease in, 2, 12; illegality of, 140; internal qualities, 176; and obstacles, 8; and opportunities, 8; and parenthood, 160; positive evaluations of, 7; in publication productivity, 12–157; resulting from marriage, 158; and scientific success, 148; in social interaction, 157
glass ceiling, 11–13
graduate education, 9–10; financial support for, 9

heredity, and gender-specific differences, 3
hiring, discrimination in, 10

identity: formation of, 5; male, 5; professional, 151–152, 178
individuation, 5
integrity, 155
intelligence, 3
interactions: collaborative, 147; collegial, 142; combative styles of, 9; effect on career, 142–143; father/daughter, 8; and gender, 142, 149; men's styles of, 9; mentor and student, 143; personal style, 147; sexual tension in, 142; social, 141–143, 156, 160, 177; styles of, 147

labor, division of, 4
luck, 173, 182–183, 188

marginalization, 5, 7, 143–144, 156, 157, 184
marriage, 157–163; to another scientist, 11, 159; as barrier to career, 11; career advantages in, 159, 161; collaboration in, 159; commuter, 159; mobility restrictions in, 159, 161; styles of, 161; "trailing spouse," 161–162; and "two-body" problem, 11, 176
men: attrition rates, 12; career priority given to, 11, 161; double standards for, 143; effect of family background on career, 165–166; epistemological style, 5; goals of, 3, 149; interaction styles, 4
mentors, 9, 184; access to, 2; as career

advantage, 174–175; interactions with students, 9, 143; lack of, 168, 171; women's opportunities for, 8–9
motivation, 4, 8, 181

objectivity, 5
obstacles; attitudinal, 157; external, 139; formal, 2, 139; funding for research, 172; and gender differences, 8; handling, 145; informal, 2, 139, 141–144; innate, 3; internal, 146; job market, 172; marriage as, 157; persistence in overcoming, 176; structural, 2, 6, 9, 10, 11, 157
opportunity, restrictions on, 2

parenthood, 158, 160, 161
perfectionism, 152–153
personality, effect on career success, 146
power, 149–150
promotion, obstacles to, 10
publication: productivity, 11, 180; quality of, 12; of research results, 174; women's output, 12, 153

rationality, 5
research: comprehensiveness in, 155; effect of gender on choice of, 148; enthusiasm for, 149–150; focus of, 174; funding for, 2, 172; high-risk, 174; integrity in, 155; niche approach, 151–152; presentation of, 155; publication of, 174; styles, 12; topic choice and success, 174
resilience, 183–185
role: expectations, 11; gender, 3, 4, 5, 6, 8; models, 5, 168

school(s): all-female, 166, 169; effect on choice of science as career, 166–169; effect on gender roles, 8
science: androcentrism in, 5, 6; avoidance of as career, 3; culture of, 170–171; early encounters with, 169; gender gap in, 12; gender neutrality in, 148; male-oriented attitudes in, 4; policy in, 13–15, 189–196; politics of, 168, 174, 175, 183; social reform

of, 7; social system of, 141–144, 160, 186–189; specialization in, 174; styles of doing, 147–157; underrepresentation of women, 13, 14; women's initial interest in, 2–3; and women's ways of thinking, 4

self-confidence, 8, 10, 144, 145, 177, 181

separation, 5

sexism, 139, 171, 178

sexual harassment, 139, 140–141, 171

social: bonding, 149; exclusion, 141–143; ineptitude, 167; interaction, 141–143, 156, 160, 177; isolation, 2, 9, 156, 157, 167, 191; marginalization, 157; networks, 2; ostracism, 167; reform, 7; skills, 188; support, 146

socialization: cultural patterns of, 14; differences, 145–147; gender role, 3, 4, 6, 8; gender-specific, 4; patterns, 6, 158; and professional success, 4

stereotypes, 5; of creativity, 154; cultural, 179; of female students, 10; gender, 5

styles: collaborative, 12, 143–144; of doing science, 147–157; of interactions, 4, 5, 9; marriage, 161; research, 12; working, 143–144

tenure, 178; and attrition, 170; denial of, 170; discrimination in, 2, 10, 139; effect on career, 172–173

tokenism, 2

university: admission, 2; male faculty in, 8; pressures on women in, 8–9

values: cultural, 3; women's, 6

women('s): academic ranks of, 12; and accumulation of advantages and disadvantages, 11; areas of responsibility, 4; attrition rates, 12, 14; collaboration styles, 143–144; and cultural rules, 149; double standards for, 143; effect of family background on career, 165–166; elements of success for, 175–179; epistemological style, 5; and family imagery, 147; and family policy, 193; feeling of inadequacy, 10; fellowship opportunities, 183; financial support for, 9, 168; geographical restrictions on careers, 11, 13; goals of, 3, 149; hints for success, 187; holistic thinking in, 152; initial interest in science, 2–3; interactional styles, 4, 5, 142; lack of role models for, 5, 168; marginalization of, 5, 7, 143–144, 156, 157; methodology, 152–157; and mother's employment history, 8; movement, 141, 176; niche approach in research, 151–152; obstacles to career success, 2–13; in "outer circle," 2; participation in graduate studies, 9; and perfectionism, 152–157; persistence of, 176; policy arguments for inclusion in science, 13–15; policy measures affecting, 189–196; problem selection of, 151–152; professional conduct of, 148–151; professional identity, 151–152; publication productivity, 12, 153, 192; range of acceptable options, 4; role expectations, 11; socialization patterns, 4, 6; social support systems, 146; stereotypes of, 10; supportive role, 4; underrepresentation in science, 13, 14; values, 6; ways of thinking, 4, 5, 148

ABOUT THE AUTHORS

Gerhard Sonnert studied sociology, history, and geography in Germany and the United Kingdom. He received his doctorate in sociology from the University of Erlangen, Germany, in 1986, and a Master of Public Administration degree from Harvard in 1988. Since then he has worked at Harvard for Project Access, a large-scale research project on scientists' career patterns.

Gerald Holton is Professor of Physics and Professor of the History of Science at Harvard University. His research into the scientific, social, and epistemological roots of the achievements and failures of major twentieth-century scientists led him to initiate this research project on the careers of scientists today.